# Literacy and language in the primary years

~~als for

teacher ~~
these essential sk~~s~~
a classroom environment in w~~

The book responds to recent chang~~
constructive way. It is written not only in the ~~
nationally-prescribed curriculum, but also in response to ~~
developments in language and literacy research – particularly the renewed emphasis on the collaborative, social context of learning and the whole language approach which stresses the interlinking of reading, writing, speaking and listening processes. Included are chapters on the phenomenon of language, the role of stories, literacy across the curriculum, new technology and assessment. Each chapter is linked to a component of the National Curriculum Programme and contains a section of points of interest, sources of further information and suggestions for follow-up activities in the classroom.

This exceptionally practical and engaging book will be invaluable to teachers in training, experienced teachers and language specialists.

**David Wray** entered higher education after several years' teaching and lecturing experience. In 1988 he took up his present position as Lecturer in Education at the University of Exeter.

**Jane Medwell** currently teaches at The Grove Primary School, Devon, and prior to this has held a number of teaching positions. She has also been a Lecturer in Education at the University of Wales, Cardiff.

# Literacy and language in the primary years

Jane Meaw...

London and New York

First published 1991
by Routledge
11 New Fetter Lane, London EC4P 4EE

Simultaneously published in the USA and Canada
by Routledge
29 West 35th Street, New York, NY 10001

Reprinted 1992, 1993 (twice), 1995, 1997 (twice), 1999 (twice), 2000, 2001

Reprinted 2002 by RoutledgeFalmer

*RoutledgeFalmer is an imprint of the Taylor & Francis Group*

© 1991 David Wray and Jane Medwell

Typeset in Times by
LaserScript Limited, Mitcham, Surrey
Printed and bound in Great Britain by
TJ International Ltd, Padstow, Cornwall

*British Library Cataloguing in Publication Data*
A catalogue record for this book is available from the British Library

*Library of Congress Cataloguing in Publication Data*
A catalogue record for this book is available from the Library of Congress

ISBN 0-415-04211-9

# Contents

vii

# List of figures

66

# Introduction

... always been at the

though ...
than under the title 'language ...
widespread during the 1970s and 80s.

Perhaps because of the central importance of literacy and language, they occasion and always have occasioned a great deal of research and scholarship, as well as spawning a vast amount of professional literature, probably more than any other aspect of primary school work. Literacy and language have been read about, written about, talked and listened about a great deal, in a great many different ways and in a world-wide variety of places. Yet there are always new things to say about them. New findings emerge from research, new insights are given by fresh minds, and new developments arise in schools and classrooms. This results in constant renewal of ideas and re-evaluation of teaching practices and materials. It is little wonder that practitioners, teachers in classrooms, sometimes find it difficult to keep up to date with the latest insights and trends.

Although developments in this crucial field have continually been made, several factors have come together to make the past few years see almost revolutionary changes in the ways we view and teach literacy and language. Of the three factors we shall mention here, two have been shifts in our understandings about the processes involved which have come from research and thinking on an international basis. One has been more locally based, but perhaps even more telling in its effects, both actual and potential. This has, of course, been the advent of a nationally prescribed curriculum, which threatens to become the most powerful agent for curriculum change we have yet seen. The present book is written in the context of the National Curriculum, as prescribed for 'English', and at the end of this introduction we include a summary of how the chapters in the book relate to the National Curriculum programmes of study. First, however, we shall briefly outline the two other important developments which have influenced theory and practice in literacy and language teaching.

The first factor has been the rediscovery, in a far more powerful way than previously, of the social dimension to learning. Established theories of learning had tended to stress the attempts of the individual to adapt to the demands of the environment, and described in great detail the cognitive mechanisms of individual learners. More recent work on learning, inspired by a reappraisal of the work of the Russian psychologist, Vygotsky, has highlighted the fact that these cognitive mechanisms are generated in a social context. Learners interact with other people as they are learning, which not only provides a richer source of input, but also makes possible particular kinds of learning. It is a noticeable fact that groups collaborating on a particular problem can often achieve results which none of their members could have achieved individually. This works with groups of adults as well as groups of children. During this collaboration the groups are constructing what might be termed a shared consciousness, which outstrips each of their individual consciousnesses. Following the collaboration they each take away a substantial part of this shared consciousness as their own learning.

A variation on this learning takes place when a learner works on a problem alongside a more advanced partner (an adult or more developed child). Here again the learner can operate at a superior level to individual capacity by 'borrowing' understanding from the partner. The partner provides a kind of prop, or 'scaffolding', for the learner's understanding. Vygotsky, and others building upon his ideas, argued that this borrowed understanding was a necessary precursor to later individual understanding. 'What a child can do in collaboration today, he can do by himself tomorrow.' The gap between individual functioning level and collaborative functioning level, the so-called 'zone of proximal development', is the area with the most productive teaching potential.

This emphasis upon the social character of learning has, of course, major implications for the teaching of language and literacy, the most obvious of which is the importance of collaborative work and discussion. Working together is seen as more than merely a context for enhancing learning: collaboration is itself learning. Groups of children in discussion are actually learning as they attempt to articulate their ideas to share them with others, as we outline in Chapter 1. Less obvious, but equally important, is the support a social view of learning gives to so-called 'apprenticeship' approaches to the development of literacy. In ＿＿＿ work alongside more experienced ＿＿ the

in isolation, ＿＿ ＿＿＿ it makes far more sense to treat them ＿＿＿＿＿ , therefore has become to look for parallels between the processes. Work on reading and listening has emphasised their similarities as receptive language processes; the role of oracy in the acquisition of literacy has begun to be studied; the links between reading and writing have been emphasised to such an extent that it is now normal to see them referred to as 'literacy'. In Australia, New Zealand, the United States and, more recently, in this country, a great deal of attention has been given to a philosophy of language teaching generally referred to as 'whole language'.

In this book we try to take a holistic approach to literacy and language learning and continually stress the links between processes and the cross-curricular nature of development. This latter aspect we discuss specifically in Chapters 8 and 9.

As we mentioned earlier, the literacy and language field is a vast one and no single volume can provide all the insights needed by teachers or students in training. Although we attempt as comprehensive a treatment as possible, an important aspect of the book is the presence of detailed notes to each chapter, giving extra points of interest, references to the source of ideas and research, and suggestions for further reading. Each chapter also has several suggestions for follow-up activities, usually classroom-based, which we hope will take readers on in their understanding of the issues raised in each chapter.

The book begins with a discussion of the role of talk in the classroom, especially the place of group discussion. In Chapter 2 we step back and look at language as a phenomenon in its own right, in particular the issues of language variation and awareness and the implications these have for teaching. In Chapter 3 we examine a central feature of whole language approaches, the place of story and children's literature. Chapters 4 and 5 look at the very earliest stages of literacy development, first linking this with the acquisition of language and then moving on to consider the initial teaching of literacy in schools. Chapters 6 and 7 discuss the central processes of literacy, the teaching of reading and writing. They both attempt to consider the processes involved in some detail before going on to look at classroom procedures and the role of the teacher. Chapters 8 and 9 take literacy out into the rest of the curriculum and discuss ways of developing it across the primary curriculum and as part of integrated project or topic work. Chapter 10 considers the place of new technology in language and literacy teaching, and Chapter 11 attempts to unravel some of the complex issues involved in assessment before suggesting some approaches to the assessment which is certain to occupy a much more central place in teachers' lives as a result of the introduction of the National Curriculum. We conclude by outlining some of the chief themes which emerge from our treatment of the extremely wide area of language and literacy development.

### Relating to the National Curriculum

The following chart details the relationships between the chapters in this book and the National Curriculum Programmes of Study as specified in *English for ages 5 to 16*:

| Chapter | National Curriculum Programmes of Study (References to D.E.S. 1989b) |
|---|---|
| 1 Talk in the classroom | 15.26–15.29, 15.33–15.34. |
| 2 Celebrating language diversity | 15.30, 15.34, 16.29, 17.43. (See also Chapters 4, 5 and 6) |

# Chapter 1

# Classroom talk

## INTRODUCTION

The National Curriculum for English makes it clear that reading and writing are no longer to be the sole focus of concern for primary teachers. Speaking and listening, for a long time neglected aspects in the teaching of language development, are given equal importance with the traditional first two Rs.[1] In assessing children's achievements in English at ages 7 and 11 all three profile components – Reading, Writing, and Speaking and Listening – are given equal weighting. In many respects this represents a considerable challenge to primary school teachers who, while generally running more talk-orientated classrooms than their secondary colleagues, have, in the main, given little real concentration to the role and development of oracy in these classrooms. Yet by the age of 11 (level 5 in National Curriculum terms) children will be expected to be achieve a series of attainment targets including:

1 Give a well-organised and sustained account of an event, a personal experience or an activity.
2 Contribute to and respond constructively in discussion or debate, advocating and justifying a particular point of view.
3 Use transactional language effectively in a straightforward situation.
4 Plan and participate in a presentation.
5 Talk about variations in vocabulary between different regional or social groups.

For teachers to achieve these things will demand two things of them. First, it will demand that they have some understanding of how oracy develops, its role in learning, and possible strategies for assisting this development. Second, it demands that teachers provide opportunities for children to develop their speaking and listening. This chapter is intended to give some guidance on both these issues. We cannot pretend, however, that the development of classrooms which foster oracy is unproblematic.

The major problem with a curriculum in which children achieve much of their learning through talking is that it produces classrooms which do not conform to many people's (teachers included) stereotypes of what a good classroom should be like. The picture of a 'good' classroom which most non-teachers and many teachers have is one where children get on with their work in as quiet an atmosphere as possible (they concentrate better that ... ... ... place it is closely controlled by the

... ...
lot were noisy this morning, Miss Smith. I nearly came ... ... ... them a talking to, only I saw you were with them.'

The problem with this picture of classrooms is that the underlying view of talking that it embodies is negative. Talk is unavoidable, but really the less there is of it, the more real learning will take place. The National Curriculum (and an almost overwhelming weight of evidence and theoretical argument) makes it essential that teachers give talk a much more prominent role in their classrooms than this.[2]

The chapter begins by examining the role of talking in the learning process, before going on to examine some of the salient features of talk in classrooms. The central part of the chapter concentrates upon group talk and its organisation, and we conclude by examining the corollary of talk, the even more neglected listening.

## TALK IN THE LEARNING PROCESS

What does talk actually do for us? Or, more exactly, what do we do with talk? The common-sense answer to this question is that we use talk to communicate with other people. In this view of talk it is the message which is important, and the talk itself is simply a vehicle. While talk obviously does have this function, it is unlikely to be quite as 'transparent' as the description would suggest. Talk is more than a vehicle. To see this more clearly we can examine some instances in which talk is used.

*Example 1:*
Two women are walking along a street and pass each other. The following exchange takes place: 'Good morning. How are you?' 'I'm fine, thank you. How are you?' 'Oh, fine, thank you.'

*Example 2:*
A man gets into his car on a frosty morning. He tries to start the car, but it refuses, making laboured sounds. He begins to talk: 'Oh start, damn you! Come on! Oh goodness, what a useless heap of metal!'

*Example 3:*
One man is explaining to another how an event happened. He says: 'Well, we were walking along the path. I saw this lad in the field. Goodness knows how he got there. I suppose he could have climbed the gate, but... no. The gate was covered in barbed wire. He must have got through the fence somehow. Perhaps there's a gap.'

On the face of it, Example 1 looks like an instance of communication, but what actually has been communicated? The exchange is so ritual it is unlikely that either of the participants really thinks about what she says. Either of them might have been suffering from minor illnesses, but still have said the same things. The function of their talk was not to communicate anything in particular, but simply to interact socially. This interactive function operates a great deal more often than we might think. Sometimes, as in this example, it replaces the communicative function. More often, it accompanies it . We regularly use phrases in conversation such as, 'Well, you know...', 'Really? Well I never!' and so on, which carry little message but do act to maintain the social relationship between speakers.

It would be difficult to argue that Example 2 showed communication (unless we assume some malicious intelligence in the car). The talk here is serving the function of emotional expression, and it is interesting that talk is used universally to 'let off steam' in this way. This expressive function is seen equally in conversation. Given the many ways speakers could choose to phrase their messages, the exact phrasing they do choose reflects elements of their feelings towards what they are talking about.

In Example 3 there clearly is some communication, with a message being passed between the speakers. But something else is happening here as well. The speaker has come to a conclusion about something as he is speaking. At the end of his speech he knows something he did not know at the beginning. This is characteristic of a great deal of talk, and is a feature which can completely change our view of learning. It suggests that talking about something is a way of learning about it. If learning is seen as ͏the modification of existing ways of conceiving the

when we discuss issues with other people. We rarely come to those discussions with our ideas fully formed and rehearsed. Instead, we take note of what others say and reshape our ideas in the light of others' contributions. To discuss is to think, and through the effort of 'thinking on our feet' we develop our ideas. In other words, we learn. The process also occurs when we teach. Many teachers will testify that the first time they really understood some things was when they tried to explain them to children. The act of trying to express ideas clarifies them.

Of the four functions of talk we have discussed, the communicative, the social, the expressive and the learning, it is the latter whose importance has tended to be the most underestimated in the past. Yet its potential is enormous.

To examine these functions of talk in action, let us look at the following extract from a classroom conversation in which a class of 6 year olds discuss with their teacher a bird's nest they have outside their classroom.[4] The teacher opens the conversation.

1  Teacher: I've got something to tell you. Mr Jackson found the shell of one broken egg on the ground the other day. [Cries of Ah!

Oh!] And he thought, 'There's one baby bird, because here's the shell that's broken now.' Mr Jackson thought there was only one baby bird, but really there are ...?

2  Pupil: Three.

3  Teacher: Three babies. How do you know there are three?

4  Pupil: Because I saw all their heads pop up.

5  Teacher: What did we see yesterday?

6  Pupil: All their heads popped up. And they all made a noise. And they all went... and two went down. No. One went down and... they both they stayed up... And for a little while they both popped down again.

7  Teacher: And when they popped their heads up, what did they do? Can you tell us about it, Gary?

8  Gary: When I was at home, I saw this egg. And it was broken. And there was a little baby bird laying there dead.

9  Teacher: Yes. They sometimes fall out of the nest don't they?

10  Pupil: What?

11  Gary: The egg was broken.

12  Pupil: What happened?

13  Gary: The egg was broken. It must have been the bird was out. And he fell on the ground and was dead.

14  Pupil: It must have been cracking open. It must have rolled over and he must have fell.

15  Pupil: I know. A cat must have had it.

16  Teacher: Who else has got something to tell us about our bird? Lise?

17  Lise: When I was going out in my garden, I went on this slide and... and this... I was going down the slope. And I heard birds whistling. And I looked on the seat where you sit to slide down... and I saw a bird's nest. It had six eggs in it 'cos it was a great big one... and I saw a bird sitting on 'em.

18  Pupil: Was it a pigeon?

Talk is clearly being used here for communication. The class are talking about something they share, and passing on their individual insights into the event. They respond to each other's contributions and ideas, as when two children react to Gary's story about the broken egg (14, 15). They ask each other questions and give each other answers. The teacher has created an environment in which individual contributions are valued and children listen to each other's ideas. The talk is thus also serving the social function of encouraging co-operation and sharing. It is also expressive of the children's attitudes towards its subject, from the overt Ahs and Ohs when they learn of the broken egg, to the underlying message of regret in the tone of Gary's 'There was a little baby bird laying there dead' (8).

In terms of learning, the extract illustrates several interesting processes. First, there are a couple of examples of children thinking aloud in their talk; creating their own knowledge as they express ideas. In (6) the child is not only recalling experience, but shaping and clarifying it through talk. Lise, in her long speech (17), seems to sharpen up her story as she tells it, producing some very precise descriptions – 'I looked on the seat where you sit to

... ... ... ... ... ... ... ... planned in detail before the children

as definitive as might be implied by the use of ...... , more like suggestions of possibilities. The children offer up potential solutions to the problem posed by Gary of how the egg was broken, which again indicates that they are engaging with the ideas and attempting to contribute to them.

A final feature of this extract, which is a powerful indicator of learning, is the role of anecdotes. Both Gary (8) and Lise (17), when asked by the teacher to comment on the school bird, prefer instead to tell a story about their experiences out of school. This 'talking at a tangent' is typical of children of this age (and indeed of most children if left to talk unsupervised) and is often thought by their teachers to be undesirable because it takes them off the point. It can, however, be itself seen as a learning process. If the definition of learning given earlier (the expansion and modification of existing ways of conceiving the world in the light of alternative ways) is accepted, it suggests that a crucial element is the linking of new experience with previously held ideas. Anecdotes which are sparked off by new ideas represent precisely the places where this linking is taking place. The teller, by telling an anecdote, is showing where his or her personal links are.

Learning is an idiosyncratic process; different learners make the links in different ways and at different points. It is difficult, therefore, for teachers to be aware of the learning needs of individuals *unless* they listen carefully to the anecdotes which new ideas set off.

This is only a very brief extract. The processes referred to above happen all the time in discussion. All of them have implications for learning and together they suggest that teachers need to give very careful consideration to the place of talk in their classrooms. But what are the typical characteristics of talk in classrooms?

## TALK IN CLASSROOMS

The most obvious characteristic of the talk which takes place in classrooms is that it is different from that which takes place outside school. Teachers often feel this very keenly and, although 'talking like a teacher' can have its advantages in conflict situations, it can also produce adverse reactions in non-school settings. 'Teacher talk' has been satirised, and while Joyce Grenfell's speaking style is clearly an exaggeration, it contains sufficient truth to embarrass many teacher listeners.

Children, likewise, tend not to talk in classrooms in the same way as they do outside. They may be asked to produce a more completed style of speech, and they will almost certainly devote a good deal of their talking time to the answering of questions posed by the teacher. Some studies have suggested that up to two-thirds of children's talk in classrooms tends to be of this kind.[5]

For both children and teachers, talking in classrooms seems to be an activity which is governed by sets of rules. It has been referred to as the 'language game of teaching', which implies, as in any game, a rule-governed system of actions.[6] Of course, in the case of classroom talk, it is unlikely that any of the participants can explicitly describe what the rules are, in the same way that no user of language can fully describe the grammatical rules of that language. The important fact is, though, that participants act *as if they knew the rules*. It is comparatively rare for users of language, or talkers in classrooms, to break the rules which pertain to that activity. What are the rules of classroom talk, and how do classroom participants come to know them?

The second part of this question is fairly easy to answer. Participants learn the rules of classroom discourse by engaging in the game. This process seems to begin very early on in children's school careers. Marked differences have been found between the kinds of discourse children engage in with their parents at home and with their first teachers in nursery and infant schools.[7] The fact that these teachers have responsibility for managing not one but, perhaps, thirty children's attempts to contribute to classroom discourse is probably sufficient explanation for the early dominance of teachers as they attempt to establish working procedures in the classroom.

Teachers gradually persuade children to answer to their names at register time and to sit quietly while others answer to theirs (probably the more difficult feat); to speak when they are ⸺ ⸺ ⸺ hands when they have something to

generally be ignored and appropriate behaviour ⸺⸺ example, when there is a clamour of children wanting to speak at once the teacher may say, 'Oh Jamie, there's a good boy sitting quietly with his hand up. What do you want to tell us?', which hopefully has the effect of getting the rest of the group also to sit quietly with their hands up.

Teachers, then, initiate children into the language game from the very beginning. Usually, by the time these children reach the junior school, they have internalised the rules and are full players in the game. These rules, by and large, are universal, although they vary in the rigidity with which they are enforced. They consist of rules about the context of classroom talk and rules about its content. In terms of context, the following things seem generally to be true:

(a) Teachers decide who will speak and for how long.
(b) Teachers plan and run the system by which those who wish to speak can have the opportunity to do so. This is usually the 'hands-up' system, although teachers have the power to bypass this, for instance by asking children without their hands up.

(c) Teachers have the final say over the acceptability of particular contributions. They can indicate their approval, or lack of it, verbally or non-verbally.

(d) Teachers can alter any of the rules at their discretion. They may, 'for instance, allow greater freedom of talking in certain lessons (e.g. art), or on certain occasions (e.g. discussion times).[9]

The rules about the content of talk can be deduced from an examination of the salient features of classroom talk. We shall do this by looking closely at an extract from an R.E. lesson given to second-year junior children. As with all extracts, it can be argued that this does not present a typical picture, which is probably true (anti-semitism is not a normal feature of R.E. lessons), but from the point of view of the patterns of talk, it illustrates several features which are suggested by research studies.

In the extract the teacher is dealing with the biblical story of Jericho.

1 Teacher: What happened to Jericho?... David Smith?

2 Pupil: It was put on fire.

3 Teacher: It was put on fire. Yes, what before it was put on fire?

4 Pupil: The walls of Jericho fell down.

5 Teacher: The walls of Jericho fell down. We don't know if it was because of all the movement around the outside (Where's your R.E. book?) causing the foundations to shake and everybody... was everybody put to the sword? Jones? Was everybody killed?

6 Pupil: No, sir.

7 Teacher: Well who, or whom, was not killed?

8 Pupil: Rahab and her family.

9 Teacher: Rahab and her family. Why wasn't she killed? Lisa?

10 Pupil: Because she had helped the spies to escape.

11 Teacher: Because she had helped the spies to escape. Right, how did they know... which house to go into? Rebecca? Rahab's house (that's a maths book. An orange one.) Ian Morgan.

12 Pupil: Er, she had, they saw scarlet ...

13 Teacher: A red ribbon or a scarlet ribbon. (Bailey... Go and get one) Right, and who was the leader now, of the Israelites? Because Moses had died, and who was it now?

14 Pupil: Joshua.

15 Teacher: Joshua. So we're now onto Joshua and the Hivites.. H..I..V..I..T..E This is another tribe of people, another tribe of

people in the promised land. Though God had promised Canaan to be the promised land (Will you listen please, Simon Evans?) Though God had promised Canaan to the Israelite people, there were other people living there, Joanne Griffiths, so they'd to get rid of the other people first or live in harmony with them. What does living in harmony with them mean? Simon?

16 Pupil: Peace, sir.

17 Teacher: Living in peace, yes. And we know all about the Israelites. They weren't a peaceful sort of nation. They were a nation of what, Jones?

18 Pupil: Moaners.

19 Teacher: Moaners, yes. We used to call Robert Jones one of the
        ⸺ ⸺ ⸺ ⸺ Christmas A nation of moaners. If they were told

than a few seconds, and they only speak when they ⸺ ⸺ ⸺ do so.

The teacher's talk consists of three types of utterance, and, in this extract, is divided roughly equally between them. He spends some time telling the class things. This 'lecturing' occurs mainly in his longest speeches (5), (15) and (19), and functions as an information-adding device to develop the lesson. It is not his only strategy for doing this. An alternative strategy he uses is to ask questions. Every one of the teacher's speeches contains one or more questions (apart from the last, which actually continued into a question in the original). These questions provide the pupils' only ways into the dialogue, as they answer his questions, and each of them is a 'display' question, that is, a question asked not because the teacher wants to know the answer, but because he wants to know if the children do.

The third type of utterance he produces is to repeat the pupils' answers, which he does on every occasion, even, in (13), anticipating the answer the child will give. This repetition has the function of evaluating their answers. There are no examples in this extract of pupils getting answers wrong, but if there were, it is likely that the teacher's tone of voice would indicate unacceptability. The tone he uses here indicates he accepts the answers given. He is therefore providing the children with feedback on their responses to his questions.

This pattern of discourse is the one most commonly found in classrooms from infant schools to sixth forms. It has been given various names such as Solicitation – Response – Reaction, or Initiation – Response – Feedback, or, because of its characteristic to-and-fro nature, 'verbal ping-pong'. The cycle consists of three 'moves', typically:

(a) The teacher asks a question.
(b) A pupil volunteers an answer.
(c) The teacher evaluates that answer.[10]

Because in every cycle of discourse the teacher speaks twice for each child utterance, it provides a good explanation for another well-documented finding: the so-called two-thirds rule.[11] This rule states that:

> Two-thirds of classroom talk is done by the teacher,
> Two-thirds of this talk consists of asking questions.

This rule could be extended by a further statement, well illustrated in this extract:

> Two-thirds of teacher questions demand only recall.

The fact that all the teacher's questions in this extract are of this kind suggests a particular view of learning. According to this view, children, in order to learn a body of material, have to be taken through it in an orderly sequence (determined by the teacher, who already knows the material). They are 'taught' by a combination of lecturing and questioning which draws them through the desired sequence. The answers they give to the teacher's questions indicate whether or not they are 'following' the lesson. This approach to teaching and learning has been given the name 'transmission' because of its underlying view that knowledge resides outside of children and has to be transmitted inside them by the teacher. Because this knowledge is held to be an objective entity it should be transmitted in as unaltered a state as possible, feedback on which is provided by children's answers to questions.[12]

It will be appreciated that this view of learning contradicts that put forward earlier in this chapter. If we conceive of learners as active constructors of their own knowledge, we see the unlikelihood of learning proceeding through the wholesale adoption of constructions of knowledge which have been formulated by other people. Learners have to make sense of knowledge for themselves, and to do this they need the opportunity to explore, interpret, and come to terms with new information. Transmission teaching does not provide these opportunities, because it has a completely different view of the role of children's talk.

One further feature of the talk in this extract is worth pointing out because it is typical of classroom talk, no matter what view of

the teacher holds. This concerns the

characteristics of individual children and relating

lesson topic. None of this would make sense unless the class had already developed ways of thinking together, in this case almost shared jokes.

The example here is not very praiseworthy (to say the least), but it illustrates a process at work in all classrooms. All classes develop shared reference points which unite them as a class. Often the teacher will be party to these. They may take the form of routines, class jokes, habitual activities or ways of going about things. They are not imposed upon the class, although the teacher might try to do this in certain instances, for example, work routines. Rather, they are arrived at through negotiation between the class and the teacher, and the chief means of that negotiation is, of course, talk.[13]

The picture of classroom talk we have given so far seems, perhaps, rather negative. There are, of course, good reasons for the predominance of the patterns we have described. Teachers do not have the luxury of prolonged periods when they can engage in productive discussion with individual children. They have to manage large numbers of children, all of whom have needs, and one way of coping with this is to structure talk exchanges to a large degree. Teachers are also, as in the case of the teacher whose lesson we have just dissected, often under the pressure of having to 'get through' a prescribed syllabus in a limited time. As a response to this pressure, tight structuring of lesson content seems to save some time.[14]

However, a further cause of the under-use of talk as a learning medium may simply be a lack of awareness on the part of teachers of the possibilities. In the following section we shall examine some of the ways in which group talk might be used more productively in the primary classroom.

## TALKING IN GROUPS

In the light of what has already been said, it will be clear that, although exploratory talk is an important context for learning, it is extremely difficult to allow sufficient space for it in whole class discussion. There will simply not be the time for individual children to engage in sufficient exploratory talk for it to make a difference. Because of this pressure, a teacher keen to involve children in exploratory talk will almost certainly make use of some form of group activities. There are certainly plenty of benefits to be gained from group talk, that is, talk between a small group of children who are working together to solve a joint problem or make joint decisions.[15]

Engaging in this kind of group talk can give children the opportunity, first of all, to express tentative ideas and explore them in a sympathetic context. Because the group are working together and not competing for scarce speaking rights, there is less pressure on them to express only fully worked-through ideas. They have the chance to put forward tentative ideas for others in the group to support, modify or argue with. Several things follow from this. In this context children are collaborating with others rather than competing against them. Much of children's school experience will emphasise competition at the expense of co-operation, and many children, in fact, find it difficult to collaborate. Yet modern society requires citizens who can work as teams. Group work is the first step towards this.

In the context of group talk, children are forced to justify their opinions and ideas, which encourages greater reflection upon them. They can also learn to have greater confidence in their own ideas. Most people, even adults, are far more confident about expressing their ideas in front of a small group rather than a large one, especially if that small group has some sympathy with these ideas because they are all working on the same problem.

Although group talk gives children common reference points, it also brings together a range of backgrounds and perspectives. Having to work with people who see things from different points of view, and who may have different cultural backgrounds and experiences, can in itself bring about a widening of children's views of the world. It also forces children to take into account the needs of their audience as they express their ideas in talk. Egocentricity can be lessened by the need to take others' ideas into
`⋅ --- ⋅ʰⁱⁿ⅁ˢ` from others' points of view.

## ORGANISING GROUP TALK

There are various ways in which group talk can be organised. In this section we shall discuss some possibilities, first for structured group talk activities, and then for building group talk into other activities. In all these activities our idea of a group is from three to six children, who may either be voluntary members or be placed together by the teacher.

Most structured group talk activities will be linked to particular tasks, although the relationship may vary.

### Defining tasks

Children can be asked to work together to define and to set tasks, for themselves and for others. Some examples of this are as follows:

*Brainstorming.* A group explore together the possibilities in a particular topic. They begin by sharing whatever ideas they each have about the topic, while one of them tries to write down the ideas as they are generated. When several ideas have emerged, the group sorts them out, categorising them, rejecting many and adding new ideas in the process. This technique may be used at the beginning of a class or group project, or as the starting point for group composition of a story or other piece of writing.

*Planning.* A group decides on how they will tackle a particular task, for example, a science experiment. They aim to produce a checklist of 'things to do' which they can use to guide the subsequent activity. In their discussion they anticipate likely problems as well as deciding on a course of action.

*Question-setting.* A group sets some questions for another group to work on. These might range from a list of questions about a text the group have read, to a quiz about a particular topic.

## Directing tasks

Children can be asked to work together to direct and monitor the tasks in which they are engaged. They may, for instance, be involved in:

*Allocating roles.* Having worked out the extent of a particular task, the group works together to allocate particular responsibilities. They might, for example, be engaged in a project and allocate parts of the work to smaller sub-groups. Or they might be producing a piece of collaborative writing, for example, a newspaper, and allocate each other roles such as art editor, proof reader, etc.

*Consultancy.* A group might be designated as consultants for particular activities, ranging from art work to the use of the computer. Other children come to them for help. The consultant's role is to help others carry out their tasks, *not* do the tasks for them.

## Accompanying tasks

There are many tasks which are best done co-operatively, for example:

*Problem-solving.* The old adage that 'two heads are better than one' is certainly true in problem-solving. If groups of children are given problems to work on, for example, mathematical or scientific investigations, they will get a great deal of practice in shared clarification of the problem, discussion of possible solutions, and joint evaluation of these solutions.

*Working on texts.* There are a number of activities in which groups of children can work together on texts. Several of these, such as cloze procedure and sequencing, will be discussed more fully in Chapter 8. Other possibilities are group discussion of questions set about a text and group generation of questions for other groups to answer.

Group discussion can also be centred around other for example:

*Peer-reviewing.* A group can be asked specifically to evaluate and comment upon each other's work. In this kind of activity the emphasis should be upon constructive criticism, and most groups will need some help in doing this to begin with. Probably the best form of help is for the teacher to join the group and model constructive criticism for them. A demonstration is usually more effective than explanation alone.

*Redrafting.* One particular peer-reviewing activity may centre around collaborative writing. If members of the group bring first drafts of pieces of writing they are under way with, their friends can help them revise and redraft these pieces. Again, children involved in this activity will need to be made aware of the importance of constructive criticism.

### Unstructured activities

There are many other ways in which group talk can be arranged on a more informal basis, not linked to particular set tasks. There is a place for it in most classroom activities, in fact, from science investigations to art work. During activities like this children can be given the opportunity to:

(a) explore issues, putting forward tentative ideas for comment by their peers and thinking aloud as an accompaniment to their actions,
(b) compare experiences, seeing common ground between them or becoming more aware of different perspectives,
(c) share information, as they each communicate their own idiosyncratic knowledge and experience,
(d) express and share pleasure and other emotions, as they react to activities in their individual ways.

### Talk in project work

One of the most productive curriculum areas for the development of group talk is that variously known as project, topic or thematic work. This is because this kind of work invariably involves times when groups of children are working together upon particular activities, be it research in library books, making a display, writing a pamphlet or other such tasks. We discuss the way project work can be developed as a context for the development of literacy in Chapter 9, but here we shall concentrate upon the opportunities it provides for group talk.[17]

We shall assume a group work structure to the organisation of the project; that is that, after the class as a whole has discussed the project in general terms, particular areas are assigned to small groups to work upon. Thus in, for example, a project on cars, one group might decide to work on the History of Cars, another on How Cars Work, and another on Types of Cars. This organisational structure has the advantage of allowing children first to focus in on a less daunting area of research, and second to have an outlet for their particular interests.

One of the first jobs of each group, having decided upon an area of the project upon which they will concentrate, is to agree upon the actual work they will do and how it will be organised. This can be done with or without the teacher, although, if children have little experience of this kind of discussion, they may benefit from having a teacher model appropriate kinds of talk for them. This talk will include brainstorming (as a way of generating ideas), exploration of links between ideas, negotiation of precise responsibilities, planning of activities and, above all, the establishment of commitment among the participants to these planned tasks.

Whilst the project is under way, if the groups are genuinely collaborating, there will also need to be regular discussion between them. This is in addition to the inevitable talk which takes place between members of a group as they pursue tasks together: ··-- ··--- each other's ideas; exploring ideas together;

responding to questions. Uuici iiiciii.... and make helpful comments or criticisms on the work which has been done, offer their own ideas to support, extend or contradict those they hear, and discuss how the work of the group as a whole is progressing and fitting together. It is particularly valuable if children ask questions of their peers (beyond the straightforward factual questions such as 'What did you do then?') Questions which demand in response explanation ('Why did ...?'), speculation ('What if ...?') and exploration of ideas ('What does this mean?') seem to give rise to significant learning, both in the children who try to answer them and those who are grappling with ideas enough to ask them.

This kind of talk is only more formal in the sense that it may require the earmarking of particular sessions in which it can take place. Perhaps once a week the group can be asked to spend some time on a review session, which the teacher can attend even though contributing only when specifically asked to. This session can also be valuable rehearsal time for other regular 'sharing' sessions at which groups discuss their work so far with the rest of the class.

Other kinds of talk involved in a typical project can be listed as follows:

1 Discussion in order to ascertain what they already know about the subject.
2 Discussion to bring children's previous knowledge about a topic to the forefront of their minds.
3 Negotiation to produce a set of feasible goals and to organise their project. The give and take of negotiation can be quite difficult for primary children.
4 Sustaining arguments and putting forward reasons and evidence for particular points of view.
5 Brainstorming as a way of generating ideas.
6 Commenting upon each other's ideas. Learning to be sensitive to other people's feelings.
7 Exploring ideas together.
8 Sharing and commenting upon resources.
9 Jointly composing notes, stories, factual writing, etc. (We discuss collaboration in writing in Chapter 7).
10 Informing colleagues about the work done.
11 Outlining immediate future plans.
12 Responding to questions.
13 Asking questions of peers which demand explanation, speculation and exploration of ideas.
14 Asking questions of visitors.
15 Reporting back to the rest of the class.
16 Presenting work to other audiences such as other classes or parents.

Because of this range of possibilities it can readily be seen that project work has a great deal of potential as a context for purposeful talk.

## DEVELOPING LISTENING

An obvious corollary of talking is listening. It is of little use creating an atmosphere in which talk can flourish as a learning medium if children do not listen to each other. Teachers often make the statement that their children do not listen very well, and this is usually blamed upon modern living conditions, in particular the presence of background radio and television. If this were true, of course, it would also be true that children in generations before television and radio were much better listeners, yet there is little evidence of this, in fact.[18]

The first problem in discussing listening is to decide what exactly we mean by it. The term is used in several ways, each with a different set of implications.

First, there are the physical aspects of listening. Listening can ˙ˉing able to hear, or being able to pick out changes in ⁓r being able to discriminate between sounds ˊ lotter combinations. Children who ˙ˉ need some attention, ˉˡᵈ be able to ˉˡ

Seconu, ˎ
Listening is usually uₒₛᵤ ˎ
some understanding of, and reaₒₒ
area in which teachers ought, perhaps, to ᵥ̲
effect in that the development of children's understa..
central part of their job. Understanding from listening does seem to have many parallels with understanding from reading, and in teaching it many of the same things apply. The first clear principle is that for anybody to begin to understand anything, they first have to consider it worth making the effort. In other words, children need to feel that things are worth listening to. It is not, of course, a sufficient guarantee of this that the *teacher* thinks that something is worth the children listening to.

Listeners also need, as in reading, to have a body of prior understanding into which they can fit incoming material. This previous knowledge has been described as a set of 'schemata', that is, ways of conceptualising the world, into which new information can be fitted, or which need to be restructured to take account of this information.[19] It can readily be seen that listening from this point of view is a very active mental process. It is probably not the case that children best engage in it by sitting passively 'absorbing' (hopefully) what they hear. It is more likely that this process needs to be made more interactive by allowing children to comment upon what they hear, to ask questions about it and to engage with it in other ways. It is not really fair to assess them as poor listeners on the basis of their responses to passively sitting while someone else, usually the teacher, does all the talking.

The third aspect of listening is its social dimension. Listening often takes place in a group situation in which participants must listen and respond to each other. This involves not only understanding what others say, but also making a contribution to the joint understanding of the group. It is easy for teachers to underestimate children's abilities to engage in this 'interactive' listening simply because it is difficult for teachers to allow group discussion to take place. As we pointed out earlier in this chapter, there are predominant patterns to discussions between teachers and children which include teachers generally making the lion's share of the contributions, and using these contributions mainly to ask questions. Even in small-group situations, teachers tend to adopt the same discourse patterns, and it may be that a more productive way of arranging these situations would be for teachers to withdraw and allow the children to run the discussion themselves. In these circumstances, and assuming they have an interest in the topic under discussion, most children will demonstrate an adequate capability in interactive listening. Teachers can help maximise their use of this capability by giving opportunities for the group to demonstrate their achievements through their discussion. This may take the form of the group arriving at a joint product, or being asked to explain their deliberations to an audience of classmates. Again, purpose is the key.

Finally, there is the aspect of listening which involves people's willingness to do it. Teachers refer to this when they complain that their children cannot 'pay attention'. As suggested above, this is not usually because children cannot listen, but rather that they do not want to. If children's interest is not engaged by what they are listening to, most of them will 'switch off'. This should not be surprising: adults do it all the time, as anyone who has sat through a boring speech can testify. The natural reaction to being bored is to think of, or do, something more interesting. It therefore falls to the speaker, or teacher, to ensure that material is presented in such a way as to make it more likely that the audience will find it interesting.

## CONCLUSION

There is clearly much more to be said about the place and the nature of speaking and listening in the primary classroom. From this brief review, however, several important points have emerged.

First, we hope we have brought out the crucial importance of oral language in the learning process. There are immeasurable benefits to be gained from a switch from transmission methods of teaching to a style which allows learners space to interpret material for themselves. Recent insights into learning suggest that we undervalue at our peril its shared, social aspects.[20]

Second we have tried to present group discussion and learning ⁓ for teachers who have to cater for the ⁓ point in

all the other issue return to it as we discuss matters cou⁓ without good reason that Speaking and Listening are given as the *first* attainment targets in the National Curriculum for English. None of the rest would be possible without them.

## FOLLOW-UP ACTIVITIES

1  It is interesting to make tape recordings of selected lessons, and use these to examine the kinds of talk children produce. Try recording ten minute excerpts from:

(a) a whole class discussion,
(b) a small group discussion with the teacher contributing,
(c) a small teacherless group discussion.

Do you notice any differences in the ways children talk in each of these situations?

You will obviously be able to analyse things in more detail if you transcribe the extracts, but be warned that transcription of children's talk (recorded under classroom conditions) is notoriously difficult.

2 For each curriculum area that you teach, try to list some possible ways in which small group discussion might be incorporated into your teaching. Try to ensure that the discussion is a central rather than peripheral part of the activities you suggest. This will probably necessitate groups working on collaborative tasks; that is, tasks with one shared end-product rather than several individual products.

3 Take a typical day's work in your classroom and try to list the opportunities children get during the day to

(a) talk and
(b) listen.

Choose at random five each of these opportunities and, for each, try to answer the following questions:

(a) Was the physical context appropriate to this activity?
(b) Did the children clearly understand the purpose of the activity?
(c) Do you think the children made any gains in terms of their abilities in talking and listening?

# Chapter 2

# Language diversity and language awareness

chapter we shall discuss language ~~.~~ ~~.~~ ,~
within English. We shall go on to make some general suggestions
for developing language awareness in primary-aged children.

## LANGUAGE DIVERSITY

The language variety used in the majority of public institutions in
the United Kingdom is almost exclusively Standard English. This
domination is historical in origin and, indeed, accidental. Had
Harold not succeeded in defeating the Norse invasion in 1066, for
example, (or had he succeeded in repulsing the Norman forces) it
is quite likely that the dominant form of language spoken in
Britain would have been quite different. Because of this
domination, however, it is very easy to make the assumption that
the United Kingdom is a linguistically homogeneous country. This
is, in fact, far from the truth. The majority of the population do not
actually use Standard English as their most common form of
spoken language, and in certain areas of the country there are
many schools where a significant proportion of the children do
not use English as their first language at home with their parents.

Language diversity is a fact of life and as teachers we need to take account of it in our responses to and development of the linguistic competence of the children in our care. To do this we need first to understand language variation. In what ways does language vary within Britain and within English itself? Second, we need to work out our positions on the issues which stem from this variation. If there is such variation within language, is it sensible to talk about 'correct' forms of language? If children do not have full mastery of particular forms are they by that token linguistically deprived? This section will therefore first outline the ways in which language can vary in modern Britain, and will then go on to explore issues such as correctness and deprivation.

## FORMS OF VARIATION

Language varies in four major ways. First, and most obviously, there is the variation between different languages as between French and Punjabi. It is quite common, and in some parts of the country normal, for teachers to have in their classes children who use English as their language only when at school, using other languages at home.  Second, there are variations due to dialect. Children brought up in Northumberland will use different words and different language structures from children brought up in London. If teachers are not familiar with these local uses then problems can easily arise.

Third, speakers may differ in the accent they use, such as a Geordie or a Scouse accent. Although such speakers use basically the same language, they may have difficulties in being mutually intelligible. Mutual intelligibility is essential for teachers and their classes.

Finally, and most commonly of all, language may vary in terms of register. We use different styles of speaking depending upon the social context in which we find ourselves, ranging from informal to formal.

We shall look in more detail at each of these forms of variation.

### Language

It is quite surprising to realise the range of different languages spoken by inhabitants of the United Kingdom. Although a complete national picture is hard to come by, such surveys as do exist suggest an extremely complex picture. The Inner London Education Authority language census, for example, announced in 1983 that 147 different languages were used by children who were at that time in London schools. The pattern of language use varies, as one might expect, across the country.[2]

Many children will speak more than one or two languages. As an example of this, consider some 8 year olds who were found in a primary school in Cardiff. These children were of Pakistani origin and spoke Gujerati at home and with some of their friends. On occasions at home, and at Saturday school, they learnt and spoke Urdu. They were also learning Arabic for religious purposes, although this was not used conversationally. At school they used

$\quad\quad\quad\quad\quad\quad\quad\quad$ of their friends, but, because they

largely because

which it was acceptable or expected.

Of course, this range of language experience is not common. Many children do, however, cope with two distinct languages on an everyday basis. Schools often view this as a problem, although it has to be remarked that this is sometimes simply a question of perception. Children who are reasonably fluent in English, French and German, say, are usually thought of as quite clever, although the same label is sometimes not applied to children who are reasonably fluent in English, Punjabi and Urdu. Children who cope, more or less successfully, with a range of linguistic demands really should be given credit for their achievements. We shall discuss ways of celebrating this language expertise and knowledge later in the chapter.

Perhaps the most important implication of this range of linguistic expertise among children attending British schools is that the teachers in these schools need at least to be aware of the range of languages their children have. This does not mean that teachers must themselves master this range of languages. This would be impractical. It does, however, mean that they should make themselves familiar with the linguistic backgrounds of their children. If this is done there is less likelihood of teachers underestimating children's capabilities, with consequent effects upon their levels of achievement in school.[3]

## Dialect

There are many regional variations within English itself and these dialects differ from one another in terms of the vocabulary and the grammatical structures they employ. Vocabulary differences caused by dialect can be a source of some confusion but also of a great deal of amusement.

Take the following words: stream, brook, beck, burn. One of these is likely to be the natural word you use to refer to a small river, but if you use your word in an area where the dialect term is different you are likely to cause some confusion and be thought of as 'posh' or just strange. There are many examples like this.[4]

A favourite dialect variant is the word used to describe the soft, usually white, shoes which children wear on their feet for indoor physical activities. In the South East these are usually called 'plimsolls', but such a word would be thought 'posh' in Lancashire, where they are known as 'pumps'. In Newcastle upon Tyne they are often called 'sandshoes', and in the South West 'daps', whereas in Barrow-in-Furness, in Cumbria, children call them 'galoshes', a word which means something completely different elsewhere in the country. And, of course, the word 'trainers' is increasingly being adopted nationwide for these shoes. It is easy to imagine the confusion caused when a teacher asks a class to put on their 'pumps' etc., when this is not *their* word!

Dialects also differ in terms of their grammatical structure, for example:[5]

*(a) Verb forms.* Some dialects use verb forms such as: 'I goes, you goes, he goes, we goes, they goes'. Others use: 'I go, you go, he go, we go, they go'.

*(b) Negation.* Many dialects use multiple negatives such as: 'I didn't get nothing'. Others regularly use 'ain't' or 'never' as a negative form, for example: 'It ain't there.' 'I never done it.'

*(c) Demonstrative pronouns.* Standard English 'those' is often replaced, for example: 'Can you see them birds?' 'Give me they pliers.'

The important thing to note about these forms is that they are regular and consistent, not haphazard and sloppy uses of English. This means that it would be inappropriate for a teacher to admonish a child who uses these forms for simply being 'wrong'. In the child's terms, these forms are 'right', because these are what he hears at home and consistently uses. There might be occasions when these forms are not appropriate, and it is this sense of appropriateness which the teacher needs to help children develop.[6]

Standard English itself is a dialect, which has developed from the form of English spoken around the administrative centre of the country in medieval times. Because of historical change there ... ... Standard English speakers may

proni... ...
had of said that...', which is a different respo... pronunciation (children have been writing it like this for a long time!). Standard English develops and changes, like any language, which makes notions of 'correctness' more difficult to maintain.

### Accent

Accent refers to variations in language due to pronunciation. Accents may be associated with particular dialects, but this is not necessarily the case. A speaker from Edinburgh and a speaker from Hereford may both use Standard English, but pronounce their words in different ways. It is probably true to say that differences between regional dialects have declined over the past 100 years, but accent differences show no sign of diminishing. Indeed, it is much more common for people in public life to use a regional accent than it was thirty or forty years ago. Accent has become a point of pride for many people, perhaps because it is an obvious means of signalling one's 'roots'.

It is still true, however, that different accents are perceived differently by people. The most prestigious is that known as

Received Pronunciation, or RP, an extreme form of which is spoken by members of the Royal Family. Like Standard English, this accent is sometimes considered as 'correct' English, although, in fact, it is spoken naturally by relatively few people. It is not a regional accent but is associated rather with social class. Its high status stems from this. Experiments have suggested, however, that this status is specific rather than general. Speakers using RP tend to be rated highly for competence, intelligence and industriousness, but regional accent speakers rated more highly for integrity, sincerity and good-naturedness.[7]

Teachers need to be aware of the characteristics of their pupils' accents. This is necessary for effective communication, but it may also help explain some of the difficulties some children may have. To take a simple example, a teacher with a South Eastern accent needs to know that her Northern pupils may have difficulty distinguishing between her pronunciation of 'cup' and 'cap'. In their accent these two words will be pronounced completely differently and will never be confused.

In another example, a teacher in a school in Reading asked her class to write a poem. In one of the children's poems the words 'spell', 'shall' and 'owl' appeared and it was clear that the child thought of them as rhyming words. The teacher was tempted to conclude that this child did not understand the idea of rhyme, until she heard him read his poem out loud. In his accent the three words *did* rhyme!

### Register

The final form of language variation is the most common of all. All of us make changes to the way we speak depending upon the social situation in which we find ourselves. We have several registers of language open to us and choose between them to suit a particular social context. These contexts vary chiefly in their degree of formality. When we visit our solicitor, for example, we are likely to use a different register of language than when we are relaxing with our friends. The language we use in these situations will vary in several ways:

(a) *vocabulary.*  we are more likely to use slang expressions, or word-approximations such as 'thingamy' in informal contexts.

(b) *syntax.*  in formal situations we are more likely to use Standard

English forms, whereas in informal situations we will probably use such forms as contractions ('can't', 'innit'), incomplete sentences, and dialect structures.

*(c) pace.* in informal situations we tend to speak fairly quickly, whereas in formal contexts we generally use a more measured pace.

The matching of register to situation is something most of us do without really thinking about it. We simply use language in the way which 'feels right'. This ability to sense appropriateness is clearly, however, learned from experience and we would expect speakers with more limited experience to be less skilled at it. This applies particularly to children. This suggests that one of the tasks of the introduced to a broad

that which is appropr

## ISSUES ARISING FROM VARIATION

### Is one variety superior to another?

Because of these wide variations between the forms of English it follows that, when people talk about 'correct' English, they are implying that there is one form which is inherently superior to all others. This form is usually Standard English, also variously known as 'Oxford English', 'BBC English', or, most tellingly, 'Queen's English'.

Arguments for this superiority usually take two lines. One is to link 'correct' speech with clear, logical thinking, and conversely, unstandard, 'sloppy' speech with illogical thinking. A second argument is that of social currency. Because Standard English can be universally understood it is far more useful than regional dialects, speakers of which often have difficulty making themselves understood outside their own regions. Of these two lines of argument, only one can be sustained.[8]

Linguists have demonstrated beyond dispute that all language varieties are rule governed and consistent systems. The idea that dialect speech is simply sloppy, or a corruption of Standard English, is negated by this fact. There is therefore little substance to the argument that non-standard speech indicates illogical thought. Non-standard speech is just as logical as Standard English. A much-quoted example of this is the so-called 'double negative' construction common in regional dialects of Britain, for example, 'I didn't do nothing'. For some people, this is worked out like an algebra equation, and two negatives make a positive. The phrase is thus 'illogical'. The use of double negatives might, however, be perfectly logical if the rule to which a speaker conforms is 'If you want to really emphasise negativeness, put in as many negatives as you can'. Examples of this kind of use are found in the work of Shakespeare and of other renowned users of the English language.[9]

It has also been shown that speakers of non-Standard English are quite capable of logical reasoning, and nothing about their language holds them back.[10] It is true, however, that some people, many teachers included, seem to believe that because children speak in a non-standard way, they have difficulties with logical thought. It is the *perception* of non-standard speech which is the problem, rather than its reality.

The argument is also weakened by the fact that language is never static, but constantly changing. Many language forms which would have been considered wrong twenty years ago are now in common use. We certainly do not these days get so upset about splitting infinitives ('to boldly go where no man has gone before') as we used to, and the form 'whom' has almost disappeared, at least from spoken language. Many grammatical 'rules' in which large numbers of people were drilled while at school have now changed beyond recall. Grammar is now thought of more in terms of a *description* of how people actually use language as opposed to a *prescription* for how they should.

The second argument has more force. It is true that to succeed in modern society, a person needs to have command of Standard English, because, as pointed out at the beginning of this chapter, all the institutions of society rely upon it. At some point in schooling, therefore, children do need to be taught to use Standard English. There are several reservations to this argument, however.

First, Standard English is first and foremost a *written* form of language. Although there are occasions when the spoken form is required, the chief emphasis in schools should be upon children's abilities to write Standard English. The recommendations of the National Curriculum support this by stating that primary school children should learn to produce and understand written Standard English, but only to understand spoken.[11]

Second, and perhaps most importantly, developing a command of Standard English does not imply a loss of command or a denigration of the language variety children bring from home. The language people speak is closely linked with their identities, and to give them the message that their language is inadequate or inferior is simply to imply that they themselves are inferior. The

language is that of appropriateness. The expert users are those who can choose the appropriate dialect or register for the situation. This implies that part of the school's job is to develop children's abilities to use language effectively in all situations, from streets and shops to courts and town halls. Developing this language awareness would seem to be a far richer goal for schools than the narrow aim of teaching the use of Standard English.

### Language deprivation

It has been consistently demonstrated that there is a link between social class and educational achievement. Middle-class children achieve more than working-class children at all levels of the educational system. The reasons for this situation have been under investigation for many years.[12] Twenty years ago the idea emerged that the chief reason for the underachievement of working-class children might be their lack of command of the language forms necessary to succeed in school. Ideas from the new discipline of socio-linguistics, in particular the work of the sociologist, Basil

Bernstein, were taken as support for this explanation.[13] Bernstein claimed that there existed two distinct language codes. One, the restricted code, was characterised by short sentences, lack of adjectives and adverbs and a dependence upon the immediate context for its understanding. The other, the elaborated code, had much longer, more formed sentences and could be understood independently of a context. This, so far, is not particularly contentious. The two codes correspond roughly to the formal and informal registers discussed above.

Bernstein, however, went further. He claimed that there was differential access to these codes depending upon social background. Although Bernstein was often misrepresented on this point, the idea gained currency that, whereas middle-class children had access to both codes and could use each in appropriate situations, working-class children tended only to have access to the restricted code. Because school conducted its business through an elaborated code, these working-class children were handicapped and found it much harder to succeed. The idea of linguistic deprivation or deficit was formed.

Theories such as these led to attempts to improve the success rate of working-class children by compensatory education programmes which involved a great deal of attention to language. Some of these programmes tried to teach Standard English to children in ways that paralleled the teaching of foreign languages.[14] The programmes had, however, little measurable success. This was largely because of several misconceptions upon which they were based.

The first problem was with the idea that the children were deficient in their linguistic ability. Work by many researchers has challenged this view and found that there is no shortage of verbal skill among working-class children.[15] The problem is that schools tend either not to provide the right environment in which these children can and will show their skill, or not to value the forms this skill takes. Other researchers have found that children whose language in schools consisted almost entirely of one-word answers to their teachers' questions, had an extremely rich language environment at home.[16] Schools were somehow failing to provide a similarly supportive environment and were thus underestimating the capabilities of their children.

A second problem with language compensation programmes was that they seemed to expect children to abandon the language of their homes in favour of the new forms they were being taught. This was very naive, and ignored the very close link between language and identity. To expect children to abandon their natural language is to expect them to abandon their definitions of what they are. Children, quite naturally, rebel against this.

The overall problem was, and to some extent still is, that schools account for the low success rate of some groups of children by blaming the children themselves, or their homes. Terms such as 'deprived' or 'deficient' imply that the fault is within the children rather than within the school. If, however, we argue that *all* children come to school speaking logically structured and fully formed varieties of language, then the problem is rather that the ᵗʰⁱˢ and does not plan its work to take

1 Schools and teachers should be aware of the varieties of language which their children bring to school with them. This involves listening to the children and discussing things with them, but it may also involve more sustained attempts to forge links with local communities and with parents.

2 Schools need to begin to work with their children as they are, rather than as they would like them to be. This means accepting that children bring a great deal of linguistic expertise to school with them and planning programmes to make the most of this. It also means attempting to create school and classroom environments in which children can feel confident that their language will be respected and is an appropriate vehicle for learning.

3 Schools should set themselves the goal of increasing the total language awareness of all their children. This means making language itself a much more prominent feature of classroom work.

These principles lead to the idea of schools positively celebrating the language diversity within them, rather than either ignoring it

it as a problem. Celebrating diversity can have a great
ial benefits as children begin to feel that their con-
to school life are important and valued. It can also have
many benefits in terms of the development of language com-
petencies. Children can be given opportunities to use language in
a wider variety of contexts and also to step back from their use of
language to talk about it as an important object in its own right.

Several possible starting points for this celebration in primary
classrooms are given below. We shall go on to suggest that these
activities also provide a useful basis for the development of general
language awareness.

## SOME LANGUAGE ACTIVITIES

### Songs and poems

There is a wealth of recorded folk music which, by its nature, tends
to use dialects and accents which may be unfamiliar to children.
This can be listened to as part of topic work, dialect expressions
discussed and children can try to imitate the accents.

Children might be able to find recordings of songs in their own
dialects or accents. They might also make their own recordings,
perhaps involving parents or grandparents.

Children might collect playground rhymes and compare these
with those used in other parts of the country or in other countries.
The Opie's book, *The Lore and Language of Schoolchildren* will be
useful for this.[18]

These suggestions can also profitably be used with children who
have community languages other than English. Parents will be the
best source of information.

### Writing systems

Children can make and display collections of alternative writing
systems, from Hieroglyphics and Ancient Greek to Urdu, Russian,
Hindi, etc. They could collect ways of writing familiar phrases such
as 'Good morning' in as many different languages and writing
systems as they can.

They can examine different writing systems for similarities and
find out how modern systems have developed.

Counting systems can also be examined from Roman numerals to modern Arabic numbers. Children can learn to count in different languages and dialects. (In the Cumbrian dialect 'one, two, three' becomes 'yan, tyan, tethera'. Several regional versions of this exist.)

Other communications systems can be examined and their uses discussed, for example, Morse Code, Braille, Semaphore, Romany signs, etc.

### Accents and dialects

Accents and dialects can be discussed directly using recorded
............ ⎯⎯⎯'ll be able to make recordings of their

⎯⎯⎯, ⎯ ⎯
particular things. Collecting words for pinisons, pumps, sandshoes might be a good place to start.

### Topic work

Many traditional primary school topics lend themselves to work on language. For example, 'Ourselves', 'Celebrations' and 'Communication' all have strong language dimensions.

Children might begin a collection of newspapers in various languages. These can be examined for similarities in form and content. They can produce their own newspaper to relate their findings.

Topics can be planned which look directly at aspects of language. For example, 'Language around the world', 'Language in our town', 'Writing', 'The development of English', etc.

Names can be a useful focus for language work. The names of the children in the class can be investigated. What do they mean and what are their origins? What do we mean when we say a person's name 'suits him'?

### Language without words

Children can investigate ways of communicating without the use of words. Pictures, mime, facial expressions, signs and signals are all ways into this.

Communications methods in pre-literate cultures might also be investigated, as well as animal communication systems.

### LANGUAGE AWARENESS

An important underlying feature of the National Curriculum requirements for English is a greater emphasis upon children's 'knowledge about language'. This is justified in the following way:

> Two justifications for teaching pupils explicitly about language are, first, the positive effect on aspects of their use of language and second, the general value of such knowledge as an important part of their understanding of their social and cultural environment.[19]

Few people would wish to argue with the second of these points since it is clear, and has been demonstrated earlier in this chapter, how central language is to individual and cultural identity. Understanding who we are involves understanding how we use language (and how language uses us).

The first argument is more controversial since many teachers are justifiably suspicious of the value of much traditional 'grammar' work in terms of its effect upon children's subsequent use of language. The National Curriculum documents, however, explicitly reject formal grammar teaching, preferring instead a much broader approach. They recommend that knowledge about language work should cover the following material:

*(a) Language variation according to situation, purpose, language mode, regional or social group*

This would cover the dialect, accent and register differences discussed above as well as the influences of context upon language and the differences between speech and writing. Work of this nature would, it is argued, make children more tolerant of linguistic variety and more aware of the richness of language.

## (b) Language in literature

This covers the use of language for particular stylistic effects, and the implication is that explicitly studying the way writers use language may enable children to incorporate a range of stylistic devices into their own writing as well as increasing their responsiveness to literature.

## (c) Language variation across time

This would cover the ways in which language usage, both grammatical constructions and vocabulary, change historically. ⸺ ⸺ the argument is that knowledge of this would make pupils

*meta-language.* This might ⸺ ⸺ traditionally associated with formal grammar teaching, such as phrase, sentence, verb or adjective, but would need to be wider than this since it would deal with language functions as well as forms. It would need, for example, to have ways of describing the difference between, 'I'm very sorry to disturb you, but I wonder if you would mind just moving your suitcase a little?' and 'I do wish you would move this. It's really in my way.' The need for this meta-language is highlighted by the inclusion in the National Curriculum of attainment targets such as the following (all at level 5):
    Pupils should be able to:
- Talk about variations in vocabulary between different regional or social groups,
- Talk about variations in vocabulary according to purpose, topic and audience and according to whether language is spoken or written,
- Recognise and talk about the use of word play and some of the effects of the writer's choice of words in imaginative uses of English.

## CONCLUSION

The most important consideration in any work on language diversity and awareness is to ensure that children's own languages and language varieties are given appropriate respect. The role of the school is to widen children's linguistic competence and appreciation of language. It is *not* to try to convince them that the way they speak is wrong. The language children bring with them into school is a resource to be built upon and we should never forget that acquiring this language is the greatest learning feat that any child ever accomplishes. Yet there is real scope for extending children's awareness of, and hence control over, the language they use and that which is used around them. If the argument is correct that increased awareness leads to an increased ability to use language, then explicit attention to the forms and functions of language should be a liberating rather than a restricting activity.

## FOLLOW-UP ACTIVITIES

1 Make a survey of some of the words used by children with whom you have contact which are not part of your normal dialect. This might include new words which the children acquire from television and other media. Consider whether familiarity with these words is  – essential
  – useful
  – unimportant
to you as these children's teacher.

2 If you have contact with children who have distinctive dialects get them to tape-record themselves telling familiar stories using their dialects. Are the children aware they are using dialect? Suggest that they might re-record the same stories but telling them in Standard English. Are they able to do this? This activity might tell you a good deal about the children's awareness of language.

3 Ask a group of children to transcribe an extract from a tape-recorded discussion they have had. Discuss with them the ways in which they can indicate in writing particular speech features such as emphasis, exclamation, querying. This can introduce a general discussion of the differences between speech and writing.

# Chapter 3

# Children's literature and the power of stories

is the paramount reason for learning to read. ~~~~
as to argue that a thriving literature is a prerequisite for a
developed civilisation.

In this chapter we shall examine the place of literature in the
curriculum of the primary school, and discuss strategies for
enhancing it. We shall begin by attempting a rationale for the
centrality of literature by discussing the value of stories and
storying. We shall then move on to discuss the criteria by which
teachers might choose literature, both stories and poems, for
children and we then air several issues which this selection raises.
We shall conclude by outlining some strategies for encouraging
the interactions with literature which are so important in
producing children who not only *can* read, but actually *do*.

## THE VALUE OF STORIES AND STORYING

All literate cultures have left evidence of the importance they have
attached to stories. There is also evidence that pre-literate cultures
also have put great emphasis upon stories and story-telling. Certainly the place of the story-teller was an exalted one in societies

prior to the advent of mass media, and even today, with so much competition from real-life information in newspapers and on television, the importance of fiction is barely disputed. Why is there this emphasis upon stories? What, in the context of primary schools, is the value of stories? We shall begin an answer to these questions by considering what stories can do for children, but firstly we should make the point that 'stories' are defined by both their forms and their content. Both these aspects have impact and any attempt to analyse the effects of stories must pay attention to this duality.[1]

It is certainly apparent that stories can teach children both about people and about 'things'. A great deal of the information we accumulate over the years is likely to have been acquired through stories rather than through factual statements. An example of this may be our knowledge of everyday life in Britain in Victorian times. We will have built up some of our picture of this from straight study of history, but for many of us, reading the novels of Dickens may be at the base of much of our knowledge. For children also, stories are likely to be a major source of information about many things.

Stories are also a way of allowing children to see things through others' eyes. Young children are naturally egocentric in their view on the world and often find it difficult to see things from other people's points of view. Stories will always be written from another point of view which children have to be able to adapt to. This broadens their perceptions of the world and helps them 'decentre'.

Stories also act by stimulating the reader's imagination. Because they deal with events beyond the here and now they encourage creative thinking without which it is difficult to respond to novel events. The imagination is stimulated by allowing the reader's mind to create pictures and impressions of people, places and events described in the story. Without these mental images the story cannot operate at all.

They also encourage readers to engage in predictive thinking; that is, throughout a story the reader is building up sets of impressions of what has gone before and predicting a series of ways in which events may proceed. These anticipations are continually being revised in the light of the unfolding story and the response of the reader can be seen as an interplay between anticipations and retrospections.[2] This process is of wide importance. Not only is it the process of reading a story, but it can be seen as characteristic of the reading process itself. As we discuss in Chapter 6, it is no longer tenable to see the reading process as a word-by-word, sequential series of perceptions. It is much more likely that it consists of an interactive exchange between symbols on the page, previous knowledge of the reader, and expectations which are continually revised as the activity proceeds. If this is so, then it may be, as several writers have argued, that children actually learn to read by reading stories.[3]

On a different level, stories may also allow children the opportunity to develop as people. They allow the exploration of problems children may be experiencing or may experience in the future, and this exploration is done at the safety of one remove. ～～～～～～～～ take comfort from stories about

～～～～ ～～ ～
are many stories in which characters race ιαιιιγ ～～～，～ ，～
such as going to the dentist, having a new baby brother, being afraid of the dark and so on. Experience with stories like these may help demystify these experiences for children. We do need to sound a word of caution here, however. The idea of children living out problems through stories has, in some quarters, been built up almost into a science – bibliotherapy, and we would not wish to go as far as the American librarian who, when asked to recommend a book for an adolescent boy, is reputed to have replied, 'Sure, what's his problem?'

This librarian obviously believed in a very direct relationship between stories and feelings. Undoubtedly there are times when stories do influence emotions, as there are when they change their readers' values and attitudes. Several people, for instance, claim to have altered their views about spiders as a result of reading *Charlotte's Web*! The link is, however, unlikely to be so mechanistic as to allow the prescription of stories for particular ailments. If it were true that reading stories always influenced people's values and attitudes for the better, then several of the best-known 'villains' in history would have been better people than they were!

One thing stories *do* allow is the vicarious experience of seeing others do things which you have always wanted to do but never quite dared. This is one of the features which appeals to children about Enid Blyton's famous characters. These children are shown in situations most children would love to be in, but know deep down they will never be able to be. Characters like *My Naughty Little Sister* and Max in *Where the Wild Things Are* also allow full rein to children's wish fulfilment. Exactly the same is happening when adults read fictional deeds of derring-do, etc.

Experience with stories can also assist the development of the use of language in several ways. It is fairly obvious that children, and indeed adults, extend their vocabulary through exposure to new words in stories. It has been suggested that children during the school years are acquiring new vocabulary at the rate of about twenty-five words per day.[4] Most of these words will not be picked up during conversation but through experience of reading and being read to.

Experience with stories also helps familiarise children with the language of books, which is distinct from the more usual language of speech. Take the following story beginning:

> The Iron Man came to the top of the cliff. How far had he walked? Nobody knows. Where had he come from? Nobody knows. How was he made? Nobody knows. Taller than a house, the Iron Man stood at the top of the cliff, on the very brink, in the darkness.

What starts off as ordinary language quickly develops a poetic quality which marks it out as literary and special. A child once wrote, 'Bigger than a bedroom, the dinosaur swung his head. Where were his friends? He did not know. Where was his home? He did not know. What should he do now? He did not know.' He had internalised the sentence structure and order, and the use of repetition from Ted Hughes' story and later made it his own. He had also learnt that book language operates to different rules than spoken language,[5] and used these rules in his own writing. This is obviously language development, but signifies something very important. The child has shown implicit recognition of the difference between speech and writing which will, in turn, allow him to apply a series of new expectations about how language is structured to his subsequent reading. Again the child is learning how to read through reading.

Of course, to be of maximum effect in this process, the language of the stories we offer to children needs to be of an appropriate quality. We gain nothing, and lose a lot, by attempts at simplification of the rich language of stories. To see the effects of this we need only look at two extracts. The first comes from the original version of Beatrix Potter's *The Tale of Peter Rabbit* (1987 edition, Frederick Warne).

> Peter gave himself up for lost, and shed big tears; but his sobs were overheard by some friendly sparrows, who flew to him in great excitement, and implored him to exert himself.

The second comes from a 1987 version of the story produced by ～～ ᵗʰᵉ cover as 'a delightful

development more closely to speech succeeds only in ᵈᵉˢᵗʳᵒʸⁱⁿᵍ rhythm and poetry of the original. 'Don't give in!' has nothing like the power of 'implored him to exert himself', besides not being likely to teach its readers any new word or expressions.

The effect of story language has an even wider implication than this, however. The fact is that stories, by their very nature, use language in a different way than it is used in everyday transactions. Instead of referring to objects and experiences within direct experience, stories involve reference to things outside the immediate experience of their readers. In so doing they form a bridge between the concreteness of the here-and-now and the abstraction of other ways of coming to know. To benefit from their education children must somehow make that link: education necessarily involves the treatment of abstract ideas. Experience with stories can help them in this. There is some evidence that it is experience with stories that is often the crucial factor in children's educational success.[6]

Stories in the primary school can also, of course, act as useful stimuli to work in a variety of curriculum areas. Much successful and valuable project work is either set in motion by the discussion of a story, or is illuminated when in progress by appropriate literature.[7] This needs to be done with some care, however, since it must be realised that literature is rarely written specifically as source material for project work. Each story has its own *raison d'être*, and care must be taken to ensure that its presentation does full justice to it.[8]

As a final justification for the place of stories in the primary school we must state a fact which probably should have been stated at the very beginning of our discussion, namely that stories are *fun*. In our concern to find complex justifications for the place of story, we are often in danger as teachers of neglecting the pleasurable aspects of stories. All teachers can testify to the immense pleasure which stories can give children. The vast majority of children, from the moment they enter school, love having stories read to them, and those for whom the introduction to reading is a pleasant experience also quickly realise the enjoyment they can get from reading stories themselves. Such enjoyment creates its own justification, but in the classroom the experience of stories can also be a shared pleasure; a point of contact between child and child, and between children and teacher.

We have so far in our discussion concentrated on the benefits children derive from hearing and reading stories. This is only one side of the picture since children do not only read or listen to other people's stories; they also create their own, whether completely invented or adaptations of other stories they have encountered. This process is known as storying and consists of the shaping into narrative of ideas or experiences. It is a process which we all engage in. In order to shape our ideas to share them with other people we commonly make use of a narrative mode. This is such a common process that we rarely dignify it with more attention than simply to call it 'gossiping', 'joke-telling' or 'spinning a yarn', but this should not disguise its importance. It is at once a vehicle for helping us make sense of experience for ourselves, and a mechanism for conveying that experience to others. Both these functions, the self-realisatory and the communicative, also operate when children engage in storying.

Telling stories, or simply narrating events, gives children the opportunity to shape and clarify past events, to order and make sense of present experiences, and to speculate and hypothesise about possible future happenings. This is what learning actually consists of, and as storying is such a natural process children engage in it without any apparent effort. Precisely because of the naturalness of the process it is likely that we regularly underestimate its learning benefits at all stages of education. Children need opportunities to tell stories to sympathetic audiences even when these stories concern seemingly factual matters.

## CHOOSING CHILDREN'S LITERATURE

If children are to get the most from their experience with literature, both stories and poetry, it seems like common-sense to ˙ ˙ᵗ ˙ᵗʰᵉᵛ need the best literature which can be provided.
˙ ˙˙ ᵗraightforward as it seems.
˙ ˙ ˙ ˙ᵗʰᵉ

readers.

Although this is, perhaps, an argumeᵤₜ ˙˙ children choose for themselves which literature to read, in practice, teachers are likely to be more involved than this. There are several issues which need to be considered in the selection of both suitable stories and poetry for children, and we shall discuss some of these. We shall not attempt to give a list of prescriptive criteria for choice, since any such are so open to dispute.

### Stories

It is possible to outline some general criteria which seem to affect children's enjoyment of stories although there will always be debate over the importance of these, and whether enjoyment is the prime criterion in any case. There can, however, be little doubt that children are most attracted to stories with strong, action-packed plots. They are often easily put off by long descriptive passages and many teachers 'edit out' these passages when reading stories to children. They also seem to prefer plots which engender a great deal of suspense. On both these counts, of course, Enid Blyton scores highly.

Children also seem to like characters with whom they can identify (although this is true of all readers), but the characters in children's stories are not usually exactly typical of actual children, but rather of children as they would like to be. Thus it is common for these characters to have much greater power and control over the events surrounding them than real children. This 'conceit' often extends to the outwitting of the adult representatives in the story as, for instance, when the 'Famous Five' solve crimes which have baffled the local police.[9]

There is greater debate over the issue of morality in children's stories. It is generally true that stories written for children present a more black and white view of morality than is true in reality. Characters are usually either obviously good or obviously bad. Nobody doubts that the goblins in *The Hobbit* are the wicked characters and will eventually lose and that Bilbo will emerge triumphant. This clear-cut view of good and evil is, of course, not unique to children's stories and many people will recall identifying the 'baddy' in a Western film simply because he was wearing a black hat!

There is a question, however, over whether this presentation of the world actually does children much good as it fails to prepare them for the shades of grey they will find in the real world. It is impossible to resolve this debate completely, but noteworthy that some well-respected children's stories do manage to introduce questions of morality. Peter Rabbit, for example, although the hero of the story, is naughty and almost gets severely punished for it. Part of the tension in the early part of *The Iron Man* is caused by the reader not quite being sure whether the character is good or bad.

The quality of language in children's stories was mentioned earlier and this does seem an important criterion to bear in mind. Ideally we would wish children to develop their own powers of language use through reading, but we would have to allow that not every encounter with a book need be so rich and educational. If, as adults, the only books we were allowed to read were established classics, from Chaucer to Hemingway via Charlotte Brontë, we should soon protest at so rich a diet and reach for Alistair MacLean or P.D. James. Children are no different. They need opportunities to read a wide variety of books, and freedom to choose. If their choice sometimes seems undemanding this does not mean that they are wasting time. In the first place, they may need the encouragement of being able to read a book without working too hard at it. In the second, experience of a variety of books will help them work out their own criteria for choosing reading material. And in the third, it would be arrogant for adults to assume they always know what is best for children. Books which teachers place little value on may sometimes turn out to be just what particular children need at a particular time, and may indeed eventually confound their critics by becoming classics themselves.[10] The teacher who reputedly dismissed *Charlotte's Web* with 'I hate these twee stories where the animals talk', must surely have lived to regret these words!

This is not to say that there are no problems in the issue of One major problem has surfaced involving

'classics' of children which now seem worrying. A celebrated exam which contains episodes such as that where the Doctor is asked to prepare a potion to turn a black man white. The man, Prince Bumpo, wants to become white so that he will not be rejected again by Sleeping Beauty. Many adults, on re-reading this passage, claim that it did not do them any harm as children, but, of course, it is impossible to tell the effect on their views about black people. It is also impossible to tell the effect on black children's views of themselves, but must give us some cause for concern.

Similarly, a great deal of criticism has been levelled at the portrayal of female characters in books and stories, even the most traditional of tales. The subordinate female character is the norm from the helpless princess rescued by the dashing prince to the simpering girl who must not join the rough boys' games for fear she gets her clothes dirty. When female characters are strong they are often wicked too, as stepmothers or witches.

Although most people would not disagree that the predominant character in British children's fiction has been white, male and middle class, there is much more debate about what should be done about this. Some would do nothing, using the argument that no harm has really been done, and concern over these issues is only raised by extremists. Others would ban books which give messages they perceive as offensive. This view is more predominant in certain parts of the country but has certainly had an impact upon publishers. A third option is to ensure that there are sufficient books which give opposing, more positive messages to counter-balance those predominant in earlier literature. These three options can be summed up as: do nothing/censorship/ widen the choice.

For all the apparent attractiveness of the third option, none of them is without its problems. Simply to widen the choice of books available to children may mean accepting that they will encounter some books which contain worrying material, and this is a risk which not all teachers are prepared to take. These issues are certainly not straightforward.[12]

One initial step which would bring issues like these out into the open would be to discuss criteria for choice with the others involved. This could, perhaps, be the focus of a meeting with parents, and could certainly involve the children themselves.

## Poetry

The poetry teachers have used with children in the past, and the ways it has been used, have often reflected the experience of poetry these teachers have had themselves. For most people their memories of poetry are dominated by their experience of using poetry in secondary classrooms, or at college or university. This has tended to influence the kind of poetry deemed suitable for children, and the approaches used to teach it. In the latter case, poetry has often been treated as another source for comprehension exercises, the main emphasis being on getting children to 'understand' the poem. Their personal responses to it have taken second place. Lessons in which teachers present poems to children are often characterised by questions such as, 'What does that word mean?' and 'What happens in these lines?'. Teachers who go further along the road to an *explication de texte* may ask such things as 'What effect does this phrase have' or 'Why does the poet choose these words?'. It is much less common for teachers to leave small groups of children alone with a poem so that they can share their feelings about it. Other ways of encouraging response to rather than explanation of poems will be discussed later.

Because poetry for most teachers meant deep thought and hard work, there has often seemed to be a necessary seriousness about it. Thus many teachers have, in the past, tended to choose poems for children which had a serious quality about them, either in tone or in the way they were read.[13] Poetry does, of course, deal essentially with matters of life, many of which are serious, and by its nature it heightens awareness of these. More recently, however, there has emerged a new genre of poetry for children which tries to heighten awareness of everyday experience through a much more approachable structure and language.

Examine the following poem, which is taken from Michael Rosen's *Wouldn't You Like To Know* collection (published 1981 by

Why?
Because the sun's shining.
Why?
Because it's summer.
Why?
Because that's when it is.
Why?
Why don't you stop saying why?
Why?
Tea-time; That's why.
High-time-you-stopped-saying-why-time.
What?

Rosen here focuses on a situation which will have meaning for children and parents alike. The piece is concentrated, refers to an almost universal experience and allows the reader to consider this experience in a fresh way by being distanced from it. All these things are the very essence of poetry, yet the style here is far removed from what many people would consider as poetry. Instead of using 'high' language it uses phrases and a structure taken from everyday conversation. Rosen deliberately uses language like this, which he has referred to as 'memorable speech', in an attempt to make his poems accessible, and thereby more likely to have an impact.

Although not without its critics, this approach to children's poetry has had an enormous impact upon the poetry now available for primary school children.[14] Poets such as Roger McGough, Brian Patten and Kit Wright have had a great deal of success with poetry which uses everyday language and comments upon everyday experience, yet does it with freshness, some seriousness, but not a little humour. In general, it would be true to say that poetry for children has lost its 'Sunday best' image, and has become much more closely rooted in everyday life and language. There will always be a place, however, in classrooms for a wide variety of poetry.

## STRATEGIES FOR ENCOURAGING INTERACTIONS WITH LITERATURE

Encounters with children in secondary schools often suggest that there is a 'reading problem' which is more widespread than that usually considered. Many children seem to come through to secondary schooling able to read, but not especially interested in doing so. This suggests a new category of reading problem; that of the reluctant reader, that is the child who can read but does not. It is likely that reluctant readers are a product of the experiences they have had with literature, which suggests that there are strategies teachers can adopt to reduce the likelihood of producing children who do not value literature. In this section we shall discuss some possible strategies for this, centred around five key issues: choice, opportunity, atmosphere, models and sharing.

### Choice

It would be very difficult to imagine anyone becoming really excited about reading if they were continually forced to read what someone else chose for them. The development of enthusiasm and of taste depends upon the freedom to exercise some choice in what is read. This argument is largely undisputed yet many teachers, often with the very best of intentions, allow their pupils only limited choice in their reading matter. There are usually two ways in which this happens.

In one, teachers feel that children's initial experiences with literature ought to be successful and enjoyable ones, so they try to ensure that children can read reasonably fluently (using a graded reading programme) before allowing them free choice of reading matter. This view leads to classes in which there are some children who are 'free readers' and others whose reading experience is limited to reading scheme books and what the teacher reads to them. If, as earlier suggested, children learn to read by reading, such a restriction on children's reading is not likely to have beneficial effects either on their capacity to read or on their willingness.

The second way in which children's choice of reading is limited ... the teacher closely pre-selects the material from which

experiencing this range that they ...
reading matter. Furthermore, of course, there is nothing at all wrong with an adult who reads enthusiastically only pulp fiction. Some adults spend lots of their working life 'coming to terms with the human condition' and, in their leisure time, wish only to escape into a good book!

What implications do these points have for the teacher who wishes to encourage love of reading in children? First, it would seem that the earlier children can be allowed to exercise some choice in their reading material the better. This does not necessarily mean that the whole of their reading need be from self-selected books. The teacher may still want to exercise some control in the initial stages. There are, however, so many excellent picture books available for young readers that there is some room for choice, however limited a child's reading ability.[15]

The second implication is that teachers need to trust children more in allowing them choice. Some children will choose books which seem worthless, too easy, or too hard to the teacher, but as long as this produces enthusiasm there seems little wrong with it. This does not mean the teacher should abdicate all involvement

with a child's choice of book. On the contrary, there is a great deal
a teacher can do to help children choose books wisely such as
discussion, finding out a child's interests, recommending and,
above all, knowing the books well. In the end, though, children
should have the freedom to reject a teacher's suggestion.

## Opportunity

It seems logical to suggest that children will not become avid
readers unless they are given opportunities to actually read. The
same argument applies to almost any activity. Although I may learn
to drive a car during a dozen or so lessons, I do not become a
driver without much more opportunity to practise. For many
children opportunities to engage in pleasurable reading regularly
occur at home, and for these children the supportive atmosphere
of a home which values books and reading is probably sufficient to
ensure that they too will come to share these values. For others
though, school may represent the most extended opportunity to
read that they get, and so it is vital that it does actually give them
this opportunity. The National Curriculum programme of study
for reading recommends that children should 'have opportunities
to participate in all activities related to reading'.

What kind of opportunities might school provide? Many schools
and classrooms have a regular period of time in which children
read individually. These times are given various acronyms, for
example:

USSR – Uninterrupted Sustained Silent Reading,
ERIC – Everyone Reading In Class,
SQUIRT – Sit Quietly, It's Reading Time.

These times usually have several common features. They often
involve *everyone* in the class reading including the teacher, who
does not take advantage of the time to mark books, hear readers,
tidy his/her desk, etc., because that would indicate to the children
that reading, while important, is not important enough for the
teacher to do it too. (We discuss further below the issue of teacher
modelling the process.)

The times also often occur at the beginning of school sessions,
either morning or afternoon. This indicates to the children that
the teacher places high importance upon them. Having them at

the very end of the day might give the children the message that they were just winding-down times.

They also often involve the whole school. In some schools even the headteacher, the caretaker, schools secretary and dinner ladies read at these times. This again indicates to the children how important these times are. Where they happen only in individual classrooms some teachers put notices on their classroom door like:

PLEASE DO NOT DISTURB
THIS IS OUR USSR TIME

This helps to avoid the problems of interruption which are often endemic to primary schools.

In terms of physical atmosphere, comfortable book corners where limited numbers of children can browse amongst book collections or actually read. The book corner may be carpeted and may be decorated with flowers and have cushions or comfortable chairs to sit on. It will usually have items aimed at encouraging children to read such as book posters, adverts, displays and perhaps examples of the ways children have responded to books.

Even if a book corner is impossible, there are several things teachers can do to create encouraging physical environments for reading. One is to take some care over the display of books. Untidy shelves with tatty books rarely encourage anyone, and it requires some effort on the teacher's part to keep the books and shelves attractive, in which the children's help can be enlisted, of course. Another strategy for the teacher is to reflect the children's interest in books in the displays that are mounted on the classroom walls. This can be part of a general sharing of experiences with books and this will be discussed further below.

The second aspect of atmosphere is the social atmosphere of the classroom. In some classrooms the reading of books becomes a very competitive and tense thing, with children vying with each other to see who can read the most books in the shortest times. This does not help them to develop a love of reading for its own sake. It can also have the effect of limiting the range of books they choose, as competent readers choose short, easy books simply because they can get through a lot of them very quickly. It also works against reflective children who may read very thoughtfully but slowly. It is far better to put the emphasis upon the quality of children's involvement with books and allow them the space to experiment, reflect and become absorbed in the books they choose.

## Models

It is sometimes forgotten that many children will arrive in school without ever really having seen anyone deeply immersed in reading a book. They will have lots of demonstrations of literate behaviour from their parents – adults can barely exist in today's world without employing literacy in many different ways. But, unless their parents happen to be enthusiastic readers themselves, these demonstrations may not have included extended reading for pleasure. These children need to see that reading for pleasure is a thing that many adults do through choice, and the only person who can show them this is their teacher. As teachers we very often seem to expect children to do things with enthusiasm which we rarely do ourselves, and certainly not in front of them. Reading is just one example of this, but a crucial one.

As well as providing a physical example of someone reading for pleasure, reading in front of children can also have a direct influence upon the way they go about reading. There are many things teachers can model. They can show that:

(a) Sometimes you can read things that make you laugh out loud, sometimes reading makes you sad:
(b) You can become so absorbed in your reading you do not hear what people say to you.
(c) You can be bored by a particular book, and if you are there are things you can do about it, for example, skipping a few pages to see if it improves, laying it aside for a while and returning to it later, changing it for another.
(d) You can choose books because of their subject, because you

like their author and for many other reasons and there are ways of finding these things out without just starting at page 1 and reading on.

To model these things for children, the teacher will not simply read in front of them, but will also be prepared to talk to them about his/her reading, why particular books were chosen and what they were like. Reading in front of children is certainly not a soft option, but can be a very valuable teaching technique.

### Sharing

There are many ways in which children can communicate their

The obvious way, which ...

children to write reports or reviews of material they have read and then to display these in some way. If this is done well it can be a very useful technique. We mentioned earlier the possibility of the book corner displays reflecting children's responses to books they have read, and a dynamic display containing reports and other material can certainly stimulate other children to read. The danger with book reviews, however, is that they become a chore rather than a spontaneous response to a book. If children are forced to write a review after reading a book, this can act as disincentive to reading another one. If, on the other hand, children are allowed to write book reports if they wish to tell their classmates how good a book was, this can have a very positive effect.

Children can respond in ways other than by writing reports. Some of these ways are listed below, but this list is by no means exhaustive. After reading a book children can:

- write a quiz about it,
- design a new book jacket,
- make an advertising poster for the book,

- tape-record an advertisement,
- construct a hanging mobile using drawings of the characters,
- draw a strip cartoon based on the book,
- make up a play based on the book,
- write a new episode involving the characters,
- enter it into the '10 best books of all time', and make an argument for its inclusion,
- write its details on a class list of books read, and give it a star grading (* for good, *** for excellent and upwards), etc.[16]

Many of these ways of responding will involve groups of children rather than individuals. Such group response can be a very effective way of encouraging children to reflect on books and poems they have read, and need not always have any physical outcome. A group of children brought together to discuss a story or a poem they have all read can share and deepen their responses simply by their discussion. To an outside observer, this discussion may sometimes seem to range very far from the 'subject' of the story or poem, but it will almost always be led by the children's real responses, which may be fairly divergent. There is much to be gained by allowing this freedom.

On a more formal level, the teacher may also encourage the sharing of response to literature by organising a class or school book-week, when the whole of the work of the class or school is centred around books and poems. During such weeks many events can take place, such as:

- displays about books being mounted,
- story and poetry readings by teachers and children,
- an assembly about books,
- inviting local and/or nationally known authors to talk about their work with the children,
- showing films or videos of well-known books,
- a book sale,
- a sponsored book-read,
- a book trivial-pursuit competition,
- a book auction, etc.

If parents and the local community can be involved in the book-week, it is even more likely that the reading of literature will receive a very positive boost.

## CONCLUSION

The major issue arising from our discussions in this chapter is that, given the vital importance of literature in the primary classroom how can the teacher ensure that his/her children develop the most positive attitudes possible towards it? The answer to this question, we have argued, is twofold. It involves, first, making decisions about the kinds of literature children will have access to in the classroom: decisions which are more complex than might at first sight appear. Second, it involves the planning of strategies for actively encouraging the reading of and the reflection upon literature. Both these issues involve a raising of the profile of literature in the primary classroom. It has too much potential to be

and why? Share your choices with some other people. Do you have any common criteria?

2 Think back to when you were at primary school. Can you remember any book (story or poetry) which was very important to you? What influence has this book had on your life?

3 'It's fine to read stories to infants, but top juniors are really too old for that.' If a colleague said this to you, what might you say to try to convince them they were wrong?

4 'We may live more by fiction than by fact. It is living by fiction which makes the higher organisms special' (Gregory, 1977). How might you argue against a colleague who believed, contrary to Gregory, that fact was more important in education than fiction? (See Lavender, 1978, for some insights into this argument.)

# Chapter 4

# The emergence of literacy

## INTRODUCTION

One influential view of the development of literacy in young children was based around the notion of 'readiness'. According to this view there was a stage in children's lives at which they were sufficiently physically, emotionally and cognitively mature to benefit from being taught to read and write. Before this time, any such teaching would have only a negative effect, because the children were not 'ready' for it. Instead of direct teaching, children who were not ready should be given pre-reading and pre-writing activities to do, to help them reach the stage of reading or writing readiness. This view permeated the training and the practice of nursery and infant teachers, and indeed is still subscribed to by many of them.[1]

In itself it was a beneficial development on some of the practices which had preceded it. It became less frequent for 4 and 5 year old children to be drilled on letter recognition and formation, and more likely for them to be given play-like activities to help them acquire skills assumed to be necessary before the formal teaching of reading and writing could begin. Many teachers became firmly committed to this approach, sometimes to the extent that pre-reading and pre-writing activities became the very heart of what early schooling was about. One headteacher is reputed to have remarked to a parent whose child was about to start school, 'What a pity Emma can already read. She will miss out on all the lovely pre-reading games our children play.' Her heart, if not her head, was clearly in the right place!

The readiness view has been strongly challenged in recent years and, interestingly enough, this challenge has come from studies of children who do not seem to conform to the stereotype the view would suggest, but can engage comfortably in literate behaviour before they arrive in school.[2] As evidence has accumulated, it has become clear that these children are not extraordinary, but in fact representative of the majority of young children who, growing up in literate societies, pick up a great deal of literate behaviour from very early in their lives. It has become clear that the development of literacy does not begin at some mystical point of 'readiness', but is a much longer process which has its roots in the social interaction into which children are born. This process has come to be known as the 'emergence of literacy', and it has generated a great _ _ _ _ _ _ _ _ _ _ _ activity amongst both researchers and

writing in the infant school. Here, however, we _ _ _ _ _ of the insights into literacy which young children may bring to school with them, and then go on to suggest some processes which may account for these insights, and around which teachers may build responsive literacy programmes.

## WHAT DO CHILDREN KNOW?

### Writing

The following piece of 'writing' (Figure 4.1) was produced by a 4 year old girl, Sarah, who wrote it as a letter to Father Christmas asking for some presents. She read it back as, 'Dear Father Christmas, please can I have a Cindy doll and a bike. Love from Sarah.'

When examining the piece it is tempting to concentrate first of all upon what Sarah does *not* know about writing. What she produces clearly does not conform to adult standards of writing, and is deficient in several ways, for example, letter formation, letter group to word correspondence, uniformity of letter size and shape. There are ways, however, in which Sarah demonstrates in

*Figure 4.1* Letter to Father Christmas

her writing that she has a great deal of understanding about the nature and the production of writing.

She first of all shows clearly that she understands that the purpose of writing is communication. She began with a need to communicate and something to say. She knew that an appropriate way of achieving her aim was to produce a series of marks on a page of paper. She also knew that these marks had to bear a relationship to a spoken message, and had no hesitation in 'reading' what she had written. In her reading she showed a recognition that the particular message she wanted to communicate needed a particular format, and her message follows the accepted letter ... Message Closure and Signature.

afterwards by drawing lines in crayon undern... writing. These features are clearly culturally specific (Chinese or Arabic children would presumably begin to write differently), but it is most unlikely that they have been deliberately taught to Sarah. Yet she knows their importance.

Sarah also demonstrates a feature which is very common in young children's first attempts at writing: a willingness to play with letter shapes, to experiment. She does not have at her command all the letters that she requires for her message, so she does the best she can with what she has. The letters she knows are, by and large, those that make up her name (even though her 'h' is reversed and her 'a' is similar to 'o'), so she uses these for her message, trying out different sizes as she does so. Her first line gets progressively higher, and she indicates by a line that she knows this. Thereafter, her lines are much more uniform.

These three features of communication, organisation and experimentation are commonly seen in the writing of young children, and demonstrate that, in fact, they have already probably learnt more about writing than they have left to learn. What is left is really refinement upon the basic features they have already mastered.[4]

## Reading

As with writing, a great deal of energy has been expended on establishing the concepts and knowledge about the process of reading which young children lack. Three decades of research have produced the following areas of concepts about print about which many young children seem rather hazy.[5]

| Concept | Knowledge involved |
|---|---|
| Book orientation | Knowing which is the front of a book. |
| Directional rules | Knowing that when reading you progress from left to right and when you reach the end of the line you go to the left hand of the next line down. |
| Print carries the message | Knowing that it is the print not the picture that carries the story. |
| Letter concepts | Being able to point to a letter and distinguish between lower- and upper-case letters. |
| Word concepts | Being able to point to a word or two words. |
| Punctuation | Knowing what full stops, commas, etc. are for. |

Although some children may have developed an understanding of several of these concepts before they begin schooling, many will know little about them until they begin reading instruction.

Such research findings, however, while producing information vital to teachers of reading, may also cause these teachers to underestimate the understandings about reading which children may have. The concepts listed above are, in fact, those which children are most likely to acquire through reading rather than as prerequisites for reading. They are technical concepts about the way print works. (There is a strong suggestion also that the extent of children's knowledge about them is disguised by the testing situations used to elicit this knowledge.)[6]

Yet other research suggests that there are other kinds of knowledge about reading which children often do bring to school with them. This knowledge seems to be centred around the functions (rather than the precise workings) of print and the way written language works as writing. There are two major kinds of evidence which we shall briefly present: children's abilities to recognise and act upon print in their environments, and children's awareness of the language of books and stories.

A large number of studies have found children (as young as 10 weeks old!) who were clearly aware of and interested in the print around them.[7] It is not really surprising that this should be so, as print is such a prominent feature of modern society. Children grow up in an environment which is saturated with print, from food packaging to telephone directories, from newspapers to electricity bills and from television advertisements to T-shirt logos.

It is, however, not just the fact of this print's existence which

⸻ that its primary purpose is to carry

is defined as g

children are reading, even if they are not doing it in a p⸻, way that adults do, relying a good deal more on the context of the print than its precise features for their assignation of its meaning. This knowledge is an important start for them in their acquisition of literacy.

The link between the experience of stories and the acquisition of reading ability was mentioned in the previous chapter. When children have this experience before school begins, they seem much more likely to be able to 'talk like a book',[8] which in turn seems to be of critical value in becoming a competent reader. Again there are several examples in the literature of young children who show awareness of the features of stories, from their stylistic conventions to the complex narrative rules around which they are based.

As an example of this, we can examine the following spoken narrative which was produced by a 5 year old boy.[9]

but then he went out in the middle of
the night
and there was this sound going – dooo-dee
doo-dee [child sings]

> he looked all around
> nobody was there in a small street where
> it had lots of holes
> he looked down one of them
> he looked down the other
> they were all alike
> but he looked down the next one
> and what was there?
> just a surprise thing
> his Daddy was there

Clearly there is much more here than the simple narrating of an event. The child uses the story technique of building tension to engage his audience and he phrases his narration in particular ways that owe more to written language rules than to spoken. The ability to do these things is evidence of a great deal of knowledge of the way stories work and the rules of written language.

The idea has been suggested that experience with stories develops understanding of story structures and familiarity with the grammatical features and sequences of written language. These in turn enable subsequent anticipation of these structures and features which assists the reading of them. It has even been suggested, with some support from research, that this is the major way in which the particular expectations needed to cope successfully with reading develop.[10] If this is true, it is very clear 'what no bedtime story means'.[11]

The evidence suggests, therefore, that it is very likely that children arrive at school, not totally ignorant about the forms and functions of written language, but with a wide variety of insights into both writing and reading. If teachers are to build effectively upon these insights, it will be useful for them to know not only the nature of the insights, but also some of the processes by which children may acquire them. These processes may be useful bases upon which to structure an early literacy school curriculum.

## HOW CHILDREN LEARN LANGUAGE

Interesting insights into how children acquire their early knowledge about the workings of literacy can be gained from considering some of the processes through which they learn spoken language. While learning to talk may not exactly parallel learning to be literate, both processes clearly have much in common, because spoken language has much in common with written language. (Written language also differs in important ways from spoken language, and awareness of these differences is in itself an important feature of becoming literate.)

We shall examine first some of the processes by which children learn spoken language, and go on to discuss how these apply to the acquisition of literacy.[12]

All normal children, from the moment they are born, are ˙ ˙˙ spoken language. One of the most noticeable facts ˙˙˙ to them, and this begins long ˙ ˙˙˙and what was

˙˙˙

by talk. This talk is ˙˙˙ expressed in adult forms. In addition ˙˙ ˙ also surrounded by talk which is not directly addressed ˙˙ ˙ Again such talk is invariably meaningful and much of its sense is obvious from its context. Children, then, begin life bathed in meaningful talk.

Because the talk which surrounds them is meaningful, young children are receiving continual demonstrations of the functions of spoken language. If an adult says to a child, 'Who's dropped his ball then? There we are. Back again', and returns the ball, the adult is demonstrating the connection between talk and the action it refers to. When the child says, 'Daddy blow', and the adult responds with, 'Yes, daddy will blow the whistle now', the demonstration is not only of the connection between language and action, but also of an appropriate form of speech. Children receive millions of demonstrations of meaningful talk, not only directed at them, but also taking place around them. From these demonstrations they have to work out how the system of language works, so that they can begin to take part in it.

Of course, the simple fact of witnessing demonstrations of language would not be sufficient to turn children into language users unless some other factors were also present. First among these is engagement,[13] that is the desire on the part of children to take part in the language behaviour they see around them. This desire arises because children witness the power of language in the world, and want to share in it. They see, for example, that if you can ask for a biscuit rather than just scream loudly, you are more likely to get what you want. They also see that using language in ways that achieve the effects they want is not something so difficult they are unlikely to master it. On the contrary, language is presented to them from the very first as something they *can* do. This produces a crucial expectation of success which we know to be vitally important in actual achievement. There is plenty of evidence that children, both in and out of school, achieve very much what they are expected to achieve by other people.[14] It is likely that this works because children internalise others' expectations about them, and come to hold these expectations of themselves. The most familiar example of this concerns children whom adults label as 'not very clever', and who come to believe this of themselves. Because they do not believe they can 'be clever', they stop trying to be.

In the case of spoken language, however, every child is expected to be able to master it (unless some medical condition makes this impossible). Asking any parent the question, 'Do you expect your child to learn to talk?' is likely to produce only a very puzzled response. The question seems ludicrous because the answer is so obvious. Because the adults around them believe so firmly that they will become talkers, the children themselves come to believe they will do it, and they do, generally effortlessly. There is an 'absence of the expectation that learning will not take place'.[15]

When children are learning to talk, it is highly unlikely that the adult expert talkers that surround them will decide to administer a structured programme of speech training. Adults who have tried to be even a little systematic in helping children to develop language have found that it simply does not work. The following much-quoted exchange between child and care-giver is an example of what can happen.

Child: Nobody don't like me.
Mother: No, say 'Nobody likes me'.
Child: Nobody don't like me.
(Eight repetitions of this dialogue)
Mother: No, now listen carefully: say 'Nobody likes me'.
Child: Oh! Nobody don't likes me.[16]

Instead of this situation, in which the adult has tried to take responsibility for what the child should learn, it is much more usual for the child to take the responsibility. Learning to talk is the child's task, which can be supported by adults but is not sequenced, structured or taught by them. This is implicitly accepted by the majority of adults who rarely try to force the pace when children are learning to talk, but instead take their lead from the child's performance.

During this learning, nobody expects children to perform perfectly from the very beginning. If children had to wait until they had perfect control of all facets of spoken language before

l... ... any speech until at least 9 or 10

When a child ..., .

much more likely to respond with something like, ..., , saying Daddy is naughty. He's a good Daddy', rather than 'No. Say "Daddy, you are naughty"'. The adult responds to the child's attempts at fully fledged speech forms by interpreting and adding meaning, rather than by correcting them. Approximations are accepted and responded to by adults, and gradually children realise for themselves that they are approximate and how to make them more 'adult'.

Any learning, to be effective, requires a great deal of practice on the part of the learner, and learning to talk is no exception. For the vast majority of children this is no problem at all. They are constantly surrounded by talk and are expected and given chances to join in with it. Even when by themselves they carry on practising, from early babbling in which language sounds are practised to later oral accompaniments to actions such as play. Significantly this practice occurs for completely different purposes than to help children learn to talk. Adults rarely hold conversations with babies and young children because they know this is good for their language development. Nor do children talk to themselves when playing because they think this will make them better talkers. Both activities occur for more fundamental, human reasons.

Conversations take place because there is something to converse about and children are included in the conversation which accompanies everyday action from very early in their lives. Children talk to themselves because this is how they represent their actions to themselves and how they reflect upon these actions.[17] This kind of talk becomes more and more elliptical and eventually fades altogether, occurring inside the head as 'inner speech'. It is the beginning of thought.[18]

For all the importance of the above processes in children's growing capacity to produce meaningful speech, none of them would work were it not for the fact they all operate in a two-sided situation. Children are immersed in language, receive a myriad of demonstrations of it, are expected to try to emulate these and given freedom and opportunities to do it at their own pace and level of approximation, but the crucial factor is that all this happens in the context of real dialogue with other people. Adults talk, not just across children, but *to* them; they expect children to talk back to them, and when they do adults respond. This constant interaction is at the heart of growing language use. And it is the need for interaction which comes first. Relationships need to be developed and things need to be achieved together. Language comes into being as a means of helping these things happen. It is therefore learned as a means of coping with the demands of being human.[19]

Because of the interactive nature of language, learning the process inevitably involves response. Children respond to adult language, and adults respond to children's attempts at language. Such response not only reaffirms the relationship which forms the context of the talk, but also gives children feedback about their language, and, perhaps, a more elaborated model upon which to base future language.

## THE DEVELOPMENT OF INSIGHTS INTO LITERACY

The same processes which underlie the development of spoken language can also be seen to underpin the development of children's insights into and their use of literacy outside of school.

As mentioned earlier in this chapter, children are surrounded by literacy from their earliest years. Here are just a few of the manifestations of this:

- they wear print, from clothes labels to T-shirt slogans,
- they consume things covered in print, from soft drink cans to chocolate bars,
- they accompany their parents shopping in printed surroundings and come into contact with signs, from Car Parking to Frozen Food, and printed packages, from Corn Flakes to Fish Fingers,
- they watch print on television, from advertisements to news headlines,
- they see print used in their homes, from shopping lists to telephone directories, and recipes to newspapers.

- reading newsp..., laughter, anger, sadness, etc.,
- consulting telephone directories, and dialling numbers guided by print,
- reading bills and reacting with dismay,
- finding their way around supermarkets by following the signs,
- and so on.

These are illustrations that print can affect the way you feel, can act as a guide to action, or can be used for the sheer pleasure of using it. As a result of these constant demonstrations of literacy, most children come to value engagement in literacy. This shows itself in all kinds of ways. Some children learn that there is little point in saying 'I want a burger', unless you are near a shop which sells them, which you know because of the signs outside. Others will proudly produce a page covered in scribble and say, 'I've written a story'. The 3 year old girl who sat for three-quarters of an hour absorbed in the pages of a book which was on her knee, upside down, had learnt to value the literacy behaviour she had witnessed in adults, even if she had not quite yet worked out how to do it. Any reception teacher will testify to the fact that most of their new charges come to school wanting to learn to read above all things. Their engagement with literacy is high.

Before they reach school, most children have few grounds not to believe that they will be successful in their encounters with literacy. The majority of 3 year olds will cheerfully 'read' a book, even if what they say does not match the actual printed words. They will also 'write', using scribble or the letters of their name to signify meaning. Because they have received so many demonstrations of literacy in so many contexts, they come to believe that there is nothing to it. Everyone else can do it, so they can too, or even if they are aware they have not quite got the hang of it yet, it is only a matter of time until they do. It is a sad fact that the first time many children begin to doubt that they will master the activities of reading and writing is when their school experience shows them these things are difficult and failure is possible.

In the early lessons which children learn about literacy, it is unlikely that adults will make too many demands upon them to perform in particular ways. The choice whether to attend to the literacy demonstrations around them and whether to try to copy them or not is left to the children. They therefore, as with spoken language, have responsibility for their own learning. Of course, parents often do attempt more direct teaching of reading and writing with young children than they do of speaking. This is only natural, given the high status of literacy and parents' perceptions that the ability to read and write is linked with success in later life. Most parents will, however, take the lead from their children in terms of how long their teaching will last, when they have done enough, and, indeed, what this teaching will consist of. Again the child has a large amount of responsibility for the process.

Adults also rarely expect the 'reading' and 'writing' of their young children to be perfect. A 2 year old who makes up a spoken story in response to looking at a captioned picture book is more likely to receive praise for this effort than an exhortation to be more careful and get the words right. Similarly, children who present their parents with scribbled 'letters' are likely to have their attempts taken seriously, with the parents pretending to 'read' the message, and not to be admonished for their poor handwriting or spelling. In the same way that children are allowed 'baby-talk' which approximates to adult speech, they are allowed 'baby-reading' and 'baby-writing'.

In addition to being surrounded by demonstrations of literacy, many children get a great many opportunities to take part in it, at however rudimentary a level. Almost all children 'write', whether it be with pencil, felt tip, crayon, paint brush or chalk. Most of them also 'read', whether from books, comics, TV screens or advertisements. The 3 year old who proudly displays a new T-shirt with Batman on the front is using the ability to derive meaning from printed symbols. The 2 year old who picks up the tube of fruit ~~~ ~~than the indigestion tablets is making discriminations ~~~~ ~~ing and writing, in rudimentary forms, ~~~~~ ~~~tivities simply because

in the shopping ~ Corn Flakes. He says, 'Bix, Mum. don't want Corn Flakes. We want Weetabix. ~~~ has given feedback on his interpretation of print, and help~~ learn more about this process.

A father is standing at a bus stop with his 3 year old son. A bus draws up and the little boy moves forward. The father says, 'No. We want the bus for Warwick Street. This goes to Haslam Road, look.' He points to the indicator on the bus. He is demonstrating which items of print it is important to attend to.

A mother is playing 'Shops' with her 3 year old daughter. She asks to 'buy' several things, and helps her daughter find each item in the shop. Each time the child finds the right item, the mother praises her with, 'Yes. That's the toothpaste.' Again the child is being helped make links between objects and their print representations.

Of course, children vary in the quantity of interactions of this kind which they experience with their parents. Where they receive a great many, the children are in fact being treated as apprentice print users, experience which almost certainly helps them develop into independent print users later. The concept of apprenticeship is an important one in trying to understand the growth of early literacy, and essentially involves the actions of an 'expert' being copied and experimented with by a less expert apprentice.

Learning takes place naturally and almost undetectably, yet it clearly does take place.

## CONCLUSION

We do not wish to imply in what has been written so far that the experience of literacy which children get at home is sufficient to ensure they develop into fully competent experts in all the ways literacy is used in the modern world. Or, in other words, that schooling is really unnecessary. While it is true that most children make a start on the process of becoming literate before they arrive at school, there is a great deal that they still have to learn. It is unlikely that simply by remaining at home and carrying on with the same kind of experience, children would acquire sufficient awareness and expertise in the many complex and high level uses of literacy which society demands of them.

Our purpose is rather to suggest that, although school has a vital role to play in the development of literacy, it can still learn a great deal from an examination of the learning processes at work in the home which we have just discussed. The attractiveness of these processes is in their naturalness. The fact that nobody, neither parents nor children, consciously plans these processes, suggests that there is something in them which is fundamental to effective human learning. If this is so, it may be that a programme of literacy teaching in schools which was based upon these processes would have greater success than one which pulled in other directions. It is worth examining how teachers might use some of these processes as frameworks for literacy programmes; which is what we shall attempt to do in the following chapter.

## FOLLOW-UP ACTIVITIES

1 A 'literacy trail' can reveal a great deal about the literacy environment in which we all live and work. This involves walking along a route familiar to you, and making a note of the instances of reading and writing you come across. Most of these will be so familiar to you it will take some effort to even notice them. The items on your 'trail' will give you a good idea of the literacy environment in which children are brought up before they reach school.

2 Try to observe some young children (3 to 4 year olds) as they

play in a home setting. Make a note of any use of literacy that they make. These may include passing notes to each other, pretending to read stories, playing shops, etc.

3 Talk to some small children about the stories they like. Try to notice any examples of them using book-like language when they talk about the stories.

# Chapter 5

# Literacy in the early years of schooling

**FROM HOME TO SCHOOL**

We shall begin by reiterating the point that we made at the end of the previous chapter. We do not wish to argue that the kinds of experience of using literacy which children get at home are in any way sufficient for them to develop as fully literate people. Schools do have a role to play. The point we wish to make is that schools can learn a great deal from an examination of the processes by which children begin to be initiated into literate behaviour at home. We shall begin this chapter by discussing ways in which school literacy programmes can build upon these same processes. We shall try to make practical suggestions of things teachers can do in this way. After discussing these issues we shall go on to look at some important recent developments in the teaching of literacy which have their foundation in some of these very processes.

**BUILDING UPON CHILDREN'S INSIGHTS[1]**

One of the most straightforward things for teachers to do is to surround children with the sight and sounds of print. Classroom walls can be covered in labels, captions, diagrams, poems, songs or nursery rhymes on charts, and children's writing. Shelves can be filled with story, picture, poetry and information books. The children's environment can be made rich with print that they can move among and, most importantly, use, play with, and experiment with. In the past, however, many nursery and reception class teachers have almost seemed to try to banish print from their classrooms, preferring to cover their walls with colourful children's paintings, interesting posters, giant collage friezes of characters and scenes from stories, etc. This was done for the best of reasons, in order to create a vibrant, exciting environment with plenty of stimuli for lively young minds. In some instances it was also intended to be helpful to children, such as when their coat pegs and storage trays were labelled with pictures rather than names. The effect, however, of this banishment of print was significantly to distance the classroom environment from that outside, with its print richness.

One of the most sensible areas of the classroom to surround with print is that known variously as the home or play corner. Where this is a small-scale replica of a home, with model kitchen ˙ ⌐'' ᵈ ᵂⁱᵗʰ the products and tools of

- Telephone directories
- Bills, final demands(!)
- Books for children to read themselves
- Books to read to the baby (doll).

Children's play in this area can then fully involve literacy and there is evidence that when such environments are provided, children do, in fact, begin to incorporate literacy events into their play.[2]

This area of the classroom can also be transformed into various other representations of real-life places, for example, a dentist's surgery, a post office, an airport, etc. Each of these has its own place for literacy which can be reflected in the classroom. For example, a group of 4 and 5 year olds was observed playing in a pretend dentist's surgery, during which time they:

- browsed through magazines while waiting their turn,
- consulted charts to diagnose dental problems of 'patients',
- wrote prescriptions,
- used telephone directories when 'phoning' hospitals, neighbours, etc.
- filled in appointment bookings and so on.

None of these children could read or write in the accepted sense, but they were quite prepared to play at literacy as a normal part of the role play they were engaged in.

Immersing children in the sounds of written language is also possible. Teachers can read aloud to children from stories, poems, information books and so on. The beneficial effects of this have already been discussed in a previous chapter. Children can also receive this experience whenever they wish, even when it is inconvenient for the teacher, by listening to cassette tape recordings of stories, etc. A listening centre can be set up in the classroom, consisting of a cassette recorder, a set of five or six headphones, and a supply of pre-recorded cassettes. These are widely available, but teachers can also record their own, or persuade other adults such as parents to record them. One dimension to this kind of activity which is important but not obvious is the provision of models of reading aloud by adults other than just the teacher. It may be particularly important that children receive a range of such models, especially in terms of gender.[3]

Teachers can also provide an array of demonstrations of literacy in their classrooms. They are, after all, literate people who continually do literate things. All teachers need to ensure is that the demonstrations they provide are representative of the way literacy is used outside school, and that the children's attention is brought to them.

Reading a story to children is a demonstration of reading, and it can be a very effective way of modelling how to read fluently and with expression. In order to be representative it needs to be accompanied by demonstrations of the more usual way reading is done outside school, that is, silently. Teachers often feel very guilty about reading silently in front of their children, thinking that this does not really count as teaching. But, as we pointed out in Chapter 3, such a lot of important messages can be passed on to children through this activity that it can certainly be counted as very productive teaching.

Writing can also be modelled for children by their teachers. Teachers do this when they write captions under children's drawings which the children then trace or copy. If this is the only demonstration of writing the children receive, however, one of the lessons they may learn is that writing only consists of a line or two at most and it has to be done as painstakingly and as accurately as possible. None of these things is true of writing in the real world, which varies wildly in length and format, is often rushed and full of mistakes, and can be revised and rewritten.[4]

Another way of modelling writing for young children, which can accompany rather than replace existing practices, is for teachers regularly to write their own news, or stories, on large sheets of paper so that the whole class can watch them do it. By doing this, and accompanying the writing by 'thinking out loud' about what they are doing, teachers can demonstrate things such as:

- writing goes from left to right,
- it goes from top to bottom,
- ᵈ lower-case letters,
- ⸱ ᵃ⁻wards.

unison.

By immersing learners in literacy and ᵣ, ⸱ demonstrations of it in action, teachers can lay the ground for the development of children's abilities to partake in it. For this to proceed, however, something else needs to happen. This is something which has been called engagement.[5] It implies that children want to join in with the literate behaviour they see around them, and to try to emulate the demonstrations they receive. This does not necessarily follow from simple exposure to literacy, no matter how frequent. What it requires in addition is that children should value literate behaviour.

As we mentioned earlier, most children arrive at school, for whatever reason, thinking that learning to read and write is quite important and looking forward to learning how to do it. Some of them subsequently do not really manage this to any great degree. Much of this failure comes about, not because the children lack the physical or cognitive resources to succeed in literacy, although a few will, but because they lose their initial impetus to succeed. There is a well-established link between failure in literacy and lack of interest in it.[6] Why do children lose interest in literacy?

There are clearly many causes for this, but we might put forward three likely ones. First, children may come to think of themselves as 'not very good' at reading and writing. This negative self-image may come about through too much being demanded of them too soon, through teachers unwittingly responding negatively to children who do not quite meet their standards, or through the experience of being humiliated or denigrated when trying to partake in literate behaviour, such as reading aloud in a stumbling manner or writing and making a bit of a mess.

Second, the activities in which they take part may lack interest or may not even make sense to the children. It is possible to persuade children that it is important to do such things as reading 'stories' which begin,

> See, see, see.
> See Pat come.
> See, see, see.
> See Peter come.

or beginning every morning for a term by tracing their name card, or playing games in which they have to make new words by putting letters in front of –at. It is much more difficult to persuade them that these activities are intrinsically enjoyable. The problem with these activities does not lie so much in their nature as in their place in the complete literacy programme of the class. If they are balanced with other activities which have greater intrinsic interest and are more obviously related to *real* literacy, they may serve a useful direct teaching function. If, however, they are the dominant type of activity in the programme, children may begin to lose sight of why they are involved in these things in the first place.

Third, children may fail to identify with their teacher as a person whose demonstrations of literacy they want to copy. This is a difficult area, but it seems fairly clear that children will only model their actions on those of someone they actually want to be like.[7] Teachers start at an advantage in this because most children do seem to want to please them and be like them. It is all too easy though for teachers to unconsciously rebuff children, lose patience with them or be negative to them, so that the children come to reject the behaviour of the teacher as a desirable model.

To avoid all this, teachers need to try to ensure that their children:

(a) achieve some success at literacy from the very beginning, no matter how small. This might mean structuring the activities the children take part in so that they are almost always easy, so that the feeling of being successful can develop.

(b) never feel that their literacy performance is dreadfully inadequate and cause for humiliation.

(c) experience a literacy programme most of which consists of meaningful, intrinsically interesting activities which relate clearly to literacy in the world outside school.

(d) are treated in ways that convince them they are liked and valued by the teacher.

⸳ ⸻ch more likely that children will develop ⸻literacy.

⸻le of

can have ⸻ ⸻ themselves and their own cap⸻⸻

Children's self-images as learners can also be ⸻, are allowed and encouraged to take more responsibility for their own learning of literacy. It is rather sad to see children who at 4 years old came to school convinced they could write and willing to have a go, by 6 years old hardly attempting even the simplest piece of writing without besieging the teacher for spellings. Such children have lost all sense of being responsible for their learning. They have learnt that someone else always knows best. Similarly in reading there are many children who, when they meet a word they do not recognise, will wait to be told it rather than make an informed guess or read on past it to see if it becomes clear later. This again is an abdication of responsibility.

There are several things teachers can do to try to avoid this happening, such as providing a variety of sources of help in the classroom. Children can be encouraged to use word banks or simple dictionaries in their writing. A series of labelled pockets displayed on the wall of the classroom, each labelled with a letter of the alphabet and containing cards with words written on them can be the source of a great deal of useful learning. Children can be encouraged to add to the words and always to try to search for the word they want in the word bank before asking anyone else. In reading, children can be given activities such as simple cloze exercises to encourage them to make predictions according to meaning.

Underlying any actions of this kind, teachers can make it an explicit rule in their classrooms that children must make attempts to work things out for themselves before asking for any help. In writing, this might take the form of encouraging children to write what they can from the very start, inventing their own ways to represent their meanings, rather than beginning with copy-writing. Some teachers have involved children in this kind of work by giving them special writing books such as journals, in which the children and the teacher join in written dialogues with one another. Because in these dialogue journals the teacher is responding directly to what the child says, rather than to the way it is written, the child is encouraged to attempt to express ideas which otherwise may well remain unexpressed.[9]

Another activity of this kind is for children to try to write what they can, and then for the teacher to ask them what they have said so she can then 'write it in *my* way'. This reverses the familiar pattern of copy-writing, and may be less of a disincentive for children to write. The teacher still provides a model for the child of how adult writing is done, but the child is not set the laborious task of copying the writing out.

There is no reason why these activities should not take place alongside other activities such as pattern making or pencil play, which are designed to train manual movements. Such activities will still be necessary, as children need to learn efficient ways of forming letters. Because they are separate from writing activities with their emphasis on meaning rather than letter formation, however, children are less likely to receive conflicting messages about what to really attend to in a particular activity.[10]

In reading, teachers can encourage children to read collaboratively rather than only individually. Two heads are inevitably better than one, and a pair of children can often cope with texts which are too difficult for either of them individually. They can also be encouraged to read silently much earlier than is usually the case, and their time with the teacher can take the form of a conversation about what they have read rather than a performance of accurate reading.[11]

In activities such as these, accuracy is inevitably going to assume less importance. Children will make many errors. They will 'invent' incorrect spellings in their writing, they will read not what is on the page but what they think it ought to say. The way teachers view these errors is very important. They might be seen as mistakes and pointed out to the children as such, with the underlying message that they should not make them. This is an understandable view in the light of the considerable emphasis placed upon accuracy by those to whom teachers are accountable, such as many parents. But it is a view which contradicts what we know about learning. If we take the view that children are actively constructing their own knowledge about the world, and continually forming, testing, and ... hypotheses about how the world works,[12] we can see that ... of the current hypotheses ... ch

Allowing these app... extra effect of giving children more pra... writing. Children who are constrained to write accurately are likely to write less, for fear of making mistakes, and children who believe reading is primarily about accuracy are likely to read more deliberately and hence more slowly. These are sensible responses to the situations they are in, but taken together they mean that these children get less practice at using literacy. While it is true that practice alone does not guarantee development, it is a necessary ingredient in effective learning.

All the above processes take place, of course, in a social context. It is, however, impossible for teachers to duplicate the closely collaborative context in which children learn to talk and pick up their early insights about literacy. This will usually be through a one-to-one relationship, whereas teachers have responsibility for perhaps thirty children. Yet a social and collaborative context is very important for the development of literacy, to an extent which has only recently been realised. Current theories suggest that children operate at two levels of capacity: a level at which they can function completely independently, and a level at which they can perform adequately in co-operation with other, more experienced operators. The difference between these two levels, which is known as the 'zone of proximal development', is the area in which the most productive teaching can take place, since what children can do in collaboration with others today, they can do by themselves tomorrow.[13]

Teaching in this zone in a normal classroom will almost certainly involve the organisation of children into groups, although there will need to be times when one-to-one situations are arranged, for book-sharing and for writing conferences, for example, activities which we describe more fully below. Judicious use of parents and other visitors to the class can enable these situations to occur more frequently than would otherwise be the case. Yet many activities will benefit from the involvement of a group of children, whose zones of proximal development overlap. Examples include the sharing of 'big books' between the teacher and a small group of children, and the organisation of groups to write together or to share their writing with each other. In these activities the input of the teacher is spread between members of the groups.

Through collaborative activities, teachers can give children the response they need if they are to develop, and can also establish the useful principle of children giving each other helpful responses. This response takes the obvious form of feedback, from which children can revise their hypotheses about the workings of literacy, but it goes beyond feedback in including responses to intentions as well as performance. Teachers need to respond to what children try to say in their reading and writing as well as to how they do it. This can be done in very small ways such as laughing with a child at a funny passage in a book, or showing interest in the events a child wants to write about. Sometimes this kind of response replaces feedback on performance, and sometimes it accompanies it. Literacy teaching which concentrates only upon performance tends to promote a view of school literacy as separate from its use in the real world.

## LITERACY TEACHING: SOME RECENT DEVELOPMENTS

The insights which have been gained from the study of emergent literacy are at the root of some recent developments in the teaching of reading and writing.

## Reading

In the teaching of reading the apprenticeship approach has had a great deal of influence.[14] This involves children learning to read by sharing books with the teacher or other adult who gives them the support necessary to make their reading successful from the very beginning. This might include such activities as:

- the teacher reading to the child who follows the text,
- the teacher and child both reading aloud, with the child joining in where he/she decides,
- ~~----~~ ~~child~~ reading in unison,

~~--ther~~ after reading it

words said aloud to the ~~-----~~

In each of these activities the teacher is adopting ~~---~~ of explicit instructor, but of a more expert participant. By taking part in the activity of reading alongside this more experienced and knowledgeable partner, children pick up the knowledge and techniques associated with the activity. They may also be told and shown how to go about the activity more efficiently, just as in more traditional teaching approaches. What really counts here is the context of the instruction, which is never other than a complete act of reading. This completeness helps ensure meaningful experience for the children, for whom the activity is the sharing of a book and not the completion of an isolated exercise.

For this apprenticeship approach to work successfully, it demands that the books which are used for sharing are perceived as worthwhile by the children, that is, they tell real stories or have interesting things to say. This concern for the quality of the material used for reading has led to the so-called 'real books' approach, discussed in more detail in a later chapter.[16] The term 'real books' is, however, usually used to distinguish between books which are written because their authors have something interesting to say, and books which, because they are written to fit the needs of a particular scheme or sequence, are artificial even though they might contain interesting material. The real test of a 'real' book is, nevertheless, in a child's reaction to it. Books which children perceive as worthwhile reading are the books through which they will learn to read. Many of the books which form part of more modern reading programmes thus would qualify as 'real' in this sense.

In the teaching of writing, evidence from children's early attempts at writing has been used to support an approach which permits children to form and continually remodify their own beliefs about how writing works. This 'developmental' approach fits well with the shift of emphasis from writing products to the writing process which has characterised most recent research into writing.[17]

Fundamental to the approach is the provision of an environment in which children can 'write' without too early a concern for mastery of the conventions of adult writing. Most children will begin by making marks which they call writing, to distinguish them from drawing. The teacher responds to these as if they were fully formed writing, and may write down underneath what the child says the marks represent. From the model of writing thus received, and from other experience with print, the child begins to make recognisable letter shapes and later attempts some linking of these shapes with the sounds of words. Typical in children's writing of this type are sequences such as:

> W R G T T FM
> (We are going to the farm)

The use of sequences of consonants (often initial letters) to represent words shows a marked development in children's understanding about writing, as they realise that writing is an attempt to capture on paper the sounds of speech.[18] Later this insight becomes refined as they realise that sound matching is not the only consideration in writing, although 'writing it as it sounds' is a principle which influences many children's writing for some time. In Helen's letter, for example, (Fig. 5.1) we have a 6 year old showing mastery of such non-sound-related writing patterns as 'talk' and 'right', but still using the sound principle for 'farther' (father), 'raydeers' (reindeers) and 'or' (all).

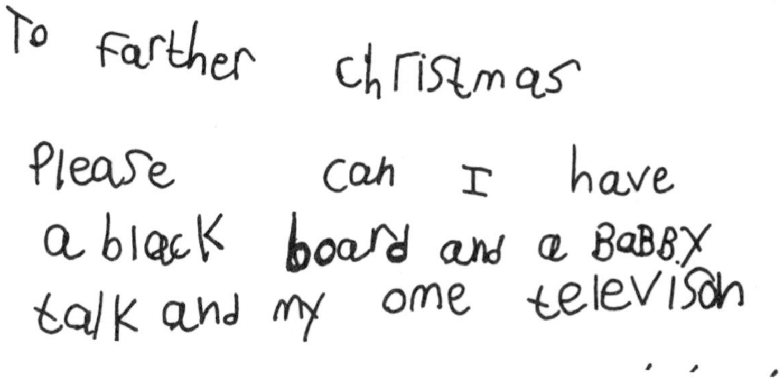

To Farther christmas

Please    can I have
a black board and a BaBBy
talk and my ome televison

          ' ' ,

*Figure 5.1* Letter to Father Christmas

Incidentally, we might speculate on how this child knows about the letter writing convention of P.S. (although she puts it in the wrong place). This certainly had not been mentioned by her teachers, who had, however, previously tried to teach Helen to begin letters with 'Dear...'. Thus we have a good example of a child deciding for herself just what she will learn and what seems unimportant.

It is important to notice that the process of gradual refinement of understandings cannot occur unless children are given the opportunity to engage in this 'creative' or 'invented' spelling. The same process of hypothesis generation and modification is seen in children's attempts to come to terms with other conventions of writing, although these have not yet been studied as closely as the development of spelling.[19]

In Figure 5.2, for example, David, who is five and a half, shows that he has realised that writing has to have full stops, but has not yet worked out their precise function. He uses them to separate words rather than sentences, which, although not the adult

David

To. father. chirStmasS. I. Waod.
. lice ∅. boxing. GlurS. AN-MaSK.
. g. Books. puZZIeS. Kite
. foot: ball. DeSK AfooE. ball. Top.
. Foot. Ball. Sute. and
. a, Jungle. Book.

*Figure 5.2* Letter to Father Christmas

convention, is still a sensible conclusion given the evidence he has.
We might also notice that he does not use capital letters
conventionally either, but neither is he random in this use. With
the exception of 'k', for which he only seems to know one form, he
only uses capitals for the beginnings of words. This again is a
hypothesis he is currently working with. (His uncertainty as to
whether 'football' is one word or two can be seen from his two
different attempts at it.)

Both the apprenticeship approach to reading and the
developmental approach to writing have in common, among other
things, a treatment of literacy behaviour as holistic and
meaningful in its own right. Teaching in these approaches only
occurs in the context of activities which are real to the children,
rather than specially devised for teaching purposes. This is
perhaps the most powerful lesson which can be learnt from the
examination of the conditions in which children learn to talk and
begin their acquisition of early insights into literacy. Neither of
these events is conceived as involving 'teaching', perhaps because
the adults involved do not class themselves as teachers. When
children arrive at school, however, teaching naturally does and
should take place, but it would seem sensible to try, as far as
possible, to fit this teaching into the context of meaningful and
meaning-creating activity which has been so successful in starting

most children on the road to becoming independent users of language and literacy. School therefore can be a continuation of development rather than a completely new start along different lines.

## FOLLOW-UP ACTIVITIES

1 Observe a child (5 to 6 years old) reading a book he has chosen for himself. How would you describe this child's reading behaviour? Can you deduce from this observation what the child thinks is involved in reading? How useful for longer-term development are these beliefs?

two possibilities). Examine it carefully. ...

you about this child's understanding of writing? Compare your analysis with that used by Newman (1984).

# Chapter 6

# The teaching of reading

## INTRODUCTION

We live in a highly literate society, in which every child needs to, and is entitled to, learn to read. It is not surprising that reading is called the first R, as most teachers see it as the most fundamental skill to be mastered in the primary years. Many children would agree with them; ask a child new to a reception class what he is going to learn at school, and the most common reply is 'to read'. Such clearly seen, shared purpose is comparatively rare in children's school learning and ought to be the best possible start to the process of learning to read. How, then, did researchers observe, 'a large number of children who find the task of learning to read a fearsome business. Some manage it only with the greatest of difficulty, some not at all'?[1]

There is no simple answer to this question and the teaching of reading has perhaps generated more controversy than any other aspect of language teaching. In the past there have been many influential theories about how children learn to read. Is it word by word, sound by sound, letter cluster by letter cluster, sentence by sentence or in some entirely different way? The debate about this has been heated, and at times acrimonious. Some of these theories have been reflected in a number of 'methods' of teaching reading and the publishing of materials to support these methods. At the moment there are materials available that are advertised as carefully structured and minutely graded, and also materials which sell precisely because they avoid grading and are comparatively unstructured. Both extremes, and all the products which take a middle position, are aimed at the same market – teachers, and it is teachers who must evaluate the theories and materials and plan a balanced start for the children in their classes. This chapter will review the main approaches to the teaching of reading, and the models that underlie them. It will then go on to consider how early reading can be organised in the classroom, and set into context as a language process.

## THE READING PROCESS

Reading is a highly complicated process, and there are a number of insights and concepts that the successful reader must develop. Some of the most basic concepts about print include the

~~~~~~~~~~~~~~~~~~~~~~~~~~~~~~~~~~~~~~~~~~~~~~~ the white spaces) are

the typeface used......

to distinguish these letters at speed. Working on a letter-by-letter basis the individual could manage to read about 30 to 40 words a minute.[2] In fact fluent readers are much faster than this, which has been taken as evidence that we perceive only the distinctive features of the letters, particularly the parts that project above the middle of the line.

In addition to recognising the letters, a reader becomes aware of the relationship between sounds and letters. The 44 sounds of English are represented by 26 letters in a way that is certainly highly patterned, but not entirely regular. A study investigating the one and two syllable vocabulary of 6 to 9 year olds claimed that the 6,092 words they knew included 211 letter-sound relationships. Of these, 166 were governed by rules and the remaining 45 were exceptions. Unfortunately the exceptions were found to occur in over 600 of the easiest words![3] Fluent readers probably construct some sort of mental image of the patterns of letters which allows them to develop expectations of letter sequences. They must also be able to distinguish morphemic units (the smallest units of meaning) and, for example, recognise that 'training', 'trained' and 'retrain' are all linked in meaning to 'train'.

The fluent reader must develop a concept of 'word' which includes a recognition that words are separated by spaces. Words must also be recognised and distinguished from one another. There are various theories which attempt to explain how readers do this.[4] According to some, it is the first and last letters which are of the greatest significance, while for others the overall word shape is the key. In any case, it is important that the reader knows that words are more than simply the sum of their letters, and can associate each word with its meaning. Even this is not as simple as it sounds as there are a great many words that have more than one meaning. Homonyms like the word 'lead' may be pronounced in more than one way and have more than one meaning. The correct one can only be located by looking at the context of the word and using clues from the surrounding text. Other words, such as the homophones 'tail' and 'tale' sound the same but have different meanings.

There is clearly more to understanding a passage than recognising the words and there is evidence to suggest that fluent readers do not need to read every word of a text in order to derive its meaning.[5] The fluent reader uses larger elements of text such as clauses and sentences and develops a high level of understanding about these. Efficient reading demands a great deal of knowledge of and familiarity with the syntax, or sentence structure, of written language.

There are a number of basic devices which make sentences hang together and run smoothly; these are known as cohesive ties.[6] Some are syntactic devices, such as the use of pronouns to refer to previously mentioned nouns, as in the following example.

The car simply refused to start. *It* had always been temperamental.

Others use vocabulary as a means of linking, as in the following example.

Some people find it hard to believe that smoking is bad for you. All the information and propaganda has had no effect upon *such doubters.*

The operation of these ties becomes second-nature knowledge to experienced readers, who have no problems in making the necessary links. For those less experienced, however, their operation can sometimes be mystifying.

Another major difficulty for young readers may be the way words are arranged as a part of these syntactic structures. Children are familiar with spoken language, and this prepares them for many of the structures they will meet, allowing prediction and anticipation of word sequences. However, written language is subtly different from speech.[7] Spoken language is looser in structure as it can rely on accompanying gestures or shared understanding of a context for its full meaning. This is not so with written language, which because it is disembedded from context has to be more clearly organised and more formal. Fairly basic written language seems to use forms that do not develop in spoken ... and will be unfamiliar to young readers. ... preparation

## MODELS OF READING

Learning to read involves learning how to make meaning from printed symbols. Different theoretical models make different assumptions about how this operates, and can be grouped according to these assumptions into three main categories: top down, bottom up and interactive models.

### Bottom-up models

Some models of the reading process assume that the process starts with the recognition and decoding of letters, clusters of letters and words, with the reader processing progressively larger units of print up to the level of the sentence, paragraph, page and finally complete text. Such models are known as bottom-up models of reading.[9] They have also been referred to as 'outside-in' models[10] since they make the assumption that reading is a process which begins outside the reader, whose task it is to transfer into his consciousness the meaning represented by the writer as graphic symbols. This model can be represented by the following diagram (Figure 6.1).

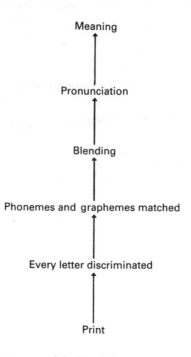

*Figure 6.1* A bottom-up model of reading

One version of a bottom-up model[11] attempted to show what happens between the time the eye fixes on a letter and the speaking of a word one second later. Again the assumption is that meaning is obtained in a step-by-step fashion going from the letter to the meaning as a sequence. The chief difficulty with models of this nature is that adults read a great deal faster than they can explain, and during this reading probably do not attend to every word or letter on the page. The model cannot explain, for example, how a fluent reader can read a sentence such as, 'iF yuo aer a fluet reodur yuo wll hve on pRblme reOdng ths sNtnce'. Strict bottom-up processing would not produce a meaningful sentence. It has generally been accepted that this model, which emphasises reading as a code-cracking activity, does not explain the full extent of reading behaviour.

## Top-down models

These models propose that the reading process begins in the mind of the reader who hypothesises about the meaning of the print to be read. The reader then samples the text to confirm or reject these hypotheses. Reading therefore does not require the processing of every letter or even of every word, but only sufficient of the text to allow the reader to gain an impression of its meaning.[12] These models have also been referred to as 'inside-out' as they assume that the most significant feature of reading is what is brought to the text from within the reader's mind.[13] The ~~diagram~~ represents this kind of model.

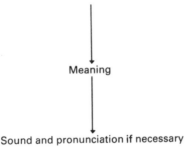

Meaning

Sound and pronunciation if necessary

*Figure 6.2* A top-down model of reading

The top-down models of Goodman and Smith have had an enormous influence on teaching practice in primary schools over the last few years. Goodman calls reading a 'psycholinguistic guessing game' in which the reader scans the text, focuses on some graphic information (print) and also uses syntactic, semantic and phonological input from his own mind to make guesses or predictions about the nature of the text. The reader then samples the text to confirm the predictions or reject them. If predictions are confirmed then reading proceeds, if not then the cycle is picked up at an earlier point.

Top-down models emphasise meaning, rather than the code of reading, and see the clause as the most significant linguistic unit rather than the word or letter. These models present reading as a parallel to listening. They assume that the child learns to read by reading and gradually picks up the parallelism between reading and listening. So the reader does not need to develop any conscious knowledge of the features of written language. One problem associated with this assumption is that research has demonstrated that the ability to segment words into phonemes (sounds) may predict later reading ability.[14] This seems to indicate that an awareness of the features of written language does have a part to play in learning to read.

### Interactive models of reading

Few people would now subscribe to an exclusively top-down or bottom-up model of reading, and attempts have been made to create models which combine the strengths of both of these. These new models can be termed interactive models and acknowledge that reading is both a perceptual and cognitive process, in which the reader uses both previous experience and the 'code' features of the text to create meaning (Figure 6.3).

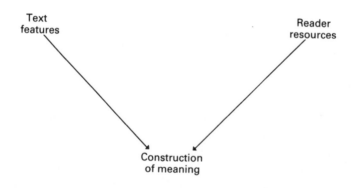

*Figure 6.3* An interactive model of reading

One model of this type is that of Rumelhart which attempts to explain the interaction of perceptual and cognitive features.[15] Rumelhart's model has at its heart a 'message centre' that deals with the input from the senses. This is constantly scanned by a number of 'knowledge sources' which contain specialised knowledge about, for example, the structure of stories and other text genres, linguistic patterns, sound-symbol relationships and the world in general. Each knowledge source scans the message centre for hypotheses relevant to that source, evaluates them and confirms or rejects them. This model has similarities to both of the other models, but is flexible in that it can focus on either top-down

that they

## APPROACHES TO TEACHING

There are a number of 'methods' of teaching reading current in British schools today, and these are based on the assumptions about reading that underlie certain models of the process. Just how particular children learn to read depends on the children, their relationship with the teacher, and the way their learning is managed.

At face value the easiest way to teach a child to read a passage seems to be to teach that child the words and this is the basis of the 'Look and Say' approach to reading. Children can learn to recognise words printed on large cards so that when a card is held up the child can say the appropriate word. This process, using flashcards, is usually done in class groups and was once a daily occurrence in many infant classes. Accompanied by practice at home, the youngster could develop the repertoire of the thirty or so words necessary to get his first book. These early books would be limited to the words already learned, and give further practice not only for recognising the words, but for recognising them in sentences. This means the reader could be confident of knowing the words, and gradually build up a sight vocabulary.

Of course, there are disadvantages associated with this approach. For some children the relationship between seeing and saying is easily grasped, for others it can be thoroughly confusing. These latter children are not always easy to spot, as they may learn to repeat what they hear from other children in the group. Nor can the teacher always be sure whether the children are attending to the print on the card, or some other feature like a thumbprint or torn corner!

Some words are easily recognised and learned, especially distinctive ones like 'hippopotamus', or words that represent familiar things. Other words are more difficult especially those that do not represent items, such as 'go', 'here' and 'it', etc. and learning a great number will place a strain on the memory. To ensure that words are thoroughly learned before presenting the child with materials which use these words will tend to limit the texts of such materials to combinations of these function words. Repetition of words will also be a significant feature. Not surprisingly some of these texts bear little relationship to real language and are likely to further confuse children, rather than grab their interest. It is doubtful whether a text which consists of versions of 'Oh, oh, oh, look Janet, look' could ever engender intrinsic interest in its child readers.

One of the most significant difficulties with 'look and say' as a method of teaching reading is that it relies on the children knowing each word individually, and getting that knowledge from the teacher. This does not provide learners with strategies which can help them to read words that they have not encountered before, nor does it place any value upon meaning as a way into word recognition.

It is unlikely that anyone could learn enough words to read in this way, and the orthography of English operates in a way that makes this feat of memory unnecessary.[16] Young children soon come to discriminate such features of written language as letters and help themselves 'crack the code'. This idea of reading as decoding also underlies phonic methods of teaching reading, which rely on children learning the sound-symbol associations of English. If children learn the sounds associated with the symbols R, E and D then they can read RED. Once all the sounds are known, then the reader should be able to decode any passage.

However there are problems associated with the use of phonics in reading. English is not a regular language and the reader has to deal with sound-symbol irregularity. For example in the word RED is the symbol E. This also appears in the word HERE; however neither of the sounds it represents in HERE are the same as in RED. The reader has to learn this through experience.

To look at another type of irregularity, the sound represented by the first E in HERE also occurs in MACHINE but is represented by I. So the same sound can be represented by different letters. In fact it is often impossible to work out the sound of a letter until you know the word. A good example of this is 'read' and 'read', words that are written with the same symbols but have different sounds.

Just as there are many phonic rules to cope with these ⁓⁓⁓ exceptions to them. Consider the

in various ways, ⁓⁓⁓ simplifications of the alphabet itself as, for ⁓⁓⁓, Teaching Alphabet. A vast range of materials has also been produced to support phonic methods, and these stress various combinations of sounds.

The approaches outlined above all emphasise certain aspects of the code of reading and the materials written to support these approaches reflect this. In an attempt to stress particular words or letter combinations in limited vocabulary texts, the language often becomes artificial and unexciting – and probably confusing to a child used to spoken language.

One approach to reading that particularly considers children's natural use of language is the language experience approach, whose basic principles are summarised below.[17]

1  What children think about they can talk about.
2  What they can talk about can be expressed in painting, writing or some other form.
3  Anything they write can be read.
4  They can read what they write and what other people write.
5  As they represent their speech sounds with symbols, they use the same symbols (letters) over and over again.

This approach to reading led to the publication of *Breakthrough to literacy* materials in 1970. These included sentence makers which held word cards and allowed the children to 'write' their own texts, word makers (with individual letter cards) and a set of books, graded by colour, that children could progress to when they had read some of their own texts. This approach allowed children to start reading with texts whose meaning was known (they had written them), and which were more relevant to the children than limited vocabulary books could be. The main advantage was that the language they were reading was naturally patterned by the child, and the children's own dialect could be respected and used as a starting point for their reading. The differences between spoken and written language and standard and non-standard dialects could be pointed out and introduced to the children gradually.

This approach to reading has the enormous advantage of emphasising the natural links between spoken language, reading and writing. It has been criticised, however, for the limitations it tends to impose upon the texts created by the children. Because of the materials used, and because it tends to involve children in copying texts, they tend not to 'write', and thus read, texts much longer than a line or two. The materials also lead to a certain amount of 'sameness' in these texts. For a child who has previously 'written', 'I went to the shops with my mum' changing this to 'I went to the park with my friend' is a lot easier than beginning a completely new structure. Recent insights into the texts children are capable of writing without these structural limitations (See Chapters 4 and 5) suggest greater potential which teachers need to build upon.

The language experience approach, as it was first used, did focus on certain aspects of the code of reading, and encouraged word recognition, but it also emphasised meaning. Children were encoding their own meanings and so were more likely to want to, and be able to read them. Criticisms of the method have resulted not in its disappearance, but rather in a broader interpretation, and its use alongside newer methods.

One of the most compatible has been the 'story method' approach to reading, which also sets the teaching of reading skills into a context of meaning.[18] This approach starts with children being read stories by teacher, parent, tape recorder, etc. until they know them and can read the stories themselves. Focus is then placed upon certain features of the story such as interesting words, phrases and other graphical features so that the child can develop knowledge to generalise to other stories. Initially this approach was accompanied by a number of carefully graded schemes which consisted not only of books, but also 'support materials' in the form of extra books, consumable workbooks etc.

In recent years, however, teachers have expressed themselves less satisfied with the story content of special schemes, and this has led to the idea of 'individualised reading'.[19] This recommended children's books and books from reading schemes that fitted into ~' ~*~~~ colour-coded stages to be used as a sort of high-quality ~~~~~~~ on matching the level of
‘ ''٠ This

some instances ٠..٠
are limited to a certain level until they ٠٠٠٠ ٠-
that level. The level of the scheme that a child has achieved may be taken to represent his ability level by the teacher, or the child. One of the most disturbing features of any graded scheme is that it may engender competition between children (and parents) in the belief that the child who progresses through the scheme faster is a better reader and will achieve more. This can result in pressure that can damage the child's self-esteem and performance.

An approach to the teaching of reading that moves still further from the code emphasis of early methods and places a greater emphasis on meaning is known as the 'real books' method.[20] This recognises the wealth of children's literature which exists today and questions the need for artificial scheme texts that stress particular elements. Proponents claim that children can develop generalised understandings about print and story from real texts.

The use of real books has gone hand in hand with the 'apprenticeship approach' to reading.[21] This approach is similar to the story book approach, but eschews a graded system of books, preferring to vest more choice in the child. The idea is that each text is read with a supportive adult until the child feels ready to take over, and even then the adult is there to fill in when necessary so that the child has complete access to the meaning of the text. The children learn to read by reading, rather than by performing the necessary component skills.

This approach is firmly based on a top-down model of reading and stresses meaning at the expense of learning about the code of written language. Most commercial materials suitable for this approach are collections of 'real' books or collections of loosely graded stories, plays and information books. This approach to the teaching of reading has been criticised for failing to help children develop concepts about the features of language in a planned or explicit way, and for the difficulties of managing such a teacher-intensive type of reading teaching. It is hardly surprising that the growth of this approach has also seen a growth in parental involvement in school reading.[22]

In looking at approaches to the teaching of reading it is clear that older methods and materials were more code based, whilst newer methods have emphasised meaning. This would seem to indicate a shift from a bottom-up to top-down model of reading. However, it cannot be said that any method or model has proved perfect or infallible, and few teachers stick rigidly to one. Today many teachers take what might be termed an eclectic approach, using the best features of a number of methods. This can be based on an interactive model of reading which stresses meaning and still attempts to develop children's awareness of the features of written language. There are a number of classroom practices that no teacher or theoretician would deny are beneficial.[23]

Reading schemes of all kinds were designed to assist teachers in the process of teaching children to read, and not to take over that responsibility. Reading schemes have been much criticised in recent years, but it is possible that too much has been expected of them. They 'work' only as well as the teacher who operates them. Teachers with a thorough understanding of the reading process should be able to choose suitable material for their approach and their children.

## MANAGEMENT AND ORGANISATION OF READING INSTRUCTION

Recent research in London infant schools[24] suggested that on average infant children spend as little as 2 per cent of their time reading, and a quarter of this 2 per cent was time spent reading to the teacher. The rest included reading alone or with others, playing reading games, using computer reading programs, etc. The same study also found that the children spent 2 per cent of their time wandering aimlessly in the class. This is time that could be used for reading without loss to any other part of the curriculum.

One way to increase reading time is to offer a balanced diet of reading activities. Children need time to flick through books and make choices; they may want to read all or parts of some books, write and read reviews and ask the opinions of their peers. Some children will want to read to themselves, some may prefer reading ~~ There should be attractive reading ~~ ~~ iduals or~~

found to be ~~ aloud. The act of hearing children read ~~ accepted practice in many schools that it is the core of reading teaching, and needs to be understood, examined, and perhaps questioned.

The origins of the practice of reading to the teacher are unclear, but the increase in this practice is certainly linked with the growth in popularity of reading schemes. Teachers have, to some extent, become operators of schemes rather than direct instructors, and hear children read to check that they have learned whatever the scheme is designed to teach at that point, be it words, or letters or sounds. The Bullock Committee[25] found that most teachers tested the child on a book before they allowed him or her to move up the scheme. This is not the only reason for the popularity of hearing children read. The rise of child-centred views about children's learning emphasised the value of learning through natural growth and discouraged such things as chanting and rote learning. In large classes, hearing children reading came to be seen as valuable individual contact time. The Bullock report suggested that all children should be heard reading several times a week, with questions to test comprehension, in order to keep a check on the progress of individual children and this advice as much as anything is responsible for the predominance of the activity in modern classrooms.[26]

There are a number of reasons why teachers hear children read aloud. First, it allows teachers to give each child valuable individual attention, which may not be easy in a class of thirty or more infants. By hearing children read, the teacher can in effect check that they can read the books, and give them specific help when and where they need it, in the context of the text they are dealing with. This function is especially important for teachers who are working on the basis of a bottom-up model of reading and feel the need to check the learning of specific sub-skills.

It has been convincingly argued that the teacher's role is to make the reading task easy,[27] and hearing children read affords the opportunity to do just this by helping children to understand what they are reading. This may involve allowing errors and omissions when appropriate, and prompting or supplying words to sustain meaning. Hearing children read can also be used for diagnosis and assessment purposes, and has further possibilities in this direction (See Chapter 11).

There are, however, difficulties associated with hearing children read that make the practice less useful than it might be. First, it rarely provides the high-quality individual contact time teachers would hope for. It has been found that most reading sessions last from two to three minutes and the average interruption-free period is only thirty seconds and it must surely be the case that little effective teaching or help can be given in such a short time.[28] In busy classrooms where a large number of children are heard reading often, it may not be only teacher attention which is scarce, but also teacher time. Two or three minutes per child a couple of times a week may use a large proportion of the teacher's time in a way that is simply not cost-effective.

Hearing children read may also encourage faulty reading strategies, particularly when using schemes which rely heavily on word recognition. The child may feel the need to read the passage absolutely accurately rather than use strategies such as guessing or re-reading which might disrupt fluent performance. This attention to accuracy may also affect the child's understanding. It is not uncommon for teachers to find that some children are able to read books aloud to their teacher but, when questioned, have derived little understanding from them. Teachers should not, perhaps, be surprised by this as, from the child's point of view, the activity often seems to demand understanding only secondarily.

The hearing of reading is an established practice which, despite certain disadvantages, has a great deal to offer. There are a number of ways of using this technique to the best advantage. First, little and often may not be the best way to hear readers. If children spend longer on the task less often, then both child and teacher are likely to get more from the experience.[29] The child could then read a whole story, or read a part and discuss the rest.

The teacher can organise the class in such a way that allows the
 ̇ ̇ ̇ ̇ ̇ ̇ ̇ receive undivided attention. This means insisting upon no
 ̇ ̇ ̇ ̇ ̇ ̇ be achieved by explaining to
 ̇ ̇ ̇ ̇ 

guesses about what  ̇ ̇ ̇ ̇
which carries important messages about reading  ̇ ̇ ̇

The activity should also involve more than listening for assessment; it should also be possible to listen for comprehension. If children read with appropriate intonation it can be taken as an indication that they have some degree of understanding. All readers make mistakes, and prompting by supplying correct words is helpful if a child has chosen a word that destroys the sense of a passage, or if a child is stuck and risks losing the flow of the story. However, teachers should avoid providing words too quickly as this prevents the child re-reading and correcting the mistake spontaneously. Adult readers frequently re-read to correct themselves or be sure of the sense. This is a technique to be encouraged in children. When children get stuck it is tempting to supply the word immediately so that the story is not lost, and to maintain the child's confidence. It may, however, be more useful in the long run to encourage young readers to guess at the meaning by using the context of the story or pictures. This develops useful strategies for the child and gives the teacher a glimpse of the child's understanding. To examine comprehension more closely the teacher may want to discuss the story with the child, examine characters, predict endings and even discuss other work by that author. This becomes a sort of reading conference and not only examines comprehension, but increases the child's involvement with the text.

When involved in these longer reading conferences, teachers will often want to make the most of the diagnostic possibilities. One structured technique for this is known as miscue analysis. This is based on the idea that children make miscues (rather than mistakes) as they learn to read, and that by looking at the miscues it is possible to tell which strategies are in need of further development. (See Chapter 11 for more detail about miscue analysis.)

By making the most of the time spent hearing children read, the teacher can increase the children's involvement and understanding of reading, and go some way towards assessing reading performance. This time should be profitable and enjoyable for teacher and child but will not be the child's entire school reading experience. As the advantages of hearing children read have been questioned, so alternative activities have been developed to replace and supplement this activity.

## ALTERNATIVE ACTIVITIES

Many of the processes that may be considered alternatives to hearing children read are best considered as additional techniques, and can be profitably combined with regular conferences about reading which may include hearing children read.

### Shared reading

One type of shared reading developed from a language experience approach.[30] This involves the use of big books supported in such a way that the teacher can turn the pages and read the book with the children, pointing to the words. This allows younger children to enjoy stories, join in with known stories and develop ideas about the relationship of sound and print. This can be further encouraged by the teacher who will discuss particular words and initial sounds, and encourage prediction of words and events using letter, word, sentence structure and meaning as cues. This sort of social reading can, of course, be extended to all sorts of classroom activities such as reading songs or reading texts composed by the children themselves. The modelling of reading by the teacher makes reading behaviour more accessible to the children.

Another type of shared reading is the type of book sharing sessions that have become associated with an apprenticeship approach to reading. This involves the following stages:

1 First the adult reads the book to the child so that the child knows the story.

~ The adult reads the story whenever possible until the child feels ·*h parts.

- ·ntil the child is reading.

~ supplying words

sharcu

sharing the whole tcx. ,

the teacher modelling reading, uis....

passage, and discussion of any decoding probiem.

arisen.[31] Some ingredients of this activity might be:

1 Teacher reads some of the text.
2 Child reads some of the text.
3 Teacher sets a reading purpose to encourage skimming and scanning.
4 The teacher asks a child to read a paragraph aloud or silently.
5 The teacher asks questions.
6 The teacher encourages the child to ask questions.
7 The teacher and the child discuss decoding problems.
8 The teacher and the child discuss content.

This sort of shared reading could be the pattern for a half-termly reading conference, and be supported by other methods such as group reading.

## Paired reading

Paired reading has been used in a number of areas of the country in recent years. It was originally designed for use by parents with their children but has also been successful when used by teachers and older children.[32] The technique has three phases:

1 The child and adult read in unison.
2 When the child feels confident enough to read for himself he knocks on the table or indicates in some other way and the adult allows him to read alone.
3 If the child is stuck on a word or makes a mistake the adult simply joins in again.

The technique has several positive points. Praise is offered regularly, and the child is never left to struggle. It also ensures that the meaning is not lost and allows the child to use reading strategies other than word recognition, in a way that might be difficult when reading alone. Above all, it can help motivation, confidence and attitude. Paired reading projects set up with parents have proved very successful, and the teacher time spent organising and helping parents has been worthwhile.

### Prepared reading[33]

This technique has been suggested as a version of paired reading. It involves four stages:

1 The teacher and child talk about the book, with the teacher outlining the story and characters.
2 The teacher reads to the child from the book.
3 The child reads the same passage silently.
4 The child reads the same passage aloud.

An essential fifth stage would be some sort of feedback about the content. This could be discussion, a review or telling another group about it. Prepared reading has some of the advantages of paired reading in that the child hears an adult reading and this can give confidence and promote understanding. This technique also encourages silent reading and could be useful for those children who are moving towards mainly silent reading.

### Group reading

In some ways group reading may be interpreted as a step backwards, as many teachers remember a form of it which involved a group of six or more children taking it in turn to read a page each of a book. This procedure seemed to create definite discipline problems as the children in the group quickly worked out which page would be theirs to read and then lost concentration as other children read, perhaps in a halting manner. Group reading has, however, regained popularity, albeit in a different form. In essence it still requires children to work in groups of six or seven reading the same book. There are a number of ways of organising the reading, with or without the presence of the teacher. With the ⁻⁻ʳ reading might follow a pattern such as the

This arrangement ᵢₙ₋
covered is increased, so that slowᵢ ₋
story rather than a short excerpt. Group reading is ᵤ.
uses less teacher time, and this time is less likely to be subject to frequent interruptions. It also allows more time to introduce and discuss the story, and the opportunity for collaborative follow-up work. This method of reading offers confidence, the support of shared reading, and time to consider word attack strategies. Some authors assert that children attain higher reading standards when they work in groups.[34]

There are, of course, other ways to organise group reading. Two children at a time might read a page together, the whole group can read together, or the teacher can read the passage then ask the children to read the same passage imitating the intonation used. Plays are ideal for group reading, or poetry with a chorus which could be read by the whole group. On the whole, group reading seems to have many advantages, and disadvantages such as lack of individual teaching time are compensated for by using it in conjunction with individual sessions.

## CONCLUSION

Reading to the teacher has been estimated to take up a very small proportion of an infant's day but a large part of a child's reading time. To increase the time spent on reading, children should have opportunities to read with other adults, such as their parents, at home. A great deal of research has indicated that programmes to involve parents in this kind of work generally produce excellent results.[35] Many schools have found positive benefits, above and beyond the improvement of children's reading, arising from the establishment of parental partnership programmes. The trend of these programmes has been a shift away from simply using parents as an extra listening ear for children to encouraging a book-sharing approach. In the process a great deal of useful parent education has taken place, but many people have been most surprised by the degree to which parents, even those previously thought incapable of or unwilling to be involved, have responded to the programmes.

It is also possible substantially to increase reading opportunities in school time. Children can get a great deal of profitable reading practice from reading games or from work with computer programs. They can also read to younger children, read with the help of tape recorders and read with other adults such as parents in the classroom. There are also, of course, many opportunities to practise reading in the other curriculum areas which make up a primary child's experience. Children learn to read by reading, and teachers must make reading accessible to them. This does not only mean providing sufficient materials at appropriate levels, but also creating meaningful opportunities in which reading can be done. In considering the teaching of reading it is necessary but not sufficient to understand the reading process. It also demands an appreciation of the importance of good reading environments. Previous chapters have made many points about these environments which are equally relevant here.

## FOLLOW-UP ACTIVITIES

1 Try to make a survey of the opportunities provided for reading in a classroom with which you are familiar. Include in your survey the opportunities children have for reading non-fiction material as well as fiction. As a result of your survey, try to suggest some implications which arise for the classroom you have looked at.

2 Choose six or so children at random from a particular class and interview them individually to find out what they think about

reading. Your interview might include questions such as:

- What do you do when you read?
- Do you ever come to difficult bits when you read? When this happens what do you do?
- Who do you know who is a good reader? What do you think this person would do if he/she came to anything difficult in reading?

As a result of these interviews you might be able to draw some conclusions about these children's concepts about the reading
~~Discuss~~ with a colleague whether this information has any
~~brought to these~~

- Are children likely to choose
  interesting or appealing?
- What messages do these books convey about reading?

It would also be interesting to discuss these books with some children. What are the children's views about books for reading?

Does this examination of reading resources have any implications for future provision?

# Chapter 7

# Writing: purpose and process

## INTRODUCTION

Primary school children spend a large proportion of their day writing. They write about what they have done and will do, they write about what they have been told, and they write to practise writing. If we ask teachers why writing is such an important classroom activity, some reply that writing is one of 'the basics'. It is a skill that we all need for effective functioning as adults in our society.

If we consider this statement a little further, it is obvious that a major way in which writing is used in modern society is as a channel of communication, a way to share ideas and information. Adults need to be able to write in an appropriate form for a particular purpose. Children, then, also need to explore and learn about the writing process and the purposes of their writing. This has implications for teachers who must consider these issues and decide how best to offer an appropriate range of writing experiences.

In this chapter we shall discuss the issue of purpose as it pertains to children's writing and outline the important role of audience. We shall also discuss the concept of repertoire and give several suggestions for ways in which children's experience of this might be widened. We shall conclude the chapter by examining the multi-faceted role of the teacher in teaching writing. We shall begin, however, with the most important issue of all: just what is this thing we call writing? An understanding of the writing process must underlie all decisions about teaching strategies and contexts.

## THE WRITING PROCESS

A common-sense view of writing is as a means of communicating information and ideas through the medium of a system of symbols. However,on closer examination it is apparent that it is not quite the simple process that this description would imply. Consider your own efforts as a writer. Writing, say, an essay will involve several stages: discovering what you want to say, ordering your ideas, expressing these on paper, revising and altering the work, putting it into final form suitable for the intended reader.

These stages do not include the pencil sharpening, false starts, coffee making and various other activities that some writers find

̇ ̇ ̇ ̇ ̇ ̇ ̇ adults are able to produce a neat, accurate piece

moulding of ideas and the creation and

Composition is, therefore, a means of learning rather than simply a way of presenting pre-formed ideas. With this in mind, writing has been referred to as 'revising inner speech'.[1] This view of composition, and writing in general, puts emphasis on the role of language as a means of making sense of one's world, 'creating worlds', rather than as a functional means of simply 'shunting information'.[2]

The writer must also *transcribe* the composition. This involves choosing an appropriate form and presenting a correct layout. Transcription also requires accuracy in spelling, grammar, punctuation and handwriting. It is clear that transcription assumes different levels of importance depending upon the purpose of and audience for the writing. A letter to a bank manager requires more care to be given to features such as spelling and handwriting than a shopping list for ourselves. Yet transcription always takes place, and always demands some of our attention in writing.

Ideally the adult should be able to co-ordinate these two dimensions of writing, but this is often not the case. Composition and transcription may inhibit one another.[3] Many adults find that they make more mistakes and changes when writing something important because their minds are so involved with composing the ideas. For children, who may have less than complete mastery of the processes involved, this co-ordination is doubly difficult.

The result of this problem of co-ordination is sometimes that children come to believe that particular parts of the writing process, usually transcription elements, are the most important and should take the lion's share of their attention. When children are asked for their views about writing, they most often express them in similar ways to Kelly, who was asked to give some advice about writing to children in the class below hers (Figure 7.1). All her references are to transcription features.

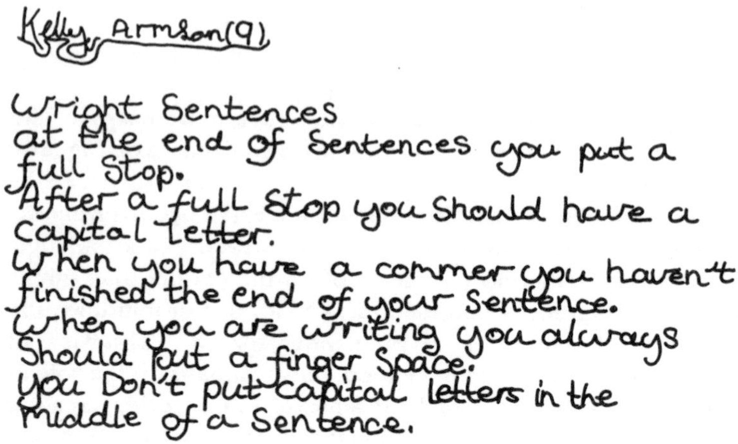

Kelly, Armson(9)

Wright Sentences
at the end of Sentences you put a
full Stop.
After a full Stop you Should have a
capital letter.
when you have a commer you haven't
finished the end of your Sentence.
when you are writing you always
Should put a finger Space.
You Don't put capital letters in the
middle of a Sentence.

*Figure 7.1* Child views on writing

One way to ease this problem is to split the composing and transcription functions of the writer, and attempt to develop them separately. One way to do this is to introduce children to the drafting process, that is going through several versions of a piece of writing. This allows the writer the freedom to concentrate first on composition, and then later to deal with transcription. Drafting, however, implies more than 'writing it in rough first'. It allows children to get to grips with three very important processes in writing: planning, revision and editing.[4]

## Planning

Many children have only the vaguest notions about planning. Elizabeth (8 years old), when asked how she plans her writing, said: 'I write the first idea, then I get another one and I write it down, and I go on until I've run out, and that's the end.' Whilst this may be appropriate in a few situations, this is not the way adult writers work nor the ideal way for children to work. Planning should enable children to generate ideas and formulate thoughts. Remembering all the ideas can be a problem for some children. Eira (7 years old) commented: 'the plan sort of helps when it ˙ ˙ˇˑ ˑˇˑ ideas I forget, and I get new ones then too.' If the ˙ ˑˇˑ ˑˇˑ child may be better able

web. This teacher ˑˑˇˑˑ butterflies; if you don't catch them quickly anu ˇˑˑˑ they soon flutter away'. Another teacher decided to introduce her class of seven year olds to planning by asking them to draw 'beginning', 'middle', and 'end' boxes and put key words into them. This focused their attention on the structure of the writing.

Many children will need this sort of help to get started, but it is important that through their school careers they experience planning in different ways, for two main reasons. First, some types of planning, like the examples above, help develop certain features only of writing. More importantly, though, teachers are aiming to give children sufficient experience to enable them to choose a form of planning most suited to their needs. The form and amount of planning necessary depends on the child and the task.

## Revision

If children are allowed to draft work they are more likely to see it as provisional, and therefore change and improve it.[5] Children, and adults, may need to reflect upon and revise their compositions several times.

It is important to realise the difference between revision and editing. Revision implies qualitative change of content, style or sequence. Although it is the most difficult aspect of the writing process to introduce, revision of drafted writing is a natural follow-on from planning. The questions writers ask themselves depend on the piece of writing, but will include:

- Does it say what I want to say?
- Is it in the right order?
- Is the form right?

Many teachers offer their children sets of questions to get them started, such as:

- Does it make sense?
- Could I add something?
- Should I leave anything out?

These can be displayed as posters or cards and children can use these independently, or with a friend (see Figure 7.2). They may

```
Go through the passage
carefully with a friend.
Read it aloud and
look at the text.

Consider:  Does it make
           sense?

           Is it
           interesting?

           Is it a good
           Length?

           Does it start and
           end well?

           Is anything
           missing?
```

*Figure 7.2* Revision instructions

be the first step towards enabling children to look critically at their work without the prompting of the teacher.

Revision may involve minor adjustments, like insertions, crossings out, etc. or it may necessitate rewriting and moving blocks. Some of these strategies are more difficult than others and it is likely that children will need a great deal of support from their teachers before they are able to use them independently.[6] There are particular techniques to which they can be introduced, such as the use of scissors to physically cut out sections to resequence writing, or the use of a coding system such as that used by one teacher of 9 year olds (see Figure 7.3).

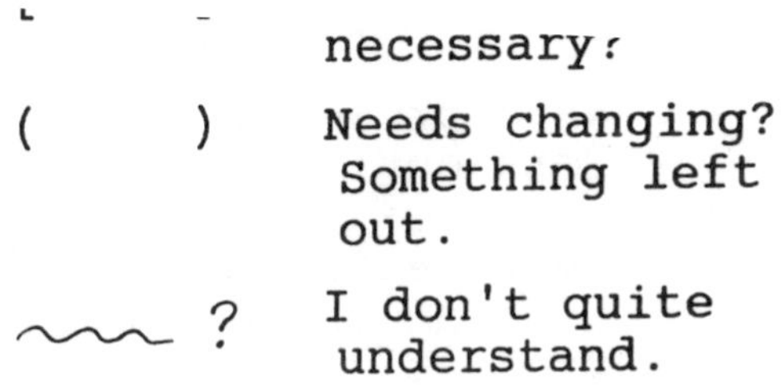

```
L        -        necessary:

(    )            Needs changing?
                  Something left
                  out.

```
 `?`            I don't quite
                  understand.

*Figure 7.3* Content editing

**Editing**

When the writing is at a stage where the author is starting to think about a final draft, then editing becomes necessary. Editing involves correcting the surface features of the text: spelling, grammar, punctuation, etc. Most children are familiar with this in the form of a teacher's 'marking'. Some teachers mark these surface features automatically, and so children set great store by them. This at least means that editing is the easiest part of the process to introduce.

These features of language are important, and although the teacher could correct them quickly and accurately, it is preferable for children to correct work themselves. This is not only a step towards independence, it also allows children to develop transferable strategies for future work.

To support the children in doing this, some teachers supply wallcharts and cards offering questions and advice (see Figure 7.4). These can be used by individuals, or more often, pairs of children. Peer editing (and indeed revision) is helpful in that it offers the child support, advice and opinions, which can be accepted or rejected depending on the author's judgement. It also allows realistic organisation of teacher time as purposeful, task-oriented discussion can take place without the teacher's presence.[7]

## Copy Editing

Go carefully through the work with a friend.

Read it aloud.

| | |
|---|---|
| ∧ | Word or letters left out. |
| ◯ | Punctuation mark missing or in the wrong place. |
| SP | Spelling error |
| \ | Space missing |
| ◯c | Capital letter in the wrong place. |

*Figure 7.4* Copy editing

## PUBLICATION AND EVALUATION

Drafting is a very powerful process that allows children to concentrate on the various elements of writing separately. The emphasis is on producing a better quality product for an audience. This means, of course, that children need to publish and evaluate their writing.

In this context publish means simply 'to make public', and this can take many forms. Some work may be read out to a teacher friend, group or class, perhaps in a designated 'sharing time'. Publication could also mean displaying work so that it becomes reading material in a real sense, from a single piece of writing on ~~· · · ·──···──  for~~ younger children by a group. In all

children are enabled to develop ~~their awareness~~ ─ ─ has an effect upon both the composition and transcription processes which children need to begin to take account of early in their writing experience. They need, in general, to have experience of writing for a range of purposes.

## PURPOSES FOR WRITING

As adults we write for a number of purposes: a letter may be written to a friend, forms are filled in to give information to the tax man, shopping lists remind us of what to buy. Most adult purposes for writing involve communication of ideas and information. This communication is a two-way activity. One person is communicating, and another is receiving the communication, and therefore acting as an audience. This idea of audience is central to adult writing, and yet has tended to be overlooked in school.

A piece of writing has an effect upon its audience. This may be behavioural, cognitive or affective. The reader may act as a result of the communication by, say, buying the right goods. A cognitive response may be that the reader learns something as a result of reading the piece. On an affective level a piece of writing may stimulate emotion or change a person's feelings.

Just as the writing affects the audience, so the audience has an effect on the writing. Let us for a moment compare this with speech. When speaking, the accent, dialect and register we use will depend on the listener, and children soon learn to talk in different ways to their friends and teachers. When writing, the style, form and content of the piece will depend on the intended audience and children need to learn how to control and manipulate these factors to suit their purpose and audience. This growth of control comes about through practice, and will best develop if we can offer children as wide a range of audiences for their writing as early as possible.

Classrooms can offer a range of audiences that can be roughly classified as:

(a) oneself
(b) the teacher
(c) a wider, known audience
(d) a wider, unknown audience.[9]

These will be considered in turn to point out the ways they can be used to develop children's writing.

*a) Writing for self*

Although we do not often write to ourselves, except in diaries and reminders, we do often talk to ourselves, aloud or mentally, to work out ideas and reason things out. Sometimes we use conversation with others as a way of sorting out ideas, and discussion becomes a sort of thinking out loud. The expression of ideas makes them clearer to us. This is a powerful argument for encouraging exploratory talk about new concepts presented in class. Real discussion, rather than one-word answers to a teacher's questions, is vital if concepts are to be properly understood.

Perhaps the most powerful way of getting to grips with new ideas is to explain them to others in writing, and anyone who has written an essay will confirm that putting ideas into words forces us to consider them more carefully. We have to make that knowledge our own in order to present it to others. For adults this involves trying things out on paper before producing a document.

However, children rarely have the chance to do this sort of exploratory writing; to try out ideas they are unsure of and, perhaps come to terms with them. So how can we offer children more opportunity to do this? Here are some possible ways:

(i)   Offer plenty of stimuli and introduction to new ideas.
(ii)  Allow free discussion, preferably before suggesting writing.
(iii) Allow greater scope for children to pursue self-selected topics in writing.
(iv)  When setting a writing topic, allow time, perhaps even a day or so, to elapse before writing. In this time a strong stimulus may ᵼ ᵼ ᵼ discussed.

teacher as an audience.

*b) Writing for the teacher*

For many children the teacher is the most frequent, and most important, audience for their writing. There are two extremes of audience role that the teacher can adopt. At one end of the continuum is the teacher in the role of a trusted adult. Whatever the audience which writing is intended for, teachers will usually be the first people to read what is written and their reaction to it is crucial. The teacher must give the impression of being concerned about what is written, rather than the accuracy of the writing, and that experimentation is encouraged. The first response, therefore, must be to the content of the passage, to show the teacher values the work. A teacher question such as 'Tell me about your writing' may give the right kind of starting point for an appropriate and constructive response. Children need to have confidence in their teacher, knowing that they will be offered advice, support and constructive criticism. For the teacher to attend only to surface features and accuracy is the surest way to destroy this confidence. This brings us to the other extreme of the teacher's role.

At the other end of the continuum is the teacher in the role as an examiner of children's writing, and for too many children this is the dominant role they experience. Many teachers feel under pressure from colleagues, parents and inspectors to display accurate and beautifully presented writing, and to be able to prove that they have marked every piece of work. Not surprisingly this can lead to superficial 'red penning' of writing at the level of spelling, punctuation and neatness. This can give children the impression that accuracy is all, and make many of them fear writing.

This is not to argue, of course, that accuracy and presentation are unimportant, or that teachers should not attempt to assess their children's writing. Assessment is vital to monitor progress and plan future input and experiences. As part of the National Curriculum teachers will be assessing children's writing on the basis of 70 per cent content, and 30 per cent transcription features. It is important that the children know that composition and experimentation are valued and assessed. Teachers introducing drafting can make it clear that planning and revision are as important as editing. Editing for accuracy can be attended to at the end by the children themselves, or in collaboration with other children or the teacher.

### c) Writing for other, known audiences

Any school can provide a wealth of opportunities for children to write for wider, known audiences.[11] Some examples, used by many teachers, include:

(i)   Letters to other children in equivalent classes in other parts of the country.
(ii)  Reports of work done for a topic. This can be a report for the rest of the school, or a booklet for a specific age group in the class.
(iii) Story books for other children to read, perhaps with an accompanying tape of the story.
(iv)  Reports of a class trip for other members of the school to read.
(v)   Requests for information from companies or official bodies.

Any teacher will be able to think of many such opportunities of writing for a known audience. The benefits, however, are not confined to giving the children an incentive to do something with their writing, important as this is. An audience of this type is often accessible to the children, enabling them to investigate overtly the demands it makes. A junior class writing for infant children might profitably spend some time looking at infant stories and talking to some of the intended audience before producing an initial draft of their story. In one class of 9/10 year olds, the children 'adopted' an infant child each. They spent some time talking to 'their' children, finding out their interests and what they liked to read about. As a result of this they composed an initial draft of a story ~h:~h was particular to individual infant children. This they shared ~d ~~ined sufficient feedback to enable ~ ~~ries were

### d) Writing for wider, unknown audiences

There will be occasions when children will write for audiences they do not know. Writing for display may fall into this category, as the children do not know who will see the work. Other instances will be:

(i)   posters for local events,
(ii)  competition entries,
(iii) reports for local and parish newspapers,
(iv)  booklets about a particular topic for storage in the library.

This sort of task asks the child to deal with a very abstract type of audience, and may seem difficult. Children can profitably be involved in initial discussion of the needs of an audience so as to sharpen their awareness.

### REPERTOIRE

'This morning,' cries Miss Creedle,
'We're all going to use our imaginations,

We're going to close our eyes 3W and imagine.
Are we ready to imagine Darren?
I'm going to count to three.
At one, we wipe our brains completely clean;
At two, we close our eyes;
And at three, we imagine.
Are we all imagining? Good.
Here is a piece of music by Beethoven to help us.'
                        (from 'Miss Creedle teaches creative writing',
                                            by Gareth Owen.)

Most of us will be familiar with the idea of 'creative' writing which this poem by Gareth Owen satirises. The teacher provides a stimulus of some sort and the children write their impressions or imaginings.[12] This sort of experience was offered to many children in the 60s and 70s until doubt began to be expressed about the value of this type of 'creative writing'. The suggestion was made that children need a wider range of writing experience.[13] In order to decide what this range should include we need to look for some sort of classification of writing. Attempts have been made to do this in various ways, involving one or more of four dimensions:

    mode
    function
    purpose
    form.

Some writers refer to modes of writing which can include narration, description, exposition and argument. Another way to see this has been to cite genres such as fiction, poetry, personal narrative, argument and exposition. This is a difficult classification in many ways, and the terminology is not consistent. It is perhaps sufficient that teachers should be aware of the different dimensions of writing.

    Another way to attempt a classification is by function. One very influential classification sees the styles and functions of writing on a continuum.[14]

                        expressive

        transactional - - - - - - - - - - - - - - - - - poetic

Expressive writing is the form nearest to speech, and therefore the most natural for younger children and the first to develop. Transactional writing is the more impersonal type of writing used to convey information, such as might be used for a notice, record or report. At the other end of the continuum is poetic writing, which focuses on form and shape first and information second. Poetic writing is used not only for poetry, but also for narrative and other forms. Poetic and transactional writing, it is argued, develop gradually from expressive writing.[15]

In the past, transactional writing has been neglected in primary schools, and yet is the dominant mode of writing in secondary schools. Children are expected to develop towards this type of ........................ they need to help

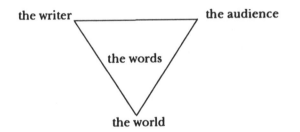

Each element of the triangle might have writing which is aimed primarily at satisfying its needs. Translating this into writing aims gives the following model:

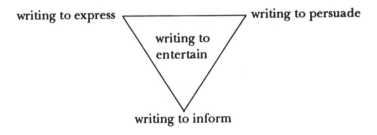

Thus writing done primarily to satisfy the needs of the writer and clarify thoughts is chiefly expressive in its aims. This is rather different from Britton's expressive writing, which refers rather to a particular style. Writing to entertain is essentially literary. The concentration is not only on content but also on the form of the writing. Writing that acts on a particular audience may have persuasive aims, and writing whose express purpose is to convey information may be said to have referential aims. This sort of writing broadly corresponds to the transactional category of the earlier model.

Naturally there is a great deal of overlap between aims. A story about a personal experience may, ostensibly, have literary aims, but it can also be expressive for the writer, and it will be written to inform the reader.

It is useful to consider the purposes and forms of writing that might be included within these four main functions of writing. For each function we shall give some brief suggestions for writing purposes and forms.

### Writing to express

Children can find expression for their feelings, hopes and fears through a range of forms.

| Purpose | Form |
|---|---|
| To clarify thinking | note-taking |
| | explanations of graphs, etc. |
| To amuse or entertain | personal anecdotes |
| | stories |
| To confide | diaries |
| | dialogue journals |
| To record feelings and impressions | poems |
| | jottings of sensory impressions |
| | personal letters |
| To predict and hypothesise | endings for stories |
| | predictions about practical work |

## Writing to entertain

This is essentially literary writing, which concentrates particularly on form and shape.

| Purpose | Form |
|---------|------|
| To amuse or entertain | Jokes riddles puzzles anecdotes poems play-scripts |

also have the effect of making children .....
persuasive writing they read.

| Purpose | Form |
|---------|------|
| To persuade | advertisements scripts for commercials cartoons book reviews |
| To present an argument | letters to the editor notes for a debate pamphlets |

## Writing to inform

This referential writing represents the majority of adult writing, and the primary school offers plenty of opportunities for children to use writing in this way.

| *Purpose* | *Form* |
|---|---|
| To command or direct | recipes<br>directions to places<br>instructions<br>stage directions<br>sets of rules for games |
| To inform and advise | posters<br>news scripts<br>invitations<br>minutes of meetings |
| To describe | labels and captions<br>reports of events<br>character portraits<br>book jackets |
| To make comparisons | charts<br>note-taking<br>graphs and diagrams<br>descriptions |
| To explore and maintain relationships | notices of<br>   congratulations<br>greetings cards<br>making requests<br>questionnaires |

Clearly, particular forms, and even purposes may have more than one function, and not all are represented here.

Mode, function, purpose and form are not only interrelated, but dependent upon each other. There is no precise way to define these elements. We must, however be aware of them if we are to offer children the experiences which will develop a wide repertoire of writing skills. It takes time to achieve this sort of range within a class, probably the whole year. This certainly highlights the inadequacies of 'a story a week', whilst underlining some of the possibilities for writing offered by a cross curricular topic.

## THE ROLE OF THE TEACHER

In supporting and developing children's writing, the teacher plays many vital roles, as organiser, activity-setter, reader, assessor and fellow-practitioner. These roles will be considered in turn.

### Teacher as organiser

The teacher creates the conditions within which children are expected to write. She must organise time, setting and resources to support writing.

All composition needs time both for discussion before writing and for planning before a draft is attempted. False starts may make the first draft slow going. The child may then need time to reflect on and make changes, edit and produce the piece. Very often time will be needed to present the work to others and evaluate it.

When David (aged 8) was asked how long it took him to write a story he replied, 'I'm best at adventures, I love them. At home I ˈ‑ ʰⁱᵗ ᵗʰⁱⁿᵏⁱⁿᵍ about it, but it only takes a half

on a rotating system. For some cⁱⁱⁱⁱⁱⁱⁱⁱ ... ___
sessions can be useful, as Elizabeth commented, 'When you go back you see the empty ideas better.' Obviously, this way of working would be impossible if children were working to a dead-line of 'a story each week', and the teacher will find it necessary to sacrifice some quantity of product for a greater depth of involvement in the process.

The physical organisation of the classroom can be helpful to the writer. Some teachers create a 'writing area' in the class. This is a relatively quiet area within which children can work individually or with others, and where the tools of a writer are available – a variety of writing implements, paper of various types, dictionaries, and a thesaurus. Some classes have typewriters or word-processors in the writing area. Although a writing area will not be possible in all classes, any classroom can be a supportive environment where writing is valued and given a high profile. This means that not only writing, but also reading, should be encouraged as a useful and enjoyable activity.[17]

Children grow up surrounded by writing, and this can also be the case in schools. We must, however, avoid the temptation to see class walls merely as a gallery. Writing in the environment serves definite purposes and this should be reflected in school. Children should be aware of the purposes of writing in the school environment, i.e. to convey information, to persuade and to entertain, and so extend their perceptions of the purposes of writing outside.

Writing can be displayed to convey information. Children will look at team lists, sports results, school dates and announcements, notices about the trip and so on. They can both read and write this informative writing and add it to displays about class topics, models, photographs and artwork. There are many opportunities for the children to be involved in their own work at the display stage.

The obvious example of persuasive writing which can be put on display is the advertisement. This can be for imaginary items, or real items like book clubs, school sweat shirts, P.T.A. meetings, open days and the like. This not only involves the children more closely in their school, it also gives them a real audience, and often provides feedback for their writing.

Writing should also be displayed to entertain. Most children and visitors enjoy reading stories, accounts and poems, and the authors may be justly proud. This need not stop with the children, though. A display of book reviews might start with the teacher writing and displaying her choice. Letters in connection with topic work may feature in a display, as may letters from children abroad. Letters from favourite authors are always a focus of interest and often stimulate writing themselves. Visitors, too, can be encouraged to contribute. On a recent visit to a school, David very politely said to one of us, 'Well, it's very nice of you to look at our writing and tell us what you think, and we know you now... do you think we can have a look at some of yours?'

It is important that writing be attractively displayed, at a height where children can read it. Displays may not consist only of final copies; some teachers display work in progress to allow the author to collect reactions, and this celebrates not only the content, but the process of writing. Other ideas include experimentation with lettering, displays of handwriting and of other languages and orthographies. Reading and writing are intimately related, and when creating an atmosphere for writing we need to consider how we can encourage reading. Attention to literacy through writing trails and book weeks can generate enthusiasm. The child who sees himself as a reader is in a position to begin to understand authorship.

A further aspect of the teacher's role as organiser is the provision and organisation of materials. Some children write in exercise books, which may include 'rough' or 'drafting' books. Others use loose paper which is kept in a file, as this can be more flexible. In either case several pieces of writing may be in progress at any time, and it is useful to have some way of monitoring this. Charts attached to the covers of books or folders can list work in progress, both in response to tasks and self-sponsored writing. The chart can record the stage each piece has reached, so that teacher and child can keep track. Larger productions, such as school magazines and papers, will require careful planning and ~~~otiation of tasks. Once these are allocated it will be useful to h~th teacher and

probably form a large p~.~ --
majority of writing tasks tend to be set by the teacher. These must be carefully considered with the child's ability, interests and experience in mind. As outlined above, there are many forms and audiences available to choose from. The same tasks may not suit all children and the teacher should accept that not all writing may reach a final, published stage. Even with this in mind the teacher must be aware of how the task is presented. One teacher was recently observed setting work for a group. The children had done factual work about pirates and to follow this up he asked a group to write 'really exciting and interesting pirate stories'. Some time later the teacher marked the stories by correcting spellings and punctuation, adding a tick and asking for it to be written out in best. Not surprisingly the children involved did not look at the marking in detail, and it did not really help the children make the stories more exciting or interesting. For many children this problem arises – the teacher asks for one thing, yet marks for something else. This means that for the child a large part of the activity is working out the real extent of the task by guessing 'what is in the teacher's mind'. When setting tasks, the teacher needs to make clear what is required and, when possible, for what audience.

If the teacher has considered the aims of the task, then marking can be appropriate and useful.

## Teacher as reader

The next role for the teacher is that of reader. It is always difficult to judge the amount and type of teacher intervention that is useful. One way of organising this is by conferencing, which involves the teacher setting aside a time to discuss writing with each child. The teacher and child can sit together and look at any work in progress with the aim of engaging in real conversation about what the child is doing, and for the teacher to read and comment on the work as a reader rather than an examiner. In this way the child can become more aware that writing is a complex process to be improved, and that the writer needs to consider the reader. The child is less likely to see assessment as a process involving simple rights and wrongs.

Initially conferences will start with fairly open questions to encourage the child to learn to discuss his work and talk about writing. The child can gradually gain confidence and build up a vocabulary of terms. Conferencing allows the teacher to support and encourage experimentation, and strengthens the relationship between child and teacher. Obviously conferencing is very time consuming and will not take place too often, but for teachers who take the idea of a partnership in writing seriously it is an essential form of contact.

## Teacher as assessor

Each teacher has a role to play as a marker and assessor of the child's work. Conferencing allows the teacher to assess the child's performance and progress, and to pinpoint difficulties where they arise. This permits effective intervention and help when it is relevant. The conference also gives the teacher a much fuller picture of the child's abilities, which will contribute to record keeping and assessment. Some teachers will wish to supplement conferencing with less time-consuming 'marking'. When possible this should be done alongside the child, as feedback then is immediate and useful. When looking at a piece of work, it is rather too easy to focus on what the child does not know, especially features such as spelling, etc. It is usually more profitable for the teacher to try to see what the child *does* know about style, appropriate form, and so on. Children learn by experimenting, and this naturally involves making mistakes. Of course, writing conventions must be learned, and teachers should not just ignore errors, but in many cases to correct every error would destroy the work. It is more productive to look for patterns of errors. Are there words or letter sequences which the child consistently spells wrongly? What is the likely explanation for a child making a particular spelling error? Is the use of punctuation random, or does the child appear to be using a rule of some kind, even if this is not the conventional one? Where error patterns like these are ʾ ʾ-ʾⁿ can be given, rather than simply offering

1ᴾ

saʿʿ-ʿⁿ

it. Co-operative writing wⁿⁿ-

model, but for many children the teacher ⁱˢ ---

effective writing. Some teachers will write alongside or in front of the children. This does not imply that they have to be expert, fluent writers, as modelling may involve sharing the difficulties and frustrations as well as the triumphs.[20]

The teacher can go about modelling the writing process in two main ways: either writing for the same task alongside the class, and being prepared to share the results with them, or writing in front of the class on a overhead projector or large sheet of paper. The children can be encouraged to comment on the writing, and the teacher can make her thoughts about it known.

The first time this occurs can be nerve-racking for the teacher, as it feels very exposed, but this is a salutary experience of what children do so often in their school lives. It also allows the teacher to demonstrate writing behaviours which many children see as 'wrong' until the teacher uses them. These include:

- making rough notes
- making false starts
- writing rough drafts
- crossing out

- re-ordering sentences and paragraphs
- writing unevenly – fast at times, slowly at others, not always using best handwriting

The teacher can also show how a writer:

- gets ideas
- shapes the ideas
- follows a line of thought
- plans
- revises
- edits
- evaluates the piece.

Simply to explain to children how these are done is not as effective as actually showing them.

Above and beyond this, of course, for children to see their teacher writing can have a marked effect upon their attitudes to the process. They must, after all, get a strange message if teachers tell them that writing is such an important thing to do they must spend most of their time in school doing it, but these teachers never actually do it themselves.

## CONCLUSION

The range of material which has been covered in this chapter makes it clear that there are many issues to consider in children's writing, many of which have only recently begun to be explored. As writing occupies such a central place in children's experience of schooling, and in all curriculum areas, it deserves very serious consideration by teachers.

## FOLLOW-UP ACTIVITIES

1 Think back to a piece of writing you have recently done. This may be anything from a personal letter to an essay. Outline the stages through which your writing went, from the first thoughts you had about it to the production of the final draft. Has your analysis of this process any implications for your teaching of writing in school?

2 Follow one child through a period of at least a week and make a record of the writing he/she does. (Your record, to be complete, would need to include writing done at home as well as at school, but practical considerations may limit it to school writing.)

Categorise the child's writing in terms of purpose, format, audience and process. Do the results of this survey have any implications for the future writing diet you might provide for this child or others in the class?

3 Select one piece of children's writing which you class as good, one piece you class as poor and one piece you feel is average. Try to list some of the criteria you have used to distinguish between these pieces. Compare your list with those of colleagues.

# Chapter 8

# Developing literacy across the curriculum

## INTRODUCTION

In this chapter we shall examine some of the ways in which literacy might be developed and used across a range of curriculum areas. Reading and writing are central activities in the primary curriculum, even though they have tended in the past to receive little attention from teachers of junior children. A belief has often seemed to underlie junior school teaching practice, and the preparation of teachers for this age range, that reading and writing were essentially topics for consideration in the early years, and should have been mastered by the time children arrived in junior classes.[1] Even a cursory consideration of the use of reading and writing across almost the whole curriculum in the junior school indicates the mistakenness of this belief.

We shall begin this chapter by examining ways in which teachers might try to develop their children's abilities to understand what they read, since this lies at the heart of their use of literacy. In the second half of the chapter we shall look at the ways in which literacy is important in the curriculum areas of science, mathematics and the humanities, and examine strategies teachers might employ to ensure their pupils get the most from work in these areas.

## READING FOR UNDERSTANDING

Most teachers will see a large part of their role in developing reading as being concerned with developing children's abilities to understand and learn from written materials. Often, however, views of this role have not been helped by the terms used to describe these abilities. They have been described as 'higher-order' or 'advanced' reading skills, terms which carry the implication that these skills are relevant only to the oldest or the most able children.[2] If, however, these skills are defined as those involved in the understanding of written material, it seems clear that it is impossible to do any teaching of reading without incorporating them in some way. Understanding is, after all, the whole point of reading, and the National Curriculum sets the attainment target that children of 6 to 7 years old should be able to 'read a range of material with some independence, fluency, accuracy and understanding'.[3]

Activities to develop the understanding of reading have

The chanks vos blunging trewiy beaeng aie ..........
chanks vos unred but the other chanks vos unredder. They vos all polket and rather chiglop so they did not mekle the spuler. A few were unstametick.

Questions:
1  What were the chanks doing?
2  How well did they blunge?
3  Where were they blunging?
4  In what ways were the chanks the same and in which ways were they different?
5  Were any chanks stametick?

You should have found it reasonably easy to provide acceptable answers to these questions, but you will certainly feel that you do not, even now, understand this passage. What *is* a chank, and what *were* they doing?

You are able to solve problems like this because you are a competent language user, and are able to apply your intuitive knowledge of language structures to the task. You know, for example, that the answer to a 'How well...?' question will usually be an adverb (even if you do not know the actual grammatical term), and you also know that most adverbs in English end in '–ly'. If you can solve problems like this, there must be a possibility that primary children may also be able to, especially as it is reasonably well established that children themselves are competent language users by the age of 7. This casts grave doubt on the effectiveness of comprehension exercises as a means of developing or assessing children's abilities to understand their reading. Fortunately, there are some alternative activities which can be used with children which are much more likely to involve real understanding.

As we discussed in Chapter 6, reading involves an interaction between the ideas brought to a text by the reader and the ideas expressed by the writer. This being so, any activities which we use to develop children's understanding from text should emphasise this interaction.

Several activities which do emphasise this have been given the common title of DARTs: Directed Activities Relating to Texts.[4] These include group cloze, group prediction, group sequencing, and modelling, and all these activities have applicability across the curriculum, not just in reading lessons. We shall look briefly at each of these.

### GROUP CLOZE

The cloze exercise consists of a text with several deletions which children have to work together to complete. The following brief example will illustrate the activity.

> John was a very lucky boy. He had been given lots of presents for his birthday and had a —— birthday party. He was still rather sad, though, because the thing he had wished for —— all had not happened. He had wanted so much to have a real —— of his own; perhaps a dog, or even a cat. But Mum and Dad had said that there was no room in the flat, and John knew they were ——. He was still disappointed, though.

The solution to these deletions lies in the combination and application of information found elsewhere in the text and in the reader's previous experiences. It also involves the application of understanding about syntactic structures. The reader has sometimes to read on past deletions, and also to have some kind of affective response to the story. In attempting to complete the problem posed by the text, the reader has to give it detailed concentration and respond to its meaning. If the problem is tackled by a group of readers, then it is even more likely that learning will take place as each reader puts forward tentative solutions and these are affirmed, questioned or extended by other members of the group.

Cloze involves much more than simple guesswork. At best it involves the systematic application of context cues, a sensitivity to nuances of meaning and to style, and the articulation of tentative hypotheses about texts. As will be seen later, it can also be a way of introducing content knowledge to children. There are a few guiding principles to its use which can help to ensure the

(ii) Leave a ~~....  ... p....  o    .~~ children the chance to develop some feel for the style of the passage they are working on.

(iii) Have children work on the text in groups of three or four. They may try to complete it individually before discussing their solutions, or complete it as a group straightaway. In either case they should be told to try to achieve an agreed version as this forces them to argue for or against particular suggestions.

(iv) If the children have never used cloze before, they will benefit from working as a group with a teacher. The teacher should not supply correct answers but should rather demonstrate the most useful process of working. Procedures such as listening attentively to another's suggestions, justifying your own ideas, and not being satisfied with the first solution which comes to mind can all be impressed upon the children by the teacher's example.

## GROUP PREDICTION

The prediction activity involves a group of children discussing, together with their teacher, a text of which they all have a copy.

The discussion should be guided by three principles:[5]

*Establishing purposes for reading.*  The children should be reading to actually find something out, whether it be to confirm a guess as to what would happen in the story or to find evidence in the story for their opinions about events or characters.

*Reasoning while reading.*  The readers should make reasoned deductions from the information presented in the story, balancing together various facts, statements, hints and possibilities, and checking them against their knowledge of the world and its likelihoods.

*Testing predictions.*  The readers should test out predictions they make on the basis of what they read, by checking them against the actual information in the text.

In order to do these things the group are given the text one instalment at a time. As they receive each instalment they are asked to:

- explain what is happening,
- predict what may be going to happen next,
- predict how the text will end,
- revise their earlier predictions in the light of new reading.

Any comments or predictions they make have to be supported by reference to the text in front of them.

The process is thus one of shared hypothesis-development and evaluation. The group are required to formulate hypotheses on the basis of what they have read and then to check these hypotheses by reference to later instalments of the text. They are involved in the anticipation/retrospection process which we described in Chapter 3 as being at the heart of responsive reading.

A text which has been found successful for using as a group prediction activity is given below.

1 I stood watching as four men came into the darkened room. They walked round slowly stopping before and inspecting each piece of furniture. Two of the men showed great interest in the sideboard. Drawers were taken out. The contents spilled onto the floor. Silver knives, forks and spoons clattered into a heap. One man immediately bent down and started sorting them out.

All were wrapped and stacked into a box. He worked quickly and quietly.

2 Meanwhile the other two men were busy emptying a corner cupboard. The teapot rattled as it was carried across to the table. The best cups, saucers and plates were also stacked on the table. The door of the cupboard swung open showing the empty shelves. No longer did the shelves hold the treasures collected over the years.

3 One of the men started to unscrew the cupboard from the wall. One side came undone easily and the cupboard hung crazily askew. After all the screws had been taken out the cupboard was lifted down and set on the carpet. Valuable

    ᵃ⁻ ⁱ ᵃˡˡ ᵃⁿᵈ ᵖʳᵒᵖᵖᵉᵈ against the

ᶜᵘᵍᵉᵘ ʳᵒ.ᵘ.ᵘ ᵘ. ᵖ.
over 100 years had never been so bare. I alone remaineᵈ.

5 Two men approached and roughly got hold of my back. I rocked unsteadily on my feet. My face was covered. My outstretched hands were turned to point downwards.

6 I felt myself being tilted onto my back. In this strange position I was carried downstairs and out into the fresh air. Minutes later I was aware of being carried up a slope and put in a corner of a large van. A strong rope was tied around me. As soon as the engine started, I was glad of the security of the rope.

7 After several hours journey we reached our destination. I was untied and carried into a hall where I was placed in a sunny corner. My face was uncovered. My weights were replaced so that movement could begin again. My hands were put at the right time, and I settled down to tick away the years in my new home, glad that removal day was over.

## GROUP SEQUENCING

The group sequencing activity is based upon the same principles as group prediction in that it involves a group of children formulating hypotheses about a text and evaluating these with reference to the information the text contains. It is also similar to cloze procedure in that it involves children in checking the language they read against their own intuitive knowledge of language structure. The activity involves presenting a text to a group of children in sections, but giving them no overt clues as to how the sections should ideally be arranged. The children have to re-arrange the sections into an order which makes sense, and which they can justify by reference to the conceptual or linguistic flow of the text. The text may be split into:-

(i)  paragraphs: which will focus readers' attention onto the flow of meaning within a text,
(ii)  sentences: which will also concentrate attention onto the flow of meaning, but will introduce the importance of linguistic cues, for example, sequence words such as 'next', 'afterwards', or causal words such as 'therefore' and 'because'.
(iii) lines: which will shift attention to predominantly structural cues, especially punctuation and noun/pronoun relationships.

The following sequencing text will give you an idea of how the activity works. (You will appreciate that the activity works much better if you can physically move around the sections.)

Someone had injected his arm with a needle.

His body seemed to be floating and his head ached; a dull, creaking sort of ache.

'Don't worry, Professor. It will be alright soon.'

Yes!

One minute he was dreaming; vague, unpleasant dreams, and the next minute he was wide awake.

It had hurt, but the voices around him had not been unkind.

A needle!

He struggled to clear his thoughts.

He must try to remember the rest.

In a flash he knew what was wrong.

He knew something was wrong.

Just before he sank into unconsciousness, a girl's voice had whispered,

He was frightened because he couldn't think what it was.

He had felt that pain before.

He woke suddenly.

He lay back and suddenly, the fear sprang at him again.

He could feel it, faintly, in the back of his mind.

He knew.

A sudden cramp pierced his leg like a needle.

purposeful reading. An example

with 9 year old children on 'Holidays'. The children first of all listed all the features they would look for in a good holiday resort. This list included sunshine, safe swimming, good shops, sailing, etc. They then listed some holiday resorts they wished to visit, such as Majorca, Blackpool, Brittany, etc. These two lists were then drawn up as a matrix.

| RESORTS / ATTRACTIONS | Majorca | Blackpool | Brittany | etc. |
|---|---|---|---|---|
| Sunshine | | | | |
| Safe swimming | | | | |
| Mountains to climb | | | | |
| Good shops | | | | |
| Sailing | | | | |
| etc. | | | | |

The children then read widely in reference books, holiday brochures and travel books in order to fill in the relevant boxes with ticks or crosses.

Another way of using this technique is to ask a group of children to read a text and to represent its ideas by means of a diagram. An example of this is given below.

A group of 9 and 10 year old children was given the following text.

> Most people are very kind to animals – but some people who like animals sometimes have to kill them. Some people kill animals because they are pests – rats, rabbits and foxes, for instance. Some people kill animals to provide us with food. And some hunt animals for sport. Some hunt animals they can eat, some hunt pests, and some just hunt for pleasure.

They discussed the text and came up with the following model:

|       | kill for food | kill for sport | kill as pests       | kill to be kind   |
|-------|---------------|----------------|---------------------|-------------------|
| kind  | farmers       | —              | farmers foresters   | vets foresters    |
| cruel |               | huntsmen       |                     | —                 |

(When a box is left blank it means the children could not think of anything to put in it. When it contains — it means they decided that nothing could go in it.)

The children who did this activity clearly added to the text, and read 'beyond the lines'.[7] By this act of bringing information they already knew to the text which they were reading, it is likely that they learnt a considerable amount from the activity.

Of course, not every text will lend itself to this treatment, but it is surprising how useful this technique can be. Several narrative texts, for example, can be represented by means of annotated maps or plans. In the case of expository texts, trying to model them in this way can sometimes reveal to the readers instances of confusion in the text's expression or in their own minds. The technique can also reveal the depth of readers' understanding of texts. The following three models were produced by three different children as a result of reading an account of the ways coal is used in industry (Figures 8.1, 8.2, 8.3).

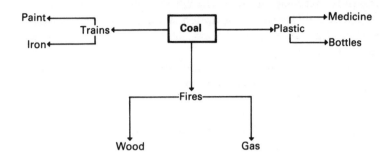

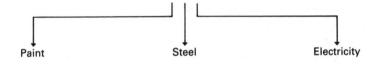

*Figure 8.2* Coal model

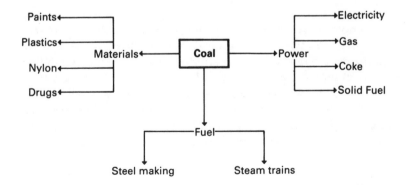

*Figure 8.3* Coal model

The three models show different levels of understanding. The first shows a very vague grasp of the ideas, with several literal misunderstandings of the relationships implied.

The second shows a basic understanding. The content has been extracted accurately, but no awareness of relationships between items is shown.

The third, on the other hand, shows not only an accurate representation of the content, but also a realisation that it is structured. The child has also gone beyond the information actually given and has incorporated her own ideas into her structure. This shows evidence of real learning.

## GENERAL POINTS

Activities such as these, all of which can easily be adapted for use with children of a wide range of ages, have several features in common. They are essentially group activities and the discussion which accompanies them is perhaps their most valuable dimension. They involve readers in active problem-solving, during the course of which they have to generate and test hypotheses. They lay stress upon interaction with texts, and the construction rather than simple reception of meaning. Finally, they generate intrinsic interest among readers. Children by and large find them exciting and fun activities. They are certainly a long way from the dull routine of the traditional comprehension exercise.

## READING AND WRITING ACROSS THE CURRICULUM

Clearly, reading and writing have a role to play in learning across the whole of the primary curriculum, and not simply in those areas in which attention is specifically devoted to them. An observation of the experiences of primary children as they move through their curriculum will show a very wide use of literacy, especially of writing, in most curriculum areas. In this section we shall examine the literacy dimension of several areas of the primary curriculum, and the particular demands that these might make. The areas we shall look at are science, mathematics and the humanities.

### Science

We need to begin by asking a number of questions about the

literacy experiences which take place when children tackle science activities. Questions such as the following might be asked:

1 In carrying out a science activity what kind of reading material do the children have to deal with?
2 What would be an ideal method of approaching this material, and how do the children actually approach it?
3 What style and format of writing are the children expected to produce, and what do they actually produce?
4 Are they given any help with the reading and writing elements of the activity? If so, what does it focus upon?

following uses of literacy may occur,

| Writing: | records of activities and observations, reports of work undertaken and results found, explanations of results, predictions of future outcomes, generalisations from work done. |
|---|---|

It is noticeable that the kind of reading and writing done in science activities tends to involve texts of a different character from those used in other areas of the curriculum. Children's experience of literacy elsewhere may be largely, if not entirely, confined to experience with narrative texts. They read and write stories. The texts they have to read and write in science are generally not narrative, being logical rather than chronological in structure.[9] It can be very difficult for children to adapt their strategies for dealing with texts to the different genres. They clearly need some kind of assistance with this. Yet the assistance they get with their science activities may often be confined to a concentration on their science content, rather than on the reading and writing involved in handling this content.

How might the teacher help children deal with the literacy demands of science activities? There are a number of strategies the teacher might introduce, examples of which will be given below. Underpinning these, however, and the key to effective help, is extended discussion – both between teachers and children, and between children. Teachers often discuss stories with children, both those they read and those they write, and this discussion helps children deal more effectively with the demands of these tasks. This same discussion can also help children come to terms with the problems of handling new text structures, and can be started very early in a child's school career by the teacher occasionally using non-narrative text with children as a variant on the narrative text which usually occupies storytime. Later, activities such as sequencing and modelling, as described earlier, can be used as a focus for discussion specifically concerned with the structure of texts. In writing, teachers can encourage children to stand back from their planning, composition and revision to discuss what they are producing in terms of its structure and the needs of its audience.

Reading and writing activities, each involving discussion, which may help children's understanding of science include the use of DARTS, and writing in tight formats. We shall illustrate these by the use of some example activities.

### Using sequencing

A group of children were given the instructions for an investigation into the workings of small electric circuits. Each separate instruction was given to them on a separate piece of card and their first task was to place the instructions into an order which they thought was sensible. In debating this the group were not only forced to use a range of textual cues, but also to elaborate upon their existing understanding of the scientific principles involved in what they were doing. The activity thus had the effect of heightening their awareness of the science involved so that when they actually carried out their investigation they were able to learn more from it than they otherwise might.

### Using modelling

A group of children studying the weather were asked to read

several items about the rain cycle, and then to try to show the cycle by means of a diagram. The group setting for this task meant that the children had to work together, each actively contributing ideas and weighing alternatives and together agreeing on an acceptable end-product. To achieve this they had to refer carefully to written text from several sources, decide on what was essential and non-essential information, interpret textual information into another medium, and produce something intelligible to other readers.

*Format writing*

~~~~~~~~~~ to find what

~~~~~~~~ ~~~ ~~~ ~,

During this activity the children had not only been engaged in scientific discovery, but had also had to think very carefully about the ways they wrote their results.

## Mathematics

Many of the same points which have been made about reading and writing in science apply equally to mathematics. Coping with alternative text structures can, in fact, be more of a problem, partially because there is a tendency for text in mathematics materials to be a disguised form of narrative. A familiar type of mathematics problem might read like this:

> Mary had 12 conkers, John had 9 and Ann had 6. They decided to share the conkers out equally between the three of them. How many conkers would they each get?

This looks like a piece of narrative, but children reading it have to treat it in a completely different way to narrative, calculating rather than appreciating. Not only that, but several children are likely to classify this kind of thing as completely divorced from real life on the grounds that nobody in their right minds would actually give away conkers without getting something in return!

It is useful to examine some pages from a mathematics textbook with particular concentration on the reading which children have to do on these pages. The following questions might be useful:

• Are the instructions given completely unambiguous?
• Can you think of alternative ways of giving them? (If you can, you might like to try these on children to see if it improves their performance on the mathematics.)
• Is there a set format for children's responses?
• Is this clearly explained?

If possible, watch some children using these pages and note any points of difficulty they have.

It is often observed by teachers that children who can actually cope quite easily with the mathematics involved in an activity find it difficult because of the reading they have to do.[10] Which, for example, of the following questions do you think children would find most difficult? You might like to try this out with some children.

• What is 32 divided by 4?
• Mr Jones, the Games teacher, wanted to play two games of football with his class of 32 children. This meant he would need four equal-sized teams. How many children would there be in each team?
• Mary had 32 pence. She wanted to share it evenly between her four friends. How much did they get each?

The mathematics involved in each of these questions is exactly the same. The facility with which children solve the mathematics is, however, greatly affected by the density to which the information is buried in text. Notice also that the two text versions of the question use a form which looks like narrative, but which children have to treat in a totally different way to narrative. With stories they can sit back and enjoy the flow of the language. Here, in contrast, they have to ignore the flow and concentrate on picking out exactly those few pieces of information which matter.

What should the teacher's reaction to this be? It is tempting to reason that, if it is the density of text which causes the problem, then children should be given mathematics questions in a straightforward format, unembedded in text. Unfortunately, of course, mathematics does not occur in real life in neatly separated 'sums', but always embedded in real contexts. We must, therefore, try to ensure that children get experience of dealing with it in this way, and help them with the problems caused by the text. Again, discussion is likely to be the key to helping them towards understanding. A great deal of learning can take place if children are given time to discuss problems they are faced with in mathematics.

Another strategy the teacher can employ is to avoid the temptation to bypass the text when children have problems. ... children who claim they cannot

... them to ... almost always best overcome by facing them directly rather than by skirting round them.

**Humanities**

By the humanities here we are referring to those areas of the curriculum traditionally called history and geography, or, more modernly, environmental and social studies. Most primary schools cover these areas through project work, which is dealt with more specifically in the following chapter, 'Literacy for learning'. At this point we should like to examine briefly the way in which the teaching of literacy can be grounded in humanities content by the use of DARTS, described earlier in this chapter.

*Using cloze*

You might like to try to complete the following text. Remember that it is more beneficial to work on texts like this in groups rather than individually. As you work through the text, try to be aware of the strategies you are using to solve the problems set by the deletions. If you can, and it is appropriate, you might also give a copy to a group of top juniors to work on.

> Some of the oldest buildings in the north of England are the —— left behind from the days of the Romans and Normans. The houses built by the —— people have disappeared although if you walk through some of our oldest —— like Lincoln and Chester you will find buildings which are —— of years old.
>
> When the —— settlers came to the north they had to build some form of —— against the cold and damp climate. They naturally used the building —— which was easily obtainable and that was ——. The very first homes would have looked something like a —— of sticks covered with grass and ——.

In order to complete the text you have to use a variety of clues from the words surrounding the deletions. In doing this you actually increase your knowledge about the subject. Sometimes textual clues lead you to conclusions about content, and at others you may have been forced to look for information elsewhere or draw upon what you already know about this subject. This activity is a good example of the 'interactive reading' we referred to earlier. It develops both the ability to read for understanding *and* subject knowledge.

### Using modelling

Read the following text and try to show the information it contains by means of a diagram. Again this will work best if you do it as a group. You might find that the activity causes a great deal of argument between you, during the course of which you have to refer constantly to the text as justification for your ideas. Again, as you do the activity, try to be alert to the kinds of strategies you are using.

> By 1066, the system was elaborate and stable. There were many social strata. At the bottom were serfs and slaves; next cottagers or cottars; then villeins, who farmed as much perhaps as 50 acres; then thanes, who drew rents in kind from the villeins; then earls, each ruling one of the six great earldoms that covered the country; and, above all, the King.... None of these people could claim absolute ownership of the land. The villeins, to use the old phrase, 'held their land of' the thanes, the thanes

held it of an earl or the church or the King, and the King held it all of God's grace. And each of them, without exception, owed duties to the others above and below him.

It is very likely that, as you designed your diagram, you found yourself adding to the text, reading beyond the lines in the way which was described earlier. By this act of bringing information you already know to a text and using it sometimes as a framework for information in the text and sometimes to fill in frameworks provided by the text, you are engaged in learning with this text.

These two activities are only examples of the wide range of applications of DARTs to the humanities area. They have the ⋯ ⋯ ⋯ of developing at one and the same time the

and write and, when they master these to a certain ⋯ ⋯ then simply use them to learn other subjects. What in fact happens is that the learning of reading and writing and the learning of subjects go hand in hand through the primary school, and indeed beyond. We need, as teachers, to be aware of both the literacy demands of the whole of the curriculum, and of the need to embed our teaching of literacy into meaningful contexts. Without this twin realisation, there is a danger that the teaching of reading and writing can become an isolated activity which is perceived by children as having little relevance to the rest of their 'real' learning.

## FOLLOW-UP ACTIVITIES

1 Design some DARTs which you might use in various areas of the primary curriculum. Try them out with some groups of children. You might find it useful to tape-record their discussions so that you can listen carefully for any evidence of learning.
2 Observe a maths or a science lesson and try to concentrate on the reading and writing done by children during the lesson. Note

any problems which children seem to have with this reading and writing. Can you make any suggestions as to how these might be avoided in future?

3 In this chapter we have dealt with only three areas of the curriculum. You might discuss the role of reading and writing in other areas, for example art, music, physical education, design and technology. Can you suggest ways in which literacy might be developed through these areas also?

# Chapter 9

# Literacy for learning

part of this
documents, formed an attainment target in its own right.

The issues raised by this statement are, however, somewhat wider than might appear at first glance – in three ways.

1  Reading for the purposes of study involves more than the use of information-retrieval strategies. These strategies are only one part of a process of locating and handling information.
2  Study involves more than just reading. The activity of writing makes an important contribution to learning.
3  The skills implied in this statement have a wider usage than simply study. We handle information in every part of our lives and it is as much part of the school's role to prepare children to deal with information as, say, a consumer, as it is as a student.

The first part of this chapter will try to explore some of these issues, and examine what it is that teachers need to be teaching to satisfy the full implications of this attainment target.

The second part of the chapter will explore some strategies for the teaching of these skills and processes, and will focus particularly upon the potential of project work as a meaningful context for this teaching and learning.

## PART 1. READING FOR THE PURPOSES OF STUDY

In place of the term 'information-retrieval strategies' it is more revealing to use the term 'information skills'. This makes it clear that handling information involves a process consisting of a number of skills. Weaknesses in these skills tend to manifest themselves quite clearly in children. Children who leaf through reference books page by page hoping to find what they are looking for by chance, children whose project work consists of sections copied word for word from these reference books, and children who after the project is done cannot actually tell you much about what they have written in their work, or what they have learnt, are all likely candidates for weaknesses in information skills.

In order to develop effective mastery of these skills in children, it is necessary first of all to define what the information process consists of. This process can be thought of in six stages, each with its constituent skills.[2]

### Stage 1
### Defining the subject and the purpose

The beginning of the process involves specifying what information is required and why. It is obviously impossible to proceed unless this is done. When primary school children do this, however, this stage often consists of nothing more than a vague statement such as 'I want to find out about dinosaurs (or birds, or trains, etc.)', which is certainly not precise enough to be useful to them. Statements like this have two logical consequences. First, they give no criteria for judging the usefulness of any information which is found. If it is about dinosaurs (or birds, etc.) then it must be relevant. Second, there is no indication of when the process of finding information should stop. Children could go on for ever finding information about dinosaurs (etc.) and still be no nearer satisfying this vague purpose.

Children need to be encouraged to specify as precisely as possible what it is they want to find out, and what they will do with that information when they have found it. They may be asked to draw up a list of questions to which they want to find answers, or tasks which they aim to complete. A more useful purpose might be something like this: 'I want to find out the relative sizes of the most common dinosaurs so I can draw scale pictures of them on a wall chart.' This defines the area and clearly specifies what they will do with the information once they have found it.

One of the National Curriculum statements of attainment for level 3 states that children should 'Devise a clear set of questions that will enable them to select and use appropriate information sources and reference books from the class and school library.'[3]

in. To this list must also be added the skills of using the various tools of information technology to retrieve needed information. Teletext televisions, viewdata systems (such as Prestel) and computer data-bases are all extremely useful sources of information in the classroom, but not unless the children possess the requisite skills for using them. For the National Curriculum statement of attainment, level 4 children should be able to 'Locate books or magazines in the class or school library by using the classification system or catalogue, and use simple information-retrieval strategies when pursuing a line of enquiry.'[4]

These location skills are not actually terribly complicated, yet children and adults alike often seem to have difficulties in using them. A common situation is for children to be able to explain perfectly well how to use an index to a book, for example, but then, when left to their own devices, to prefer to leaf through a book instead.[5] This is possibly because these things had been taught to the children in a theoretical rather than practical way, and the children had just not made the transfer.

## Stage 3
### Selecting information

This means choosing the specific information required to meet the purpose identified earlier. Children very often find it very difficult to be selective in the information they extract from books in particular, often resorting to wholesale copying of large extracts. They need to be shown how to match their particular information requirements with what is available, and how to take note of information rather than copy it. One way of doing this, and lessening the incidence of copying, is to encourage children to formulate specific questions to which they wish to find answers. These questions need not simply be factual, they can also be interpretative. They might, for example, want to know why a particular event took place. The point is that they are unlikely to find answers to these questions neatly encapsulated in a few words, and so are forced to be selective in what they read. At this point the skills of skimming a text to gain a general impression and scanning to glean specific points are very useful, and can also be most effectively taught.

## Stage 4
### Organising information

The next stage of the process involves synthesising the information found into a full answer to the original question. Pulling together information from a range of sources can be a very demanding task. (It is not mentioned until level 8 of the National Curriculum statements of attainment for reading). It is, however, made a good deal easier if the information need is defined very precisely, as suggested in stage one above. If children have formulated precise questions before beginning their information search, then these questions will form a structure for their note-taking, so that they note down things they want to know, rather than every piece of information they come across. Children need also to be positively encouraged to consult a range of information sources in their quest, and then to look for common points, or instances of disagreement in their notes.

## Stage 5
### Evaluating information

If they do find conflicting information in their sources, children should be able to use a variety of criteria to judge the accuracy, relevance and status of the information they find. Children will naturally tend to believe, as will many adults, that everything they read in books is bound to be true. Yet they will constantly come across examples of misleading, incorrect, intentionally or unintentionally biased information, and they need to know how to recognise this and what to do about it.[6] The teacher may need to

deliberately with examples of incorrect or biased

is to be encouraged.

in the

results is needed. This may ...

personal purposes or presenting it to others. ..

encouraged to think of a definite audience for their finished work, then it will be possible to get them to assess the work's appropriateness for this audience by actually having their work read. The example of this which immediately springs to mind is that of older junior children preparing information booklets for younger children in the same school, although there are many possibilities available for children to prepare reports of particular information-finding activities to pass on to other readers.

Children also need to ensure that the means of presentation they choose is compatible with their original purposes, and with the nature of the information they have collected. From an analysis of the information process it is clear that more than 'information-retrieval strategies' are being used here. Retrieving information is, in fact, only one stage of a much more involved process, and children need to develop their abilities to handle the whole process if they are to be fully competent at information handling. Neither is it true that reading is the only aspect of literacy which is involved in information handling, as the next section makes clear.

## THE PLACE OF WRITING

Traditionally, children's writing has been seen as a demonstration of learning rather than a contributor to it. The most frequent end-product to a piece of investigation work, a project or any activity was a piece of writing. Teachers would look at this writing in order to assess the degree to which the child had learnt anything from the activity. Writing was seen, then, as a product resulting from a process of learning which had taken place elsewhere.

This view of writing as a product has been dramatically challenged as we describe in Chapter 7. Much more attention is now given to the process of writing, that is, how writers get from the stage of not knowing what they will write to finishing a piece. The journey has become more interesting than the finishing point. It has also become clear that during this journey writers are involved in learning. The traditional model of writing has looked like this:

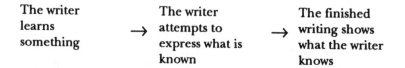

An alternative model, more usually held these days, would give the act of writing a more pervasive role.

According to this model, learning comes into being through the act of trying to write. This may include the elaboration and extension of previous ideas or the 'aha' experience of arriving at completely new ones. Anyone who writes has had the experience of being led in an unexpected direction by the impetus of the writing, with ideas seemingly coming from nowhere. Another common experience is that of trying to express ideas which are felt to be familiar, but which the act of expressing causes one to rethink.

If writing has this learning function, what strategies might be adopted to help children use it effectively in the information process? Several useful strategies for this, such as drafting, writing for publication, aiming at an audience, teacher modelling the process and conferencing have already been described in Chapter 7. Here we shall concentrate on a few suggestions which may prove particularly useful in assisting children to handle information in the process described above.

## 2 Brainstorming

Children can be given a limited time to write down, without any attempt at order or classification, as many words, phrases and images connected with a topic as they can. They can then work in small groups to order these ideas into common themes. This, like the next suggestion, helps children articulate a 'map' of their existing ideas, and can also produce several unexpected insights.

## 3 Concept Mapping

This is a more structured version of brainstorming and involves children, either individually or in small groups, writing down a linked series of ideas about their topic. They begin by putting the topic title in the centre of the page. They then note down any ideas which this title brings to mind. These ideas then trigger off other ideas which are noted down, and the process continues. A finished concept map can look rather like a spider's web, and the technique is sometimes referred to as 'webbing'. An example of a completed map is given below.

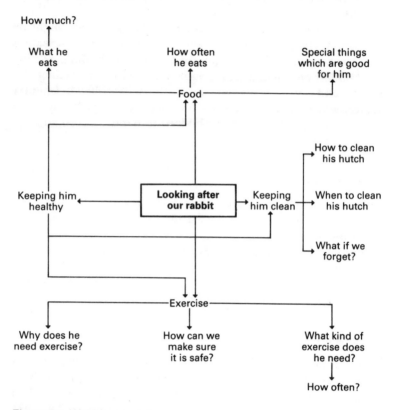

*Figure 9.1* Webbing model

**4 Explanations**

Children can be asked to take a topic or a process and write an explanation of it for other children. Examples include such things as a guide to school rules for new children, a guide to how to use the school library, suggestions for a topic on the school garden and so on. In trying to explain things for others, children have to clarify their own knowledge about these things.

**5 Instructions**

Children can write instructions or directions for others to follow. This may include such things as how to play certain playground games, how to do particular science experiments, how to make a model and so on. The instructions can be tried out by other children and refined until they are totally comprehensible and effective.

### 6 Rewriting

Children can be asked to take a text which they are currently using in connection with a topic and rewrite all or part of it for another audience. This may be for younger children, or simply other children who have not become as familiar with the ideas in that

[illegible] they involve

It is a truism to say that the use [illegible]
lives as adults. There is, of course, a very important affective side [illegible] this. Many of us use literacy as a source of pleasure and emotional enrichment. But the majority of our encounters with literacy in the world involve the handling of information. The ability to do this effectively has come to be called 'functional literacy', and it should not be forgotten that part of the job of the school is to enable children to cope with the demands, in this case the literacy demands, of the real world outside school.[8] It is important to note that this is more complex than it might seem. Schooling, at whatever age, is not just a preparation for what comes after it, but it should also concern itself with helping children to deal effectively with the demands of the world they currently inhabit. Children are involved in the use of literacy and the handling of information from long before they go to school. School should support them in this.

What does this functional literacy involve? This has been classified in several ways, each with its own merits. One particularly influential piece of research into the life of some American communities found literacy being used for seven socially orientated purposes, by adults and children alike.[9]

1 *Instrumental.* Literacy provided information about the practical problems of everyday life, e.g. bills, traffic signs, price tickets, etc.

2 *Social interactional.* Literacy provided information needed to maintain social relationships, e.g. letters, cards, cartoons, etc.

3 *News-related.* Literacy provided information about distant events, e.g. newspapers, newsletters, etc.

4 *Memory-supportive.* Literacy served as an aid to memory, e.g. notes, telephone directories, address books, etc.

5 *Substitutes for oral messages.* Literacy was used when direct oral contact was impossible, e.g. messages, notes to school, etc.

6 *Provision of permanent record.* Literacy was used when records were required for legal purposes, e.g. tax forms, certificates, etc.

7 *Confirmation.* Literacy provided support for ideas already held, e.g. settling disagreements, checking against recipes, etc.

This classification may be of some use in the planning of information-handling activities in school. Each of these uses of literacy suggests areas of experience which might be provided for children. There are many opportunities for these kinds of activity to be incorporated into primary school life.

## PART 2. DEVISING TEACHING STRATEGIES

The second part of this chapter will deal with the devising of suitable approaches to teach the skills discussed in the first part. Opportunities need to be taken to teach information skills across a wide variety of curriculum areas. This may well mean engineering teaching situations in which these skills can be developed. Three considerations need to be borne in mind.

### 1 The context of the teaching

Teaching information skills is often, if it is done at all, carried out in separate lessons with such names as 'library lessons' or 'study skill lessons'. It often employs books of exercises or workcards with such titles as 'Using an index' or 'Using the library'. These, however, because they are not placed into really meaningful contexts, are often less effective than they might be. Such exercises may have their place, as will be suggested later, but there is a danger that they can become ends in themselves. If this happens it will be difficult for children to apply what they learn through these exercises to real-life information-handling situations. It is likely to be more effective if the teaching of information skills can be integrated into a variety of curriculum areas.

of the teaching

school. T up

some instruction in the use of encyclopaedias, but there will be a marked difference in the sophistication of their usage.

### 3 The content of the teaching

It would seem to be insufficient to teach these skills through explanation alone. Children need guided *practical* instruction. The most effective means of instruction will probably be to put children in a situation where they have to use the skills to find and handle information which interests them. This will give them essential practice in using these skills and will also show them that they have a real purpose and benefit.

## PROJECT WORK – A MEANINGFUL CONTEXT

With these three considerations in mind, one of the most useful opportunities for teaching information skills would seem to be during some form of project work. The project approach is very commonly used in primary schools but has often been heavily criticised for producing nothing more than 'uninvolved copying'.

It does, however, offer a superb context for the exercise of the whole range of information skills. The teaching of these skills within a context meaningful to the children is of the utmost importance, and project work can provide a highly motivating and child-centred set of activities in which effective skill development can take place. A project to be of maximum benefit needs to be organised according to a systematic plan and one means of such organisation is given below, described in the context of one particular project which was carried out with third-year junior school children.

The system involves four stages, each of which should involve teacher and children working together, rather than the teacher simply imposing ideas upon the children. This negotiation is essential if maximum advantage is to be made of the children's interest in the project, and also if they are to eventually become independent enough to plan and execute their own self-sponsored and monitored projects. The four stages are:

1  Goal-setting – determining the aims of the project, i.e. what will be produced, in what format and who will it be aimed at?
2  Planning – making plans to achieve these goals, i.e. what resources will be needed, where will they be obtained, how much time will be given to the project, how will the classroom be organised, where will direct teaching, independent research, group discussion, etc. fit in?
3  Implementation – carrying out, or adapting, plans, including direct teaching, group research, etc.
4  Development – teacher and children evaluating success, and using this evaluation to review the process for the next time.[10]

The project was entitled 'Holidays', and arose through interest generated in the class by the children's sharing of their plans for holidays during the coming vacation. Not all the activities undertaken will be described, but only sufficient to give a flavour of the approach.

*(a) Devising goals.* The first step was for the children, under the guidance but not domination of the teacher, to decide upon what they hoped to achieve during the project. (It was felt important to give the children as much responsibility for planning and running the project as possible. Their commitment was felt to be crucial if

the aim of setting skill teaching within a meaningful context was to be achieved.) Two of the goals which were specified for the project were for the children to produce their own holiday brochures for places they had visited on holiday, and their own passports.

(b) *Making plans.* The next step was to decide, again teacher and pupils together, how to set about achieving the specified aims. It was decided that examples of holiday brochures would have to be obtained as well as other information about specific holiday areas. This involved making arrangements to visit travel agents as well as the local and school libraries. It was also decided that a real passport would be needed and after some discussion one of the

............................................... ᵇ⁻⁻⁻ ⁻⁻⁻⁻ made to visit

(c) *Implementing plans.* In carrying out the plans that had been made, the children had to exercise a whole range of location and selection skills. They had to obtain information from books and other printed materials and also by asking questions of people. They had physically to go to where the information they wanted was to be found, be it in libraries, post offices or travel agents, and they then had to get the information and bring it back to school. They then had to evaluate the information and put it together into an appropriate form. They had to fill in forms (monitoring each other to ensure they did it correctly), design their passports, and join together descriptive prose and appropriate pictures to produce holiday brochures which retailed information in an accurate and attractive way. All these activities were done with the benefit (but sometimes the hindrance) of peer advice.

(d) *Evaluating progress.* The children and the teacher were continually evaluating the success of the process. Regular sessions were held in which groups reported back on their progress. Their form-filling was monitored by other children, and those responsible for obtaining things like printed brochures from travel agents were under a good deal of pressure from their classmates to deliver the goods on time. At the end of the project other children were allowed to read the completed brochures and were asked their opinions as to whether these gave sufficient information to enable a choice of holiday resort to be made and also whether they presented the resorts in a suitably attractive light. Criticisms were taken serious note of by the authors, several of whom subsequently asked if they could work further on their pieces to improve them in the light of these criticisms.

During the project there were several opportunities for instruction in information skills, particularly those of evaluating and synthesising information from a range of sources. Occasionally groups were brought together who seemed to be having similar problems and direct instruction was employed. Twice the whole class was brought together for some work on critical reading, using a selection of advertisements and newspaper reports. On many more occasions, individual children's difficulties were highlighted and attempts made to deal with them on the spot, using a variety of resources. Commercially produced books of exercises on such topics as 'using an index' or 'skimming' were found very useful for this. It was felt that instruction during the project was more likely to have had lasting effect because it was set within a meaningful context. Children could, it was felt, see a purpose in this instruction simply because it was helping them achieve better results in a project in which they were very interested.

The integrated approach to teaching information skills, whether through project work or other areas of the curriculum, makes certain demands on the teacher. He/she needs to have readily available substantial collections of suitable skill-development activities. Also vitally necessary is the ability to spot the points at which instruction is most likely to be effective. Thus the approach can be extremely demanding on the teacher. However, the potential for purposeful and productive learning is vastly increased, and it is also much more likely that skills learnt in this way will transfer to other areas.

## CONCLUSION

This chapter has tried to suggest that there is an intimate relationship between literacy and learning, and to explore some of the ways in which the two might be brought more closely together in primary school teaching. The central role of project work has been dwelt upon because this seems to offer perhaps the most beneficial context in which the use of literacy to learn can be developed. Any learning will, of course, be enhanced if children can see clearly why they are doing it, and if they are genuinely interested in it.

## FOLLOW-UP ACTIVITIES

1 Think back to a piece of project work you have done with a class -- which you have seen someone else do. Try to specify points                                                        children were

information in a library.

about their task in the most efficient way, or are there other ways in which they should have proceeded? What would your task now be as these children's teacher, and how would you set about it?

# Chapter 10

# The use of the computer to develop language and literacy

## INTRODUCTION

Computers have undoubtedly made an impact upon schools and children since they first began to appear in classrooms and homes. Their impact upon teachers, however, has, with some notable exceptions, been less marked. Many teachers still feel very suspicious about the new technology, and this suspicion has been exacerbated by the feeling that often their pupils know more about it than they do. In some primary schools the computer rarely ventures from the cupboard and in others it is employed running low-level drills. As an example of this consider the following classroom activity.

Two children are sitting in front of a computer on which they see a list of words such as 'little', 'was', and 'with'. Below this list appears in larger type an anagram of one of these words. The children have to work out what the original word is and type it in the space provided on the screen. In this case the anagram spells out 'aws'. The children decide the word must be 'was' and type a 'w'. The computer beeps at them and will not accept this letter. The children are puzzled and ask their teacher what is wrong. She looks at the screen and tells them to try a different word. They eventually try 's', which the computer accepts. They complete the word 'saw' and the computer rewards them by a trilling noise and printing on its screen 'Three cheers'. It then sets them another anagram.

What is the problem with activities like this? The major one seems to concern the relationship between the children and the computer. The computer is acting like a very didactic teacher and knows all the answers. The children do not so much have to work out the answers as to guess what is in the computer's memory. The activity then is completely closed. It is based upon a very low-level model of learning which proceeds through Stimulus – Response – Reward to try to drill particular skills. The use of flashy and appealing graphics and sound, and the obvious excitement of the children as they use this new machine should not obscure the fact that poor teaching is taking place here, if indeed one can describe it as teaching and not simply testing.

This picture of computer use is not, of course, universal, and the main aim of this chapter is to examine more productive uses. We shall do this in two ways. First, we shall put forward and enlarge ... ...dging the potential of software designed ... ...amine some

In putting ...
computer software it is important to ...
ideally be no different from those against which any teaching materials should be judged. In the early stages of the use of computers, many programs appeared in which children were asked to do activities which teachers had long ago abandoned as too limiting. The computer was a novelty and children generally were only too willing to use these programs just to get a turn on the machine. Novelty is now wearing off, however, and as children become more and more accustomed to sophisticated uses of the computer outside school, they will demand more exciting uses inside school. The very first question which should be asked about educational software is, 'Would this activity be worth doing if it did not involve using the computer?'

There are five more specific criteria we shall put forward.[1]

## 1 Openness

Most good educational materials are open-ended and do not predetermine particular linear ways of working. This criterion is particularly important for software. Open software (often termed content-free or framework software) is usually heavily emphasised by computer enthusiasts. The term is, however, often used in two ways, which can be confused. In one sense it refers to software which is content-free and simply operates as a tool upon content which is chosen by the children or the teacher. A good example of this kind of software is a word-processor, which exists solely to help users manipulate the content (writing) they supply.

In the other sense, openness can mean open-ended in the directions in which it might lead. From a fixed starting point the software might lead in several directions depending upon the interests of the teacher or the children. An example of this kind of software would be an adventure game which, even though its content will be predetermined in that children have to 'solve' its problems in a way its programmer thought legitimate, can still be used as a stimulus for a wide variety of activities in a range of curriculum areas, according to children's interests.

### 2 Stimulation of creativity and problem-solving

Good software should cause children to *think*, rather than call for a series of conditioned responses. This latter so-called 'hospital model' of learning presupposes that children learning are like patients who are ill: there is something wrong with them which needs precise diagnosis and remedy.[2] Learning, in fact, more often proceeds in a more holistic and haphazard way than this. Learners bring skills, knowledge and predispositions to situations and, in attempting to come to terms with these, extend their skills and knowledge in ways it would have been very difficult to predict exactly. This more creative view of learning can be supported very well by the use of computers. The software itself may pose problems for the learners, as in an adventure game or a simulation, or it may be a tool for solving them, like a data-handling program. The chief point is that the learners are given a degree of freedom in determining how to set about problems.

### 3 Can be used across the curriculum

It is a truism to say that language and literacy do not only develop in lessons labelled English or Reading, but they can be developed throughout the curriculum. Good computer software should encourage this use of language across the curriculum. Software which operates as a tool rather than a delimiter of content may, again, be more effective at this. A word-processor can, naturally, be used to write about anything and may be just as useful for producing the kind of non-chronological writing done in science, for example, as for the more usual narrative type of writing. A good adventure game such as DRAGON WORLD or FLOWERS OF CRYSTAL can stimulate children's work in areas ranging from science to creative arts.

### 4 Flexibility

Software, like any teaching material, is only as good as the teacher
~~~ ᵘˢᵉˢ it. and even the best software can be used
˙ ˙ ˙ 'teacher-proof

teachers determine. ᴵ˙˙˙ᵤ ᵤ˙
teaching rather than as a teacher itself is a very powerful indicator of good software.

### 5 Encourages co-operation

As we discussed in Chapter 1, co-operation and group discussion seem to be very beneficial to the development of language, and good software should provide a context in which this can flourish. This argues strongly for making small-group work the most pre-dominant context for the use of the computer. This can easily be justified on economic as well as educational grounds. Computers are too expensive to devote much of their time to use by individuals.

There are arrangements the teacher can make to maximise the discussion which occurs around the computer. Often groups of four work better than three or five because it is less likely for children to have their views swamped by being outnumbered.[3] Group composition also makes a difference, with care being needed over placing the more forceful children. No amount of organisational manipulation will make up, however, for the poor stimulus for discussion provided by some commercially available software.

## PART 2: WAYS OF USING THE COMPUTER

### 1 Adventure games

Adventure games have always been one of the most popular uses of the computer since the advent of the micro-computer, and many people have become almost addicted to their combination of fantasy and logical thinking. They also have a great potential in the classroom, especially as a focus for the development of language and literacy.[4] The prime reason for this lies in the range of problem-solving skills which players are obliged to employ during games. At every stage players are confronted with some kind of problem, some easy enough to solve, but some requiring a great deal of logical reasoning and inspired deductions. In solving these problems, players need to test out a series of hypotheses, and continually ask the question, 'What will happen if we ...?' The games thus demand a very scientific approach.

They also require the use of careful reading to progress. Often the clues as to how to proceed next are contained in on-screen text which has to be read with care for very small details, all of which are important. Children are often careless about this kind of reading and the necessity of doing it to survive in the game can be a very strong motivating factor to doing it accurately.

The use of these skills is given a further extension when we consider the context in which adventure games are most likely to be used in the classroom. It is unlikely that children will work on them as individuals but much more likely that they will work in small groups. They are therefore solving problems in collaborative situations. In observing a group working on an adventure game it quickly becomes apparent that they spend far more time interacting with each other than with the computer. The computer sets the problems and acts as an arbiter of group decisions, but the real learning potential is in the discussion which precedes each of these decisions.

The teacher can organise the work so that each group in the class gets a turn to use the game on the computer, and most adventure games have natural breaks when the users are 'sent home' or 'killed', and another group can have their turn. Off the computer, the group can write up their accounts of where they have got to, speculate on what they may have done wrong and what they should do next, or engage in any of the follow-up activities they may be pursuing. In any class use of an adventure game, all children will spend a good deal more time away from the computer than in front of it.

The potential for follow-up work is another powerful benefit in the use of adventure games. They can spark off work in a wide range of curriculum areas and many teachers have developed exciting integrated projects using an adventure game as a stimulus.

A final dimension to the adventure game is the possibility of children being involved in creating their own games for other
... This will usually involve the use of

Many teachers have been impressed by the way even quite young children quickly learn how to use word processing programs on the computer, and seem to be able to improve the quality of their writing by doing so. An example of this improvement can be seen in the following two versions of a story written by a 6 year old.

Version 1:
once upon a time there was a baby called henry and a big dragon too and a boy called tom and a girl called sarah and the baby and the big dragon took them to the world of darkness and tom was scared but sarah said its spooky and scary but the nice dragons said wheel keep you safe and that is there best one

Version 2:
Once upon a time there was a baby dragon called henry and a big dragon called peter. They had so many adventures but there best one is when they made friends with a boy called tom and a girl called sarah. The baby and the big dragon took them to the frightening world of darkness and tom was scared. Sarah said its spooky and scary but the friendly dragons said wheel keep you safe and they did. That is there best adventure.

The first version she wrote by herself on paper, and then typed into a word-processor. It is a fairly typical infant story with an unadventurous use of words, no punctuation and a plot which seems not to have been thought through. The second version, which she produced after about 20 minutes on the computer, suggests, however, that some of these judgements about her writing ability may have been harsh. Here her range of vocabulary increases, the technical aspects of her writing improve, and her plot, while still not outstanding, at least shows an attempt to take into consideration the needs of a reader. The computer allowed her space to experiment, and also to step back from her writing and read it with fresh eyes. These two features are perhaps the most significant of the benefits word-processing gives to children's writing.

Word-processors can also be used as teaching devices in the context of children's writing, with consequent improvements in quality. An example of this can be seen in the following piece written jointly by two 7 year olds. After hunting for minibeasts in the school field, the two boys wrote:

> today we went out side to look for little creatures and we found an ant and one was red and jamie russ found a big black spider and daniel jones caught it in his pot and we also caught a centipede and it was red and it went very fast and mrs wilkins caught a earwig and two caterpillars but one caretpillar escaped from the yoggat pot and we found some slugs and they made a slimy trail on the white paper

Their teacher asked them to read the piece to him, and they were all struck by the over-use of the word 'and'. The teacher used the search and replace facility of the word-processor to exchange the 'ands' for markers, and asked them to look at the writing again.

> today we went out side to look for little creatures *** we found a ant *** one was red *** jamie russ found a big black spider *** daniel jones caught it in his pot *** we also caught a centipede *** it was red *** it went very fast *** mrs wilkins caught a earwig *** two caterpillars but one caretpillar escaped from the yoggat pot *** we found some slugs *** they made a slimy trail on the white paper

This revision produced the following finished article:

Today we went out side to look for little creatures and we found ants. One of them was red. Just then Jamie Russ found a big black spider. Then daniel jones caught it in his pot. We also caught a centipede. The centipede was red like the ant. The centipede went very fast like the ant. Mrs Wilkins caught an earwig and two caterpillars but one escaped from the pot. Then we found some slugs and they made a slimy trail on the white paper.

The improvement in quality is quite clear. This may have happened without the use of the word-processor but it is doubtful if the process would have been so simple, or the children so eager

................................................... about word-processors that leads to this

.....r...

writing.

A significant reason why children may find it difficult to really accept the idea of writing as provisional when it is done on paper is the fact that, if they wish to change their writing, this will usually involve rewriting it. The sheer physical effort of this will persuade some children to adopt a much more studied, once-and-for-all approach to their writing. With a word-processor, however, alterations can be made on the screen and there is no need to rewrite. This facility for immediate error correction allows children to approach writing much more experimentally. They soon become prepared to try things out and alter them several times if need be. They also begin to be able to live with uncertainty. If, for example, they are unsure of particular spellings, they can try an approximation and check it later, without breaking the flow of their writing ideas; 'We'll do the spellings afterwards' becomes a familiar strategy.

Also, if writing is saved on a disk, children can return to it for revision at a later date. This facility to revise previously created text has a very important effect. Writing ceases to be a one-shot exercise, with everything having to be got right at one sitting.

There is, in fact, no limit to the number of times the writer can return to it, and make changes as easily as the first time. This adds to writing the important dimension of time. Ideas can be considered over time, new ideas can be taken on board, and writing can be discussed with others. This has the effect of making writing a much more thoughtful process.

Allowing children the time for the reflective editing implied by this may seem to involve the dedication of large amounts of computer time to very few children. This, however, need not be the case because of the facility to print out the writing children produce. They can then take away this printout, and work on revising it away from the computer. This can involve crossing sections out, scribbling extra ideas in, and discussing the draft with anyone they wish. They can then return to the computer when it is again free, to call up their draft and make any changes to it they feel necessary, before printing again, whereupon the process can be repeated. This idea of using hard copy for revision has an extra advantage in addition to its freeing of computer time for others to use. By altering printed text and especially by crossing out, children can begin to lose their fear of making writing messy. Because of their earlier educational experience, many children approach writing extremely reluctant to do anything to disturb the perfection of a page. A printout, however, costs them little physical effort and can always be repeated if need be. It need not, therefore, be kept perfect, a change in attitudes towards writing with great significance for children's future approach to it.

A further advantage of printed writing is its levelling effect. Many children have poor self-images of themselves as writers not because they lack ability in the composing aspects of the process, but simply because they find handwriting a strain. In word-processing, poor handwriting is no longer a problem. Children with poor physical co-ordination can write as well as those with good, and the sense of achievement these children get can be immense. This is not to argue, of course, that clear, efficient handwriting is no longer necessary. Children will still need to be taught handwriting. It does mean, though, that lack of ability in this aspect of writing need not assume the over-arching debilitating effects it often does. It also means that teachers can get beyond the presentation aspects of children's writing when attempting to make judgements about children's abilities. Most children will need help of some kind with their writing, but it is easy for teachers to concentrate this help on the physical aspect simply because this is what stands out immediately. If this aspect can be discounted, teachers can direct their help to other, more important parts of the writing process.

An extra dimension to word-processing is given by the use of desktop publishing, that is, the production of books, journals, newspapers, etc. by writers themselves, without the intermediate stage of specialist typesetting. This technology can be seen as providing extra facilities for the output of children's work on the computer. Several of these facilities have important implications.[5]

The first concerns purpose. A common use of desktop publishing in schools is in the production of class/school news-
~~~~~~ These by their nature, are intended for

magazines through desktop publishing is that these media are generally very familiar to children. They recognise their distinctive features and appreciate the facility that desktop publishing gives of emulating these 'real life' features. An important stage in the production of a class newspaper or magazine should be the close study by children of real newspapers, etc. In the course of this study many literacy skills can be taught and practised, from the critical reading of advertisements to the factors influencing the impact of headlines.

The desktop publishing environment has some features which make it particularly useful for realistic writing formats. One of the most important of these is the cut and paste facility. By using this, sections of pages can be electronically lifted from one place and moved or copied to another. Writers can resequence their writing with little effort. It is possible to achieve this with scissors and glue, but not with the same simplicity. Again this facility increases the provisionality of writing. Not only can text be changed at will, it can also be rearranged in any number of ways.

Another feature which desktop publishing makes possible, and which the available software is just beginning to make use of, is the mixing of text and pictures. Software is now available which enables users to snatch pictures from video players and cameras, and import these as digitised pictures into the desktop publishing environment. Once under the control of the computer software, these pictures can be manipulated in various ways: stretched, enlarged, reduced, rotated, reversed, chopped into pieces and overlaid or interspersed with text. This is a facility of immense potential, which enables users of small personal computers to produce pages which are almost indistinguishable from those of real newspapers. The technology to do this is, perhaps, beyond the reach of most primary schools at the moment, but the usual rule of computers will almost certainly apply: *what computers can do today, they will do better tomorrow – for less money.*

One example of what can be achieved at the moment with readily accessible hardware and very cheap software is shown below (Figure 10.1). This was produced by a group of three nine-year-olds after listening to a reading of *The Lion and Albert.* The sophisticated style and studied use of wit suggest that the computer had made it possible for these children to reflect upon their work in a way they would not otherwise have done.

*Figure 10.1* Using new technology

### 3 Information-handling

Handling information is already part of most children's experience in schools. Almost all teachers will at some point ask children to collect information and display it, an example being the project on ourselves which has as an end-product graphs of children's heights, weights, spans, etc. The computer is ideally suited to tasks of this nature, and can allow children to handle data in quantities and with results that they could not otherwise manage. The computer will store the data in a very compact way and it will also display it on request in a variety of formats, for example, graphs, Venn diagrams, scattergrams, pie charts, and so on.

~~Because it will~~ display data so easily, the computer allows

without its problems, and the children ~~quickly~~ to interrogate the computer in very precise ways if they are to get the right responses. The debate between the members of a group over how to phrase their questions has a great deal of potential for learning.

Learning how to ask the right questions of a collection of information can be done on data-bases which are already prepared. There are several of these available on such subjects as the weather for a particular area, birds of Britain, placenames, census data and so on. A great deal of work can be done on these collections. Much more learning can, however, arise when children construct their own data-bases.

This process begins with the asking of questions. The design and construction of the data-base is then done with the purpose of answering these questions. This puts the computer firmly into the role of a tool for solving problems, rather than something children should learn to handle for its own sake. The questions which children begin with determine the kind of data which will have to be collected, the way it will be stored in the data-base, and the kind of output which will be possible. An example will make this clearer.

A class of third-year juniors were beginning a project on the Egyptians. They had amassed quite a large collection of reference books which would be useful but wanted an easy way of locating suitable ones for particular parts of their work. They used a computer data-base for this purpose. They began by deciding what they would need to know about a particular book to ascertain whether it was useful at any time. They listed four features:

- Difficulty (How hard was it to read?),
- Illustrations (Were there any and were they good?),
- Topic (What was the book about?),
- Information (How much information did it give?).

Each of these was categorised:

- Difficulty – easy, medium, hard.
- Illustrations – detailed, poor, none.
- Topic – for example, The Ancient World, The Pyramids, Egypt.
- Information – detailed, stories, poor.

A computer data-base was then constructed with six fields (types of data): Author, Title, Difficulty, Illustrations, Topic, Information. Details of each of the books was then entered into the data-base by the children. An example of one record is given below.

AUTHOR: J.Smith
TITLE: Life in Ancient Egypt
DIFFICULTY: Hard
ILLUSTRATIONS: Poor
TOPIC: Ancient Egypt
INFORMATION: Detailed

Once the data-base was set up, children used it as part of their project work. If, for example, a child wanted to find a book with a good picture of the Sphinx which he could copy, he searched the data-base for books with detailed illustrations and on the topic of The Pyramids or Ancient Egypt. If another child wanted to write a piece comparing the way of life of ancient and modern Egyptians, he might search for books of medium difficulty, detailed information and on the topic of Egypt. The children were very pleased with their data-base, regularly commenting on how much more quickly they could now find the books they wanted. The computer was definitely a useful tool for them. They had also learnt a good deal, almost without realising it, about skimming books for particular purposes as they entered information into the program.

## 4 Text-manipulation

In Chapter 8 we describe cloze procedure, which is an activity designed to get children to interact with a piece of text by predicting words to complete it. The computer software which best ~nnroaches the problem-solving aspect of cloze procedure is
~~~~~~~ ~~~~~~~ children with the

```
3                  . .
4               t              t
5        t                .
```

They had been given a start by their teacher who had 'bought' all the 't's for them. They predicted the second letter of line 1, and the letter after the 'T' of line 3 to be 'h', and then predicted the following 'e's. This gave them the following:

```
1     The t          t     t t
2          '  t          't
3          '. The t          t  t
4                t             t
5        t                .
```

This caused some consternation as they realised that neither of the words they were working on were likely to be 'the' because 'there's too much space'. After a while they guessed the words must be 'then', and then decided to get a clue by buying all the 'e's. This gave them the following:

```
1        Then t e e e       t    t t e
2            ' t         e 't    e
3          e  e'. Then t e e e     t  t
4            e     t e       e  t e
5          t e           e      .
```

They were then able to guess that all the 't-e's were 'the's, and an inspired guess gave them 'elephant'.

```
1        Then the elephant      t  the
2            ' t         e 't    e
3          e  e'. Then the elephant   t
4            e      the      e    the
5          the           e    .
```

The conversation then went as follows:

Mark: I know this story. It's the elephant..
David: Yes, the elephant and the baby.
Mark: The elephant and the bad baby. It must have bad baby in there somewhere.
Philip: What's the story? We've got to find the story then it gets easier.
David: I know. The baby wouldn't say please or thank you.
Mark: What did he do?

After some further conversation and guessing the boys had:

```
1        Then the elephant said to the bad
2        baby ' t         e 't    e
3          e  e'. Then the elephant sat down
4            e      the      e    the
5        and the bad baby e     .
```

This conversation followed:

David: What did he say?
Mark: He said 'he hadn't said please'. Try 'you haven't said please'.
Philip: 'Please' will go, look. And 'haven't' here. But that's not 'you'.
Mark: No. 'You' goes there. But what's that? It's not 'and'.
Philip: 'But'. 'But'. It's 'but'. 'But you haven't said please'. What's that 'e' doing?

They now had:

1    Then the elephant said to the bad
2    baby 'But you haven't     e said
3    please'. Then the elephant sat down
4          e       the       e     the
5    and the bad baby  e      .

After a further twenty minutes' work the boys finally arrived at:

1    Then the elephant said to the bad
2    baby 'But you haven't once said
ℚ    please'. Then the elephant sat down
                           · · ' ' · · ·f the road

were also developing their ·····  ˙
apply previous knowledge to the present task, to preuici ·····
sequences and words, to search for alternative possibilities. All
these activities are part of the reading process.

The boys were also learning to co-operate. They took it in turns
to type in their guesses, and there are many examples in their
discussion of an idea from one of them being taken up and
developed by another. This again is quite significant behaviour
from infant children.

Several studies have suggested that DEVELOPING TRAY has a
great deal of potential as a language development environment.[6]

> TRAY requires high level problem-solving skills; an analysis of
> given data and other information; decision-making about
> strategies to adopt; the creation and interpretation of meaning;
> hypothesis forming and testing; evaluating data and strategies;
> imagining; referring to other sources of information;
> experimenting.[7]

It is also open in the sense that teachers can enter their own texts
for children to work on. Thus teachers can aim the work at specific
needs, or focus on specific topics.

## 5 Using LOGO

As well as being taught by or learning through the computer, children should also be given the chance to teach the computer. If this is done in a logical manner it implies some form of programming being done by the children. Possibly the computer language most suited to this is LOGO, and a great deal has been written describing the possibilities of this language as a vehicle for problem-solving and for developing a healthy attitude towards mistakes.[8]

The best known part of LOGO is turtle graphics. A small robot, known as a Turtle, can be attached to the computer and instructed to move and draw lines by the user. This turtle can also be represented on the computer screen, usually by a small triangle. This can be more convenient, but children need the experience of actually making a real turtle move and producing real pictures. The turtle is instructed by commands such as 'FORWARD 100', 'RIGHT 90', 'FORWARD 100', which will produce the following shape.

(The children are not told what numbers to use with each command, but have to discover this.)

As well as direct commands, small programs can also be constructed such as the following, which will make the turtle draw a square:

```
FORWARD 100
RIGHT 90
FORWARD 100
RIGHT 90
FORWARD 100
RIGHT 90
FORWARD 100
RIGHT 90
END
```

This can be simplified by using the REPEAT command:

```
REPEAT 4
FORWARD 100
RIGHT 90
END
```

To begin with, the turtle only knows a limited number of commands, such as FORWARD, BACKWARD, RIGHT, LEFT. The most powerful feature of LOGO, however, is that it can be taught new ones. For example, by typing in TO SQUARE, and the above program, the turtle will thereafter know the new command SQUARE and will draw one to order. Series of commands can be ⸺ ⸺le by teaching it TRIANGLE, DOOR and ⸺ ⸺ught HOUSE. It is this

to be ⸺

in in their LOGO work. In ⸺ ⸺
written, children are required to conceptualise ⸺ ⸺
the turtle to do, to break it down into smaller units, to anticipate the turtle's responses and to test hypotheses. Because their task involves the production of written instructions, it can make them very aware of the provisionality of writing and reinforce the idea of drafting which we discussed in Chapter 7.

In addition, programming the turtle will usually be done in small groups and, therefore, the children have to co-operate and share ideas. They also have to make their thinking explicit so that others can comment upon it and they can comment upon that of others. This externalisation of tentative thinking is difficult to achieve in other contexts, but can be extremely valuable both to participants as it forces them to think ideas through, and to observers as it shows any gaps or blocks in the thinking. Because of this, LOGO can be an extremely valuable language development tool as well as an environment for developing mathematical abilities.

Turtle graphics is one example of a 'Microworld'; a small, tightly defined environment in which children can explore, create and test out ideas within a set of rules. The LOGO language permits other microworlds. It can be used to produce music, to write stories, to design adventure games, to control more complex working models, etc. In all these, the computer is in the role of learner and the children in that of teachers. To teach they have to use language in precise ways, to draft and redraft instructions, to actively construct ideas rather than passively absorb them, and to develop and test hypotheses.

## CONCLUSION

We have had space in this chapter for only a limited consideration of the role of the computer in the development of language and literacy.[9] There are several promising areas of development which we have not discussed. These include the use and creation of teletext systems, the use of electronic mail and the use of spreadsheets. These uses have in common their open-endedness and their potential for creating purposeful environments for language use. In using the computer the question is not so much, 'What language and literacy skills can the computer teach children?' but rather, 'What language and literacy skills will be developed in the course of using the computer to do these activities?'. The emphasis should be upon using the computer for real purposes, which involve the use of language and literacy.

## FOLLOW-UP ACTIVITIES

1 Take a project that you might do with junior children. Try to list the ways in which the computer might be used during the various activities in this project. If, for example, your project was Flight, your list might begin like this:

| | |
|---|---|
| Types of aircraft | – use a database to store information,<br>– use the turtle to draw aeroplanes. |
| History of flight | – word-processed accounts of events,<br>– produce newspaper front page about 'The First Flight'.<br>– write TRAY texts about flight events, |
| Airports | – word-process a set of instructions for catching a plane,<br>– produce a passenger guide to the nearest airport using desktop publishing. |

2 Observe some small groups of children using the computer together, for instance, using an adventure game. Make a note of the kinds of language they use together (tape record them if you can). Is there anything about this language which surprises you? You might like to eavesdrop on the same children as they do another activity, for instance, maths. Do you notice any difference in their use of language?

3 Take one type of computer software (for instance, word-processing packages or adventure games). Using the following list of primary age ranges, try to match some appropriate software packages against each. The list below has been partially completed

packages which are available for the BBC

for using the computer throughout a primary

# Chapter 11

# Assessing language and literacy development

## INTRODUCTION

In conjunction with the establishment of the National Curriculum, a much greater emphasis has begun to be placed upon assessment, and many teachers would argue that this has been too great. The main concern of teachers, they would claim, should be with teaching rather than testing. It is difficult not to feel sympathy with this point of view and to agree that there are real dangers of the assessment tail wagging the teaching dog. Certainly assessment should be the servant of good teaching rather than the master and nobody would wish for the crude 'teaching to the test' which has occurred in earlier educational eras.

It is, nevertheless, important to realise the very close links that ideally exist between assessment and teaching. All teachers need to relate what they teach to the abilities and aptitudes of their children, and they need to have some means of ascertaining what these are. All teachers, therefore, assess, but often this is done in a very *ad hoc* way, by the forming of general impressions – impressions which are sometimes almost complete after no more than a few weeks of knowing particular children. The problem with this *ad hoc* assessment system is that important clues as to children's abilities can often be missed owing to the teacher not being organised to notice or record them. Some more systematic approach to assessment is ideally required, which goes beyond the impressionistic.

Nor is it sufficient for teachers to rely solely upon the administration of one or more tests at the end of each year, or even twice yearly. Teaching strategies can quickly be hopelessly inappropriate if this is all the information they are based upon.

Most teachers in fact realise this and make a series of informal judgements about children as they go along. Again the major need is to systematise these informal judgements.

In this chapter we shall attempt to give a firm basis for systematic assessment of language and literacy. In the latter half we shall discuss several practical strategies for assessment, but first there are several issues which need to be dealt with. These include the important question of purpose and issues related to the various approaches to assessment. We shall begin by discussing the crucial question, 'Why assess?'

WHY ASSESS?

6 to help match materials and methods to particular needs.

A further result of the use of assessment should be to increase the professional competence of teachers. In order to qualify as professionals, teachers need to be able to advance sound justifications for their actions, and assessment can be one powerful source of such justifications. Assessment is not an optional extra in teaching, but an essential, integral part of the process.

## Maintaining standards

If people outside of the teaching profession are asked to justify the place of assessment, one popular reason they will give will be 'to maintain standards'. There is obviously some force in this since schools, in order to ensure that they are producing children who can perform to an acceptable level, clearly need some kind of assessment of what this level of performance is. The maintenance of standards implies that this level of performance should at least remain the same over a period of time, and most people, teachers included, would hope it would rise.

## Making comparisons

Assessments are also used to compare pupils within particular groups, such as school or class populations, or even on a national basis. Such comparisons may be used as a means of allocating resources to particular groups. A school or a local authority may, for example, decide to provide extra teaching equipment or teaching help to a group of children who have been identified as having special needs. Another, perhaps less desirable, use of such comparisons occurs when parents look at the assessment results of two or more schools and decide to which they will send their offspring on the basis of these. Fears have been expressed that widespread national assessments will lead more frequently to this situation, which discriminates in favour of those schools who already have such advantages as a high level of resources, an experienced and able teaching force and a highly advantaged catchment area.

## Measuring progress

Assessments can also be used to measure progress. Many schools administer some form of assessment to their children at the end of set periods, such as a year or six months. They then record the results in such a way that indicates whether children have made progress over a longer period.

## Evaluating teaching approaches

One of the products of such assessments of progress might be an evaluation of the teaching methods and materials experienced by the children. Assessments of children's progress are not the only source of this evaluation. Teachers will also evaluate materials and approaches on the grounds of their complexity, ease of operation and intelligibility. The extent of children's learning is, however, an important and necessary criterion for judging the success of teaching approaches.

## Diagnosing difficulties

A further use of assessment is to identify particular difficulties which individual children may have. This can be done at several levels, from an assessment that a particular child is weaker in mathematics than other curriculum areas, to a detailed statement of precise problems.

## Matching materials to children

As a result of diagnosing children's problems, judgements may also be made as to the kinds of materials and teaching methods which would best fit individual children's needs. Teaching can therefore be tailored to these needs.

## Who is assessment for?

the above description of the

perspectives are best

form in the table below.

*Table 11.1*

| Purposes for assessment | Perspectives | | | |
| | National | Local authority | School | Teacher |
|---|---|---|---|---|
| To maintain standards | MC | MC | MC | sc |
| To compare groups | sc | MC | MC | sc |
| To measure progress | MC | MC | MC | sc |
| To evaluate approaches | | | sc | MC |
| To diagnose difficulties | | | | MC |
| To match materials to children | | | | MC |

(Key: sc = of some concern; MC = of major concern)

## National

At a national level the prime purpose of assessment is to keep a check on national standards of achievement. When national standards appear not to be making the advances they might, this is usually the signal for national government initiatives. Both the Bullock Committee in the early 1970s and the present National Curriculum were instigated as a result of concern over standards, and there have been several other examples of this happening.

National Curriculum assessment strategies also show a concern with the measurement of progress, since schools will be expected to report each year on the progress of their children through the various levels of attainment. This will, however, only be done on a group basis and the progress of individual children will not be reported. By implication, such reporting will also allow national government to make comparisons between the achievements of groups of children from different schools. The first three assessment purposes are therefore applicable at a national level.

The final three purposes are, however, not really applicable. National government does not, even under the National Curriculum, have responsibility for determining the use of particular teaching approaches. It therefore has no interest, other than a very general one which may be expressed through nationally sponsored research, in using assessments to evaluate these approaches. Neither the diagnosis of difficulties nor the matching of materials to children's needs are national concerns. These are more properly concerns at a more local level.

### Local authority

A local education authority will have similar requirements from assessment procedures to national government, but on a smaller scale. It will want to keep a check on whether standards are being maintained in its schools and will also want to know that cohorts of children are making progress. As with national government, this will only be done on a group basis and individual children's records of progress are unlikely to be kept by the local authority.

Local authorities are sometimes concerned with comparing groups of children. Some authorities still operate selection systems for post-primary education and use assessment to determine which children are given particular kinds of secondary education. More commonly, authorities often operate screening procedures, using a variety of assessment techniques, in order to identify groups of children who need extra help, usually in reading. These procedures are sometimes followed up by a diagnosis of individual difficulties, so that a basis for the extra help can be determined. Such diagnosis, although sponsored by the authority, will usually be done, however, by the teachers directly involved with the children concerned.

As with national government, it is rare for local authorities to make decisions about teaching approaches and materials. They are therefore not really concerned with the evaluation of these through assessment; neither are they concerned with the matching of materials and methods to the needs of particular children.

## School

of purposes for assess-

groups for purp

streaming is comparatively rare in primary schools, setting for sub jects such as mathematics and music is probably on the increase.

Schools may also use assessment as a means of evaluating teaching materials and approaches on a fairly wide basis. They may, for example, decide to change or abandon a reading scheme on the grounds that its use did not seem to have led to sufficient improvement in their children's abilities at reading. It is, nevertheless, more usually the case that the teaching materials a school uses are selected for reasons other than their positive effect upon children's learning.[2]

The purposes of diagnosing difficulties and matching materials to needs are only oblique concerns at the school level. On a day-to-day basis these tasks are carried out by individual teachers, who may comply with a general school policy but usually have a great deal of autonomy in their actions.

## Teacher

From teachers' points of view, all of the purposes for assessment described above have some application, although some are more central to the role of a teacher than others. Teachers are concerned with maintaining standards, yet probably do not give this attention on a daily basis, as there are other more prominent things which grab their attention. Likewise, they are concerned with the progress made by the children in their care, yet probably give this aspect attention only in special circumstances. If they have children who are giving them particular concern, they may well be aware of the progress of these children week by week, or month by month. With the majority of their pupils, however, progress will usually figure in their thoughts only at larger intervals, for example immediately following a general assessment such as a test. Teachers will also make comparisons between groups of their children, perhaps in order to assign groups to particular programmes or to allocate their own limited time, yet will often do this only at large intervals. Some teachers may continually form and re-form classroom groups as a result of on-going assessments, but they are comparatively rare.

Since teachers are directly concerned with the day-to-day administration of programmes of instruction, they need to make extensive use of assessment for purposes concerned with this. They need to diagnose particular needs and to match these needs to teaching materials and methods, as a result of which they inevitably make evaluations of these materials and methods.

It can be seen, therefore, that assessment serves a different range of purposes from each of these four perspectives. This being the case, it would seem to follow that each perspective ideally requires slightly different forms of assessment in order to satisfy its purposes. An assessment technique which satisfies the needs of national government or a local authority is unlikely to give a teacher sufficient information upon which to base a responsive teaching programme. Teachers, in particular, need to consider very carefully the information they require about their children's language and literacy development and to plan an assessment programme based upon this.

## APPROACHES TO ASSESSMENT[3]

In some circumstances assessment takes the form of a series of tests (or examinations) administered after the completion of a teaching programme. This 'summative' evaluation can provide valuable information about the effects of the total programme, and would seem to be appropriate in the case of fixed length units of teaching such as particular topics in history, science or other curriculum areas. The teaching of language and literacy, however, would seem to be far more of a long-term, developmental process. Important decisions about the methods and materials used would need to be made during the course of their use rather than only at the end of the programme. This is not to say that there is no place for summative evaluation in language and literacy teaching. There may well be some value in regular end-of-term or end-of-year summative checks on children's progress since these provide useful statements on progress made. They are not, however, par-

~~∙ ∙l--l∙ ∙∙∙eful~~ for the purpose of evaluating particular teaching

~~l ∙∙∙l∙∙∙ing~~ individual

precise time ~~oi nccu. ∙∙∙∙. __~~

outside agencies such as local authority screening ~~programmics, ∪i~~ even to school-determined assessment programmes, since it must relate precisely to individual teachers' programmes. It therefore needs to be carried out by teachers themselves, often using assessment strategies of their own design. Some guidelines for the development of these strategies will be given later in the chapter. At this point we shall try to explore what exactly we are doing when we are assessing language and literacy development.

In order to be reasonably sure of arriving at an accurate assessment of a child's language and literacy development, a teacher could investigate and observe all the instances of a child's use of language and literacy over a period of, say, a month. This would involve making judgements about each particular language and literacy task – for example, how well the child performed; which aspects of the task were found difficult and which easy; what special strengths and weaknesses there appeared to be; and what the child's attitude was towards the task. Assuming the teacher knew how to assess these things accurately and reliably, this would give a reasonably comprehensive picture of a child's capabilities. There are, however, some problems with this approach, to say the least!

It is simply not possible for a teacher to observe and assess every instance of a child's use of language and literacy. These are so integral a part of life that such an attempt would involve careful observation of almost everything the child did.

Assessment, therefore, cannot be comprehensive. A teacher's judgement of children's progress is, instead, based upon analysis of their performance at certain defined times and in certain, necessarily limited, situations. It is based, that is, upon a sample of children's language and literacy behaviour. If judgements are to be made as a result of this limited sampling of behaviour, it follows that these judgements are the more likely to be accurate the more representative this sample is of children's total language and literacy experience. In the past, assessments of progress have often failed to ensure that this was the case. It has, for example, often been assumed that a child's high score on a test of word recognition implied competence in all areas of reading, and, indeed, in all areas of the curriculum. There is plenty of evidence to suggest that this assumption does not necessarily follow.[5]

Thus teachers in assessing, that is, sampling the language and literacy behaviour of children, need to consider carefully the degree to which their sample reflects the full range of language and literacy activities in which children engage, both in and out of school. If there are areas of development not represented in the sample under consideration, then the teacher cannot make assumptions about children's development in these areas. Nor, by extension, can the teacher evaluate the effectiveness of teaching programmes designed to develop these areas. This is true even with regard to a limited field of literacy development, such as reading, which itself encompasses a wide range of activities, skills and processes.

It would seem, then, that the assessment of language and literacy needs to cover a wide range of areas. This implies the need for a wide range of assessment procedures. A single test, administered at regular intervals, will simply not provide sufficient information about all-round development. Teachers need to develop a battery of assessment strategies to cater for the multi-dimensional nature of their language and literacy teaching. Suggestions for the components of such a battery will be given later in the chapter.

## MODES OF ASSESSMENT

There are three basic modes of assessment: norm-referenced, diagnostic and criterion-referenced. We shall discuss these in turn.

### Norm-referenced assessment

In norm-referenced assessment, children are assessed on their abilities to perform specified tasks and their performance is compared with what is assumed to be the normal performance for children of their age. These assessments rank children's performances by matching them to the scores made by normal ͨ ˉˉˉ There is a wide range of such

ͨͤ ͧͣͤͤͤ ͘

measure of progress which they appear ιο ɡ·ͽͨ· ͘·ͤˉˉˉ understand the concept of 'Reading Age', which they derive from such tests, and it is an attractively simple idea to say that a child with a reading age of 7 is reading at the same level as an average child aged 7. There are, however, several drawbacks to the use of such assessment devices.

First, many of these tests, and certainly the most popular reading tests such as the Schonell, are individual. They require teachers to devote anything up to half an hour of their time to testing one child. This is a time-consuming process and during this time the teacher cannot, of course, attend to the needs of other children in the class. Because of this many teachers decide to administer tests like these during break or lunch times. If it were possible to obtain the same kind of information using less time-intensive means, it would seem sensible to do this. There are certainly several group-reading tests available, by the use of which teachers can obtain reading ages for whole classes after a fifteen or thirty minutes testing period. These group tests have, however, their own problems. Some children may react badly to testing situations and may not give of their best in these circumstances. It is more difficult to reassure these children to the same degree as in an individual test, and in consequence the results obtained may be skewed against them.

A second problem with standardised tests is that of representativeness. Because of the test situation, children's performance may not be representative of their capabilities, and the abilities actually demanded by the test may not be representative of those making up even one small area of literacy and language. The most common skill, for example, for reading tests to assess is that of recognising words out of context. It has been demonstrated that children perform differently when faced with words in context,[7] yet the tendency is for interpreters of test results to assume that children who can do the one will also be able to do the other. There are tests available which assess word recognition in context, and, to an extent, comprehension, but it is still hard to find standardised tests which focus upon the use of context, or the use of reading to handle information, much less upon other aspects of language and literacy such as writing and listening. Even within the skill areas which a test does examine, there is often little clue as to where a particular child's strengths and weaknesses lie. Two children may end up with the same score, yet have widely different skill profiles.

A further problem with norm-referenced assessment is to do with where these norms come from. By design these tests are necessarily based upon norms established in the past. They thus serve only to assess the maintenance of the status quo in literacy. In a rapidly changing society, new definitions of literacy make it vital that children's abilities be assessed in terms of the needs of the present and future rather than the standards of the past.

Tests by their nature are inevitably culturally grounded, and they discriminate against testees to the extent that these are not in tune with the same culture. As a small example of this, consider the following. The Schonell reading test includes the word 'adamant'. Children who can read it accurately should be reading at about the level of a 13 year old. In a class of 9 year olds in 1975, every child in the class could read this word. Upon investigation it transpired that a favourite television programme of all the children was about a character called 'Adam Adamant'! Five years later, in another class of the same age, a significant proportion read this word as 'Adam Ant'. Cultures change rapidly in the modern world! Another example of this occurs in the much used Neale Analysis of Reading Ability test, which has confused many otherwise perfectly literate children with its reference to a 'milkman's horse'. This cultural grounding which standardised tests have is, of course, even more serious when the children involved do not belong to mainstream British culture, and it can lead to serious under-estimation of these children's abilities.

In general it would appear that, while group standardised tests may have a value in providing reasonably quick assessments of general levels of ability, norm-referenced tests on the whole are inefficient providers of useful teaching information, when consideration is given to the time they take to administer. The ranking of children's performance against those of their peers is not particularly useful teaching information as it gives no which would benefit

other assessment devices

order to determine areas in which children are strong or in which they have weaknesses. There are several points to be made about such assessments.

First, good teachers are constantly engaged in a process of diagnosing children's difficulties through informal methods, for example, hearing a child read or marking a piece of work. Very often this informal diagnosis will be all that is needed to make an assessment of a child's strengths and weaknesses in those partic-ular skills. Only in difficult cases will more formal diagnostic tests be needed as a guide for future teaching of particular children.

Second, diagnostic assessment tends to be conducted at an individual level and hence can be very time consuming. Because of this it makes very little sense for a teacher to spend this time with a child if there are quicker ways of arriving at the same information. With most children this will be the case and informal methods of diagnosis will be adequate. With a minority, individual attention and more formal diagnoses will often pay dividends.

There are several published diagnostic tests available, but unfortunately most of them seem to test the acquisition of the beginning skills of reading, especially the use of phonics. Tests diagnosing weaknesses in, for example, the use of information skills and the writing of narratives are generally not available. It is, of course, possible for teachers to design their own tests in areas they wish to investigate, and some suggestions for ways to approach this will be given in the second half of this chapter. The problems of validity and reliability, which inevitably arise in the construction of assessment instruments, are not so serious for teachers as they would be for educational researchers, since the instruments will never be the only source of information teachers will have. As mentioned above, the teacher is constantly using a range of informal methods to diagnose children's problems, and the results from any teacher-devised formal assessment will be interpreted in the light of this background information.

Diagnostic assessment does, therefore, have an important place as part of a range of assessment procedures used by the teacher. Its main use would be to check on hypotheses already formulated by the teacher about individuals' specific strengths and weaknesses. In the classroom these hypotheses basically arise from the observed answers to a teacher's questions, such as, 'Can this child complete this piece of work satisfactorily?'. If the answer is in the negative, the teacher might go on to speculate on the reason why. Diagnostic assessment aims to provide an answer.

### Criterion-referenced assessment

In asking the question, 'Can this child complete this piece of work satisfactorily?', the teacher is setting up the piece of work as a standard against which to judge the child's performance. The child's performance is judged, not against that of other children in his age group, as with norm-referenced assessment, but against the demands of a particular task. This kind of assessment has a great application in the development of language and literacy, and underlies the specification of National Curriculum attainment targets. After all, the most vital thing for a teacher to know about a child's use of literacy is not how it compares with that of other children, but rather, whether it is of a standard that will enable the child to perform adequately in all the areas of life in which literacy is needed. In other words, the child is judged against a criterion of task difficulty, rather than against the performance of peers. There are several general points to be made about this form of assessment.

In assessing children's abilities to complete specified tasks, the teacher is clearly in a position to integrate assessment fully into the teaching programme. The tasks chosen would usually be tasks used for teaching, and hence there need be no distinction between teaching and testing. This is generally not true of norm-referenced assessment.

Criterion-referenced assessment can also quite easily serve a diagnostic purpose. If the teacher analyses the skill demands of the various elements of the tasks to be used, a reasonable assumption can then be made that a child's failure in any of these elements indicates a weakness in those particular skills. Diagnostic teaching ___ thus proceed with minimal recourse to formal testing

Criterion-referenced assessment
evaluating language and literacy development, and teaching pro-gramme effectiveness, as long as care is taken that the procedures employed do not lead to an overemphasis on constituent skills. If realistic tasks are used for assessment there is much less danger of this happening. In the rest of this chapter we shall discuss some strategies by which assessment can be embedded into such tasks.

## ASSESSMENT STRATEGIES

In devising assessment strategies for language and literacy, as for any curriculum area, there are four basic questions which need to be asked about each strategy proposed. These are:

1 Will this give me any information I do not already know?
2 Could I gain this information more easily another way?
3 Is this strategy practicable in a classroom situation?
4 How can I carry this out with a minimum of disruption of teaching time?

Only in the event of satisfactory answers to these questions should the strategy be adopted.

There are three basic strategies for assessing language and literacy development. These involve either looking at what children actually produce, or observing them while they are involved in language and literacy tasks, or asking them questions about what they are doing. We shall discuss these strategies in turn and suggest for each some appropriate techniques.

### Analysing products

Making judgements about children on the basis of what they produce has been a traditional means of assessment and most teachers develop a fair skill at doing it. Although more recent developments have tended to shift concentration onto process, there is still a great deal which can be gleaned from analyses of children's language and literacy products. We shall look closely at two aspects of this: first at a technique for analysing the product of a child's oral reading, and second at the assessment of written products.

### (a) Miscue analysis

Miscue analysis is based upon the theory that the mistakes a child makes when reading aloud from a text betray a great deal about how that child is tackling the reading task.[8] According to the theory, these mistakes are never simply random. Each mistake is caused by the interactions between a set of circumstances which include the child's general approach to reading; his/her approaches to that particular text; the context surrounding the word; and the graphic and phonic features of the word itself. What the child says is evidence that can help a teacher determine what the child was attending to at the time of reading, which may in turn indicate the beliefs about and skills in reading which the child has.

As an example, the following sentence in a reading book – 'The man got on his horse' was read by a child as 'The man got on his house'. Because the word 'house' does not make sense in this context, it is fairly safe to assume that making sense was not the chief preoccupation of this child, who seems rather to be attending to the initial letters of the word. Another child read the sentence as 'The man got on his pony'. This child seems to have been attending more to the meaning, even to the extent of ignoring what the word looked like. These two children seem to have different approaches to the task of reading, which lead them to 'miscue' in different ways.

Of course, the misreading of one word is not sufficient evidence upon which to base a complete assessment. The technique of miscue analysis, therefore, uses a child's oral reading of much longer texts and tries to point out patterns in the kinds of mis-readings which the child produces. It is usually carried out with the child reading from his/her normal book, and the teacher recording exactly what the child reads onto a copy of the text which she has in front of her. There are several suggested coding systems for this recording,[9] although the exigencies of time usually mean that the simplest possible system is most effective (it is also

. . . . . . . . . . . for later, more detailed

aloud from . . . . . . . . ,

In a hole in the ground there lived a hobbit. Not a nasty, dirty wet hole, filled with the ends of worms and an oozy smell, nor yet a dry, bare, sandy hole with nothing in it to sit down on or to eat: it was a hobbit-hole and that means comfort.

Their reading was recorded using the following system:

// ...........................pausing
behind ...................sounding out phonically
the .........................omission
on
/ ...........................addition
make
milk .......................substitution
C ............................self-correction

The record of Robert's reading is given in Figure 11.1, and that of Gary in Figure 11.2.

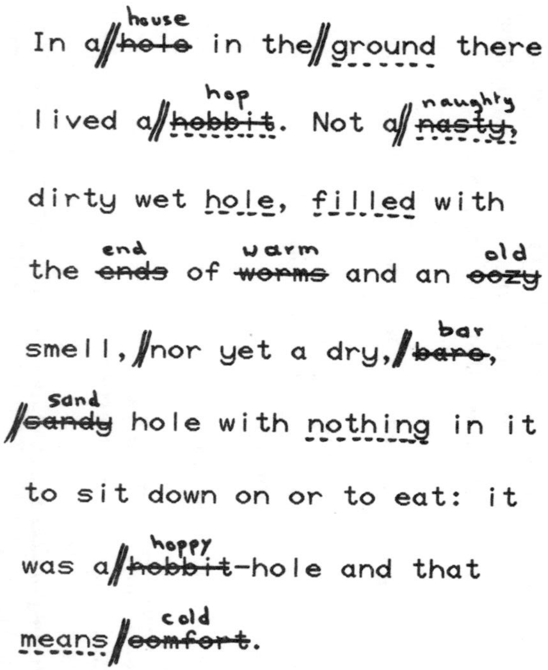

**Figure 11.1 Robert's reading record**

In a //[house]hole in the //ground there

lived a //[hop]hobbit. Not a //[naughty]nasty,

dirty wet hole, filled with

the [end]ends of [warm]worms and an [old]oozy

smell, //nor yet a dry, //[bar]bare,

//[sand]sandy hole with nothing in it

to sit down on or to eat: it

was a //[happy]hobbit-hole and that

means //[cold]comfort.

*Figure 11.1 Robert's reading record*

---

**Figure 11.2 Gary's reading record**

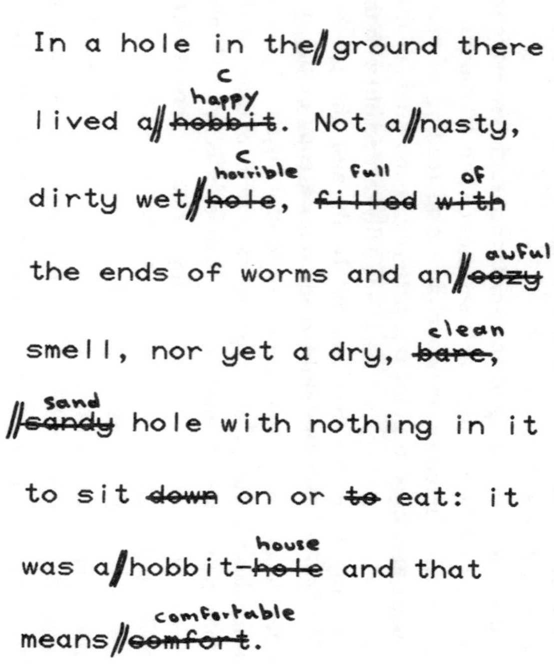

In a hole in the //ground there

lived a //[happy]hobbit. Not a //nasty. Not a //nasty.

dirty wet //[horrible]hole, [full of]filled with

the ends of worms and an //[awful]oozy

smell, nor yet a dry, [clean]bare,

//[sand]sandy hole with nothing in it

to sit down on or to eat: it

was a //[house]hobbit-hole and that

means //[comfortable]comfort.

*Figure 11.2 Gary's reading record*

For each child the teacher completed an analysis form and these are given as Figures 11.3 and 11.4. (ER on the form stands for Expected Response, that is, the original word. OR stands for Observed Response, what the child actually said.)

The teacher was now in a position to make an assessment of each child's reading and a statement about the kind of experiences they would now need. These assessments were as follows:

Robert
Robert does not appear to be reading for meaning. His miscues suggest attention to grapho-phonic cues only. This is confirmed
ding of under-breath sounding out.

Gary
Gary clearly realises that reading is chiefly about meaning. His miscues largely suggest a concern for meaning-seeking. At times he is a little cavalier about the actual words on the page, preferring his guess, albeit usually a sensible one, to looking carefully at the words.

His attention to meaning must not be disturbed, but he needs to be encouraged to look more carefully at the words on the page. We could try getting him to read some poetry, especially out loud. Getting the words exactly right is more important in poems.

This example has hopefully shown some of the very rich insights into children's reading which miscue analysis can provide. It must always be borne in mind, however, that this technique, in common with all assessment techniques, is never the sole source of information available to the teacher. Other sources, such as those described below, will be used to confirm, modify or enlarge upon the insights gained from miscue analysis. The teacher will build up a battery of assessment techniques each complementary to the other.

## Robert

| ER | OR | Possible cause of miscue |
|---|---|---|
| hole | house | Guessing from initial sound? Possibly looking forward to "lived". |
| hobbit | hop | Guessing from initial sounds. |
| nasty | naughty | Initial sounds. |
| ends | end | Only read beginning of word. |
| worms | warm | Initial sound. |
| oozy | old | Initial sound. |
| bare | bar | Initial sounds only. |
| Sandy | sand | Only read beginning. |
| hobbit | happy | Initial sounds only. |
| comfort | cold | Initial sounds only. |

General comments on reading

Very hesitant and monotone. Consistently using sounding out (under his breath) as approach to words. No self-corrections even when word did not make sense.

Remarks on comprehension

Could not retell story. Little indication that any of it had been understood.

**Figure 11.3** Robert's reading analysis form

## Gary

| ER | OR | Possible cause of miscue |
|---|---|---|
| hobbit | happy | Expecting a further noun. Self corrected when error realised. |
| hole | horrible | Initial sound? Fits tone of sentence. Corrected. |
| filled | full | Meaningful response. |
| with | so | Response to meaning of previous miscue. |
| oozy | awful | Near synonym. |
| bare | clean | Follows on from dry. Possibly opposite of "drought" earlier. |
| sandy | sand | First part of word only. Meaning preserved. |
| down | — | Preserves meaning. |
| to | — | Preserves meaning. |
| hole | house | Initial sound? Preserves meaning. |
| comfort | comfortable | Meaning preserved. |

General comments on reading

Some hesitancy but seemed to be trying to make sense of passage. Self-correcting on occasions.

Remarks on comprehension

Able to retell story. Understanding seemed good.

**Figure 11.4** Gary's reading analysis form

## (b) Assessing writing

Teachers are usually familiar with the assessment of children's writing since they get so much practice at doing it. It is worthwhile looking at the process in more detail, however. Four particular considerations must be borne in mind when assessing written products.

(i) An assessment of writing must begin with a consideration of the aims which were originally formulated for this piece of work. The product cannot be judged unless these are taken into account.
(ii) The assessment must also take into consideration the
    ˙ ˙˙˙˙˙ ˙f the children producing the work. A piece of writing
                                              ˙˙ ˙˙'s capacity.

she received and the ˙˙˙˙ ˙˙˙
outcome.

As an example of this kind of assessment, the two pieces of children's writing below (Figures 11.5 and 11.6) will be analysed in the light of these four considerations.

(i) Both pieces were produced with similar aims. As part of a project on the environment, these two third-year juniors read pamphlets from the World Wildlife Fund and Friends of the Earth about the threat of extinction to certain animal species. After discussion with their teacher, they (along with four other children) agreed that they would each write their own pamphlet about this problem, which would have the aim not only of giving its readers information, but also of encouraging them to action. These readers were to be other children in the same class.

With regard to its original aim, it can be seen that only one of these pieces really fulfils this. It is written in a very direct style which communicates information but also tries to worry its readers. The second piece conveys information, but seems to lack commitment and its style appears too bland to have real impact.

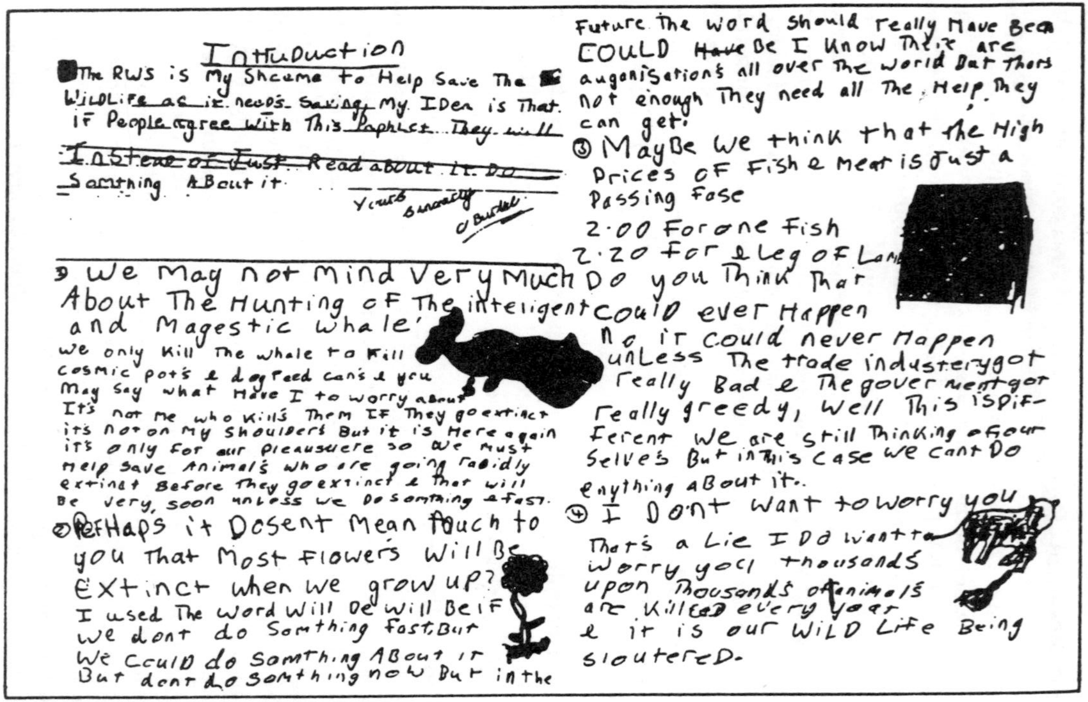

Introduction

■ The RWS is my Sceame to Help Save The Wildlife as it needs Saving. My Idea is That If People agree with This Taprist. They will.

~~Instead of this~~ Read about it Do Something About it
Yours sincerly
J. Bushell

① We May not Mind Very Much Do you Much About The Hunting of The intelligent and Magestic Whale'
We only Kill the whale to Kill cosmic pots & defred canis you may say what Hide I to worry about Its not me who kills Them If They goextract its not on my shoulders But it's Here again its only for our pleasure so we must Help Save Animals who are going Rapidly extinct Before They goextinct Or That will Be very, soon unless we do something a fast.

② Perhaps it Dosent Mean much to you That Most Flowers Will Be Extinct when we grow up? I used The word will beWill Beif we dont do Something FastBut We Could do Somthing About it But dont do something now But in the Future the word Should really Have Bea COULD Have be I know They are organisations all over the world But Thars not enough They need all The Help They can get:
③ MayBe we think that the High Prices OF Fish & meat is just a Passing Fose
2.00 For one Fish
2.20 for a Leg of Lam That Do you Think That could ever Happen No it could never Happen unless The trade industrygot really Bad & The gover neatgot really greedy, Well This isspit-ferent We are still Thinking of our selves But in This case we cant Do anything about it.
④ I Dont want to worry you That's a Lie I Do want to worry you thousonds upon Thousonds of animals are killed every year & it is our WILD Life Being sloutered.

Figure 11.5 Writing assessment piece

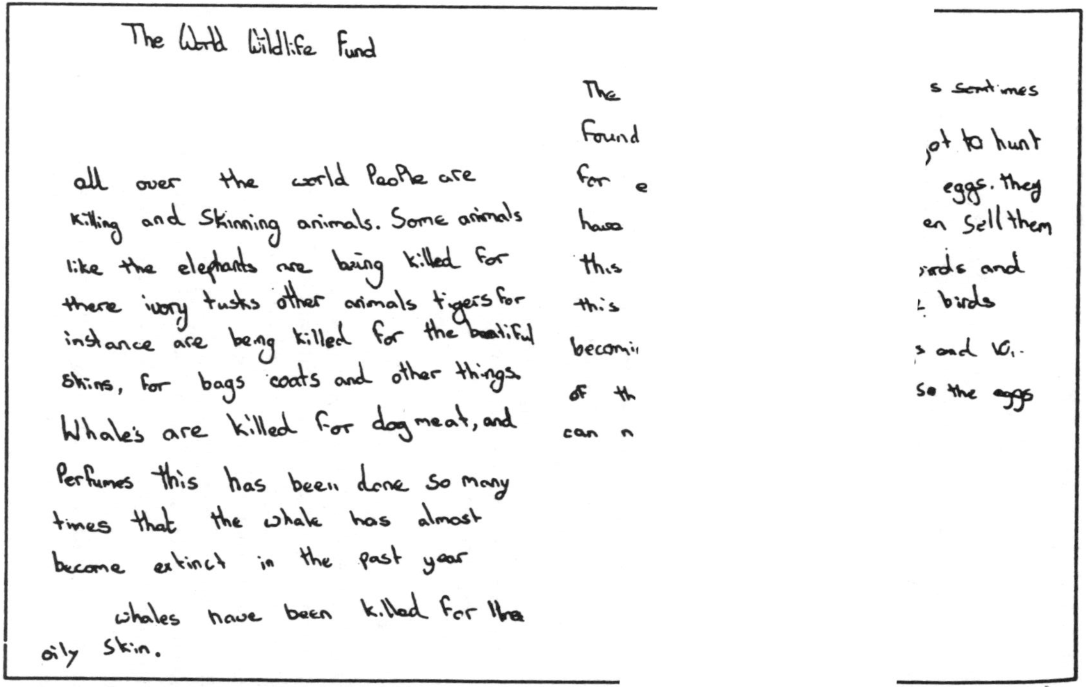

The Wold Wildlife Fund

all over the world People are
killing and Skinning animals. Some animals
like the elephants are being killed for
there ivory tusks other animals tigers for
instance are being killed for the beatiful
skins, for bags coats and other things.
Whales are killed for dog meat, and
Perfumes this has been done so many
times that the whale has almost
become extinct in the past year.

Whales have been killed for tha
oily skin.

The
found
for e
have
this
this
becomii
of th
can n

s sometimes
got to hunt
eggs. they
on sell them
rets and
t birds
s and vi
So the eggs

Figure 11.6 Writing assessment piece

(ii) The writer of the first piece was a boy who rarely shone in school work. From his conversation he was clearly bright and interested in a wide range of things, but the work he produced was invariably slipshod and rarely finished. This piece of work was one of his very best and was given great praise by his teacher.

The girl who wrote the second piece was a child who almost always excelled in her work. She worked extremely conscientiously and was universally regarded by teachers in the school as 'clever'. This piece was fairly typical of her work; reasonably tidy and accurate rather than inspired.

(iii) Both pieces of work were read by other children in the class. When choosing work for the class display on the project, the children included the first but not the second piece. They commented that the first piece 'made them angry', but insisted that it be typed on the jumbo typewriter before being put into the display, because 'the infants won't be able to read it'.

(iv) Both children had similar resources available to them for this work. Both were actually written within one lesson, and were first drafts. Neither child wished to revise what they had written.

The obvious difficulty with a piece of work like the first one is that it has to be read very carefully before its merits are appreciated. It is easy to be put off by the poor presentation and bad spellings, and not to realise that this is, in fact, a remarkable piece of writing. Writing like the second piece will often be judged more kindly because it is neater and more accurate, but it is, in fact, a much more ordinary piece.

## Observation

Teachers observe children working all the time. As a result of this observation they make assessments of children's abilities and attitudes, and plan future work. Yet, when asked about their methods of assessment, they will hardly ever count observation amongst them. Perhaps because observation is so common an activity and seems so subjective, it is very underrated in terms of the assessment information it can provide. Yet it has a great deal of potential. Its greatest strength lies in the fact that it enables assessments to be made while children are actually engaged in language work, and does not require them to be withdrawn from it into a special testing situation. It therefore enables direct analysis of the child's *process* of working, without which assessment must be incomplete.[10]

To use observation deliberately as an assessment technique requires a systematic approach. It also requires some means of recording the information gained rather than relying on memory alone. A systematic approach will involve first of all knowing exactly what one is going to be looking for. This might mean listing the skills it is hoped to assess, and preparing a checklist of them. An alternative approach is to list the activities the children will be doing, and leaving space for noted observations about their performance.

Observation can be guided by a list of points to look for, sug-gestions for which are given below. It is important to state that

be simply 'ticked off' as

(pace National ......
systematic observation.

### (i) Reading
Does the child:      select an appropriate book to read?
                     judge when a book is too difficult?
                     become absorbed in a book?
                     respond to what is read?
                     re-read favourite books?
                     re-tell stories previously read?
                     use a variety of cues in reading words?
                     read silently?
                     understand the way books and print work?
                     have an appropriate language with which
                        to talk about the way he/she reads?

### (ii) Writing
Does the child:      turn to writing as an enjoyable activity?
                     make independent attempts to write?
                     write appropriately for different purposes
                        and audiences?

revise and redraft writing with or without
the help of an adult?
collaborate with other children in writing
activities?
make attempts to spell and punctuate
correctly?
have good habits of letter-formation, etc.?

(iii) Talking and listening
Does the child:    participate in large and small group
discussion?
listen to others' points and respond to
them?
articulate ideas in a clear and appropriate
manner?
match his/her manner of talking to the
needs of an audience?

## Probing

Often simply observing what children do will not be sufficient to
really evaluate the way they are thinking about their tasks. A way of
penetrating into this can be to ask them questions about how they
performed various tasks, or what they were thinking about as they
did them. This questioning fits best into a conferencing approach,
which we discuss in terms of its contribution to the teaching of
reading in Chapter 6 and to the teaching of writing in Chapter 7.
Three types of probing questions will be found useful in this.

### 1 Looking-back questions

These are of the type, 'Can you tell me how you did that?' They can
be useful when looking at children's work alongside them. The
children's answers to this question may well reveal a great deal
about their perceptions of the processes of language. The
following extract from a conversation between a teacher and 7 year
old Clare is an example of this approach. Clare has just written her
version of the story of Red Riding Hood in which the heroine is
menaced by an alien rather than a wolf.

Teacher: Oh, that's an interesting story, Clare! Where did you get
the idea from?

Clare: From my book. We don't have wolves here any more.

T: Yes, that's right. Can you tell me how you started writing your story? What did you do first?

C: Me and Joanne talked about it and ... we just wrote it.

T: Did you write it together?

C: Well ... at first we wrote the same thing ... then Joanne wanted to change hers and I didn't. So we wrote different ones.

T: Did you change your story at all? As you were writing it?

C: I changed some words ... Emma told me how to spell them.

T: Oh, Emma helped you too? What did she do?

C: She read the story after I finished it. She told me my spellings.

T: ~~ ~~ ~~Now. Did you plan to do anything with your story when~~

and use it in another context, a ...-, -
old. She had been able to participate in discussion both in planning her writing and in editing it. She was prepared to work on her writing collaboratively although this did not survive the disagreement with her partner.

Her approach to the writing process showed some evidence of planning although this was not extensive. She was unclear about the destination and audience for her writing and saw revision purely in terms of editing spellings.

All these evaluations would require further investigation, but it is clear from this brief extract what a wealth of information the teacher was able to glean simply by asking questions which caused Clare to reflect on what she had done.

### 2 Looking-forward questions

An alternative kind of question can be of the type, 'Can you tell me how you will do that?' They ask children to think about their actions before they do them. It is, of course, possible that because they are made by the question to think through in advance what they will do, they actually perform differently than they would have done without the question. The question may therefore have a teaching role, as well as being a way of seeing whether they know what to do. Questions such as the following are of this type:

'When you go to the library to look for that book, can you tell me what you will do?'
'Now, you are going to write your report on sports day for the school newspaper. How will you start?'
'This group are going to discuss your puppet play. How are you going to make sure everyone gets a fair chance to say what they think?'

As a result of questions like these the teacher is able both to make an initial assessment of children's approaches to the process, and to prompt them in a way that may actually develop their thinking.

### 3 Thinking-out-loud questions

These are of the type, 'What are you thinking as you are doing that?' They can help make children's thinking about certain tasks explicit and alert the teacher to faulty approaches. They may include questions like:

'As you make notes from that book, can you tell me why you are choosing those things?'
'You have just written this bit about seeing the panda in the zoo. Can you tell me what you are planning to go on to now?'
'Now, is your discussion going well? Have you found any problems?'

It is quite likely that, in general, teachers ask too few questions like this. In addition to providing useful information about the way children are thinking, they can have the important effect of heightening children's awareness of the way they are using language. Developing this 'metalinguistic awareness', as we argued in Chapter 2, is an important task for the teacher of language and literacy.

## AN INTEGRATED APPROACH

Perhaps the most important point to be made about the assessment of language and literacy is that a single source of information or assessment technique will never be a sufficient basis upon which a teacher can build appropriate teaching programmes. This requires a great deal of information of many kinds and from many contexts. The teacher therefore requires an integrated approach to assessment.

This approach should include information gained from formal assessment procedures such as miscue analysis and structured observation, but it should also include the kind of day-to-day information which teachers often underrate, such as incidental conversations with children about their work. Because of the intimacy of classroom teaching, teachers are privy to a great deal
 ̄ ̄ ̄ ̄ ̄ ̄ ̄ about their children's strengths and weaknesses, to
 ̄ ̄ ̄ ̄ ̄ ̄ ̄ ̄ thus in a

which they have access.

## FOLLOW-UP ACTIVITIES

1 Collect two or three pieces of writing from the work of one child with whom you have contact. Examine these pieces carefully and try to make an assessment of this child's writing abilities on the basis of these examples.

Try to specify some points in your assessment about which you would like to have extra information. For each of these points suggest some possible ways in which this extra information might be gained.

2 Carry out a miscue analysis with two or three children. Tape-record their oral reading and use the recording as the basis for your analysis.

On the basis of your analysis try to make an interim assessment of the reading of these children, and some statement about the kinds of experience each of them now needs. Make a list of some extra information you would like about these children and suggest ways in which you might set about obtaining it.

3 For a project or piece of thematic work you are planning or have recently carried out with children, try to identify some of the opportunities in this work for the assessment of language. Your list might include such elements as:

— opportunities for systematic observation of children working,
— opportunities for holding interviews/conferences with individual children about their use of reading and/or writing,
— opportunities for examining carefully what children produce, perhaps in conjunction with the children themselves.

4 Suggest some ways in which you might involve children in making assessments of their own performance and capabilities in language.

Discuss with your colleagues the extent to which this is a desirable or feasible aim in assessment.

# Conclusion

predominant themes have
covered the substantial ground which makes up ......,
language. To conclude the book, we shall briefly review the most
important of these themes.

Perhaps the most fundamental theme, which underlies most
recent work in language, has been a conception of the nature of
the learning process which emphasises its active and, above all,
social nature. As we discussed in our introduction, the rediscovery
of the work of Vygotsky has assisted a major rethinking of the
nature of learning. This is now seen as rooted in social processes.
It is also seen as active rather than passive, involving learners
constructing their own views of the world, rather than receiving
these directly from another person. This process of construction
relies on learners interpreting new discoveries and insights in the
light of their existing cognitive structures, or schemata. It also
places language at the very heart of the learning process as the
medium through which this construction takes place. This
conception of learning leads naturally to several other important
concepts which emerge as themes throughout our book.

First, as we pointed out in the introduction, learning is seen to
be considerably enhanced by collaboration. This may involve the

development of shared consciousness as in peer collaboration, or the presence of the borrowed consciousness which Vygotsky suggests develops in novice–expert collaboration. The role of collaboration has been discussed in several places in the book, particularly in the chapters on talk, reading and writing. With regard to talk we focused particularly on the role of small-group work, which also has an important role in the learning of reading and writing. For these latter processes, however, we gave even more attention to novice–expert collaboration, looking specially at apprenticeship approaches.

A particular form of collaboration has been referred to several times in the book under the heading of conferencing. This has become a popular term used to describe the discussion between child and teacher, or child and child, of language work in progress. A reading conference might focus on issues such as children's responses to particular texts, their attitudes to reading, or their strategies for making sense of text. A writing conference might focus on children's plans for their writing, their need and scope for redrafting particular pieces, or the reactions of an audience to these pieces. In all cases the conference will be built around the notion of equality of partnership, with neither participant having more speaking or action rights than any other, and with final decisions about subsequent action being left to the child around whose work the conference has centred. Of course, the management of this kind of conference demands particular skills on the part of the teacher: skills which will probably not have been exercised or developed in the course of more traditional approaches to language teaching.

A key word for the collaborative approach we have described is 'interactive', and the concept of interaction has an important place in language and literacy work. It has been suggested as an enabling mechanism in language acquisition, and, by extension, looms large in literacy development, as our earlier remarks about collaboration suggest. Interaction does not, however, refer only to collaboration between teacher and child, or child and child. It is also used to refer to the relationship between a reader or writer and a text, whether spoken or written. In our chapter on reading we described the interactive model of the reading process and suggested that reading was characterised by the 'to-and-fro-ing' between the reader and a text, with meaning being the result of these transactions. This process is also at the heart of the reader-response theory which we described in our chapter on children's literature. We also discussed interactive listening in our chapter on talk, and small-group discussion, of course, relies on interaction. It is also possible to see writing as an interactive process, with the writer having to balance the often complex relationships between purpose for writing, audience and textual demands, which we discussed in our chapter on writing.

A theme which has emerged several times in our book as a strategy for teaching has been that of teacher-modelling. One of the conditions which we discussed for the learning of spoken language was the witnessing of demonstrations of language by the learner. ~~~~~tions are an essential element of any learning. It would
~~~~~~ ride a bicycle, to

Teachers, nevertheless, ~~~~~
of children's eyes for a large proportion of the day, anu usuany, being accepted as people who are worth imitating. By simply demonstrating language processes such as writing, responding to books, taking part in discussions and listening attentively, teachers can provide effective models from which children can and will learn a great deal. Too many teachers are dissuaded from providing these models by the concern that in simply reading, writing, listening and talking they are not actually *teaching*. Our argument is that these actions can be very effective teaching indeed.

During the course of this modelling, and also while collaboration and conferencing is going on, teachers are also provided with opportunities to do something which, although it has not been discussed directly in the book, has underlain much of what we have said. This is the making explicit of knowledge and insights which accomplished language users understand implicitly. All language users develop a great many understandings about the way language processes work simply by using these processes. Often these understandings are implicit and can be articulated only with great difficulty by their possessors. As teachers interact with children and focus upon their use of language, they constantly meet the need to refer explicitly to elements of this use. Discussion of this kind has three likely results.

First, it provides children with a model of how to think about and discuss language processes, parts of which they may pick up and begin to use themselves. An important constituent of this model will be attention to the way functions and forms interact in language. Discussion of purposes for language use will not have the effect of increasing children's language awareness unless it is closely linked to the ways in which these purposes influence actual language expression. Similarly, discussion of language forms without taking into account purpose and meaning produces only the dry, untransferable knowledge which has too often resulted in the past from grammar exercises.

Second, it offers them a language with which to discuss language. The importance of this *meta-language* we discussed briefly in our chapter on language awareness. It is difficult to imagine how discussion about language could proceed sensibly and usefully in the absence of particular ways of referring to the elements discussed, although it must be pointed out forcefully that the mere drilling of children in linguistic or grammatical terms will not be sufficient to provide them with a usable meta-language.

Third, this discussion may encourage children to express their own thoughts about their own use of language, and by this expression to reflect upon their use. Reflection should help them produce more considered language use and, in a real sense, increase their power over their own language. Through reflection they may come to appreciate such things as how to recognise when they do not understand something; how to take steps to resolve this problem; and how to shape their language productions more precisely to the needs of their purpose, context and audience.

Although we have tried to cover what appear to us to be the most significant issues in language and literacy teaching at the moment, there can be little doubt that, given the pace of change and the volume of publications now being produced in this field, important insights will continue to be derived from work in a variety of fields such as linguistics, psychology, sociology and anthropology, not to mention straight educational and curriculum research. For the teacher who wishes fully to understand the infinitely fascinating subject of language and literacy in education, our book, therefore, is only an introduction. We wish our readers very pleasurable further reading.

# Notes

(1983) gives a good introduction to tnis but Bruner ___
give perhaps the fullest account and set the learning process fully into
a social context. The constructivist view is linked closely with schema
theory, the chief architect of which has been David Rumelhart. See
Rumelhart (1980) for a particularly good account of this.

4   This extract is taken from Rosen, C. and Rosen, H. (1973).
5   For a good review of research findings into the nature of talk in
    classrooms see Edwards and Westgate (1987).
6   The term 'language game of teaching' comes from the work of Bellack
    and his colleagues, whose study (Bellack et al, 1966) was one of the
    first to analyse the 'cycles of discourse' which characterise classroom
    talk.
7   See Tizard and Hughes (1984).
8   See Willes (1981).
9   The major source of this information is Sinclair and Coulthard
    (1975). For a full review of the area, see Edwards and Westgate (1987).
10  The terms 'Solicitation – Response – Reaction' come from Bellack et
    al., (1966), and 'Initiation – Response – Feedback' from Sinclair and
    Coulthard (1975).
11  The two-thirds rule comes from Flanders (1970) whose interaction
    analysis system has had a great deal of influence upon classroom
    interaction research. Flanders does not actually classify questions, so
    the third statement in the rule, as given here, is an extension to his
    work, drawing upon copious other research.

12 The analysis of 'transmission' teaching comes from the seminal work of Barnes (1976).

13 The development of shared understandings is inevitable in classrooms, as in other long-term social situations, but they can be quite difficult for an outside researcher to penetrate, as Walker and Adelman (1976) show.

14 See Edwards and Westgate (1987), especially Chapter 2.

15 For an interesting summary of the place of purposeful group talk see Wade (1985), especially Chapters 1, 6 and 8.

16 See Fourlas and Wray (1990).

17 For a more extensive review of this area, see Chapter 8 in Wray (1990a).

18 See Tann (1990) for an extensive treatment of listening.

19 According to Rumelhart (1980) there are three major processes by which existing schemata are altered. *Accretion* is the acquisition of new knowledge which simply fits into pre-existing schemata. In *restructuring*, existing schemata are reorganised to give new insights. In *tuning*, existing skills and knowledge structures are made increasingly automatic. These three processes operate in conjunction to make up learning.

20 This is a view of learning which is becoming increasingly supported by research, such as that of Edwards and Mercer (1987) and that reported in Bruner and Haste (1987). Its founding insights, however, come from work much earlier by Vygotsky (1962). See Wertsch (1985) for a review of Vygotsky's contribution.

## 2 Language diversity and language awareness

1 See particularly Department of Education and Science (1988) (the Kingman report) and (1989b) (the second Cox report).

2 The Summary report of the Linguistic Minorities Project (1983) contains some fascinating figures relating to the pattern of language use across the country. Children in school in various Education Authorities were asked if they spoke a language other than English at home, and what it was. Some of the results are given for three areas: Bradford, Peterborough and the London Borough of Haringey.

In Bradford, of the 79,758 pupils surveyed in the age range 6 to 16, 17.8 per cent claimed to speak a language other than English at home. The most popular languages mentioned were Punjabi (by 52.7 per cent of those who did claim to speak another language), Urdu (19 per cent) and Gujerati (8.8 per cent).

In Peterborough, of 32,662 pupils surveyed, 7.4 per cent claimed to speak a language other than English at home. The most popular languages mentioned were Punjabi (24 per cent), Italian (23.7 per cent), Urdu (17.8 per cent) and Gujerati (11.5 per cent).

In Haringey, 24,140 were surveyed and 30.7 per cent claimed to speak a language other than English at home. The most popular languages mentioned were Greek (34.1 per cent), Turkish (14.7 per cent), English-based Creoles (9.3 per cent).

3 There are several sources of help for teachers who wish to become more familiar with the language diversity of their pupils. Notably useful for this, as well as for practical classroom suggestions, are Houlton (1985) and Gregory and Woollard (1985).

4 Upton, Sanderson and Widdowson (1987) provide a series of dialect 'word maps' of England which contains such fascinating detail as the geographical spread of the expressions 'cross-eyed', 'squint-eyed', 'boss-eyed' and 'cock-eyed'!

5 Edwards (undated) gives a useful summary of the most common differences between Standard English and British dialects.

6 Probably the best detailed account of this argument is still Trudgill (1975).

    -----ing work of Howard Giles is responsible for much of our       ---- people respond to accents. See Giles

           ----ment and

   IOI ---

more up-to-date u-----

11 Department of Education and Scie---

12 Douglas (1964) was a very influential study which ---- relationship between home background and educatio---- achievement. Craft (1970) contains a range of papers on various aspects of the issue.

13 Bernstein (1971), still widely available in various editions, contains his most widely quoted papers. Atkinson (1985) provides a thorough critique of Bernstein's work.

14 The teaching programme proposed by Bereiter and Engelmann (1966) is the most widely quoted (and attacked) of these. That proposed by Bernstein's colleagues (Gahagan and Gahagan, 1970) was less extreme than some.

15 Notably Labov (1969) and, more recently, Heath (1983).

16 See Tizard and Hughes (1984).

17 Bernstein himself makes this point in his article 'Education cannot compensate for society', included in the 1971 collection.

18 Opie and Opie (1959).

19 Department of Education and Science (1989b), Chapter 6.

## 3 Children's literature and the power of stories

1 An interesting discussion of the importance of taking into account both form and content will be found in Fox (1988). She criticises the line of investigation which concentrates upon form and has produced story 'grammars', for example that of Mandler and Johnson (1977),

which can then be directly taught to children (cf. Rand, 1984). This approach, Fox argues, has the effect of 'sidelining' stories as simply another language form to be analysed, instead of putting them in their rightful place at the heart of language and language production.

2   This point is made in much of the work of reader-response theorists. In particular, Iser (1978) expounds the idea of the reader imaginatively remaking a text as a result of the interaction between anticipations and retrospections. For an accessible recapitulation of reader-response theory see Chapter 1 of Benton and Fox (1985).

3   This is a familiar argument which is expressed most cogently by Frank Smith (1978) and, more recently, by Margaret Meek (1988).

4   This is a point that Frank Smith makes (Smith 1988), quoting research by Miller (1977).

5   See Perera (1984).

6   This was one of the most influential findings of the Bristol Language Study which charted the development of language of children through their early years at home and school. The director of this study, Gordon Wells, has written widely about his work, but perhaps most accessibly in Wells (1987).

7   Many useful ideas for this will be found in Jones and Buttrey (1970).

8   This point is extremely well made in Cheetham (1976).

9   Lists of criteria will be found in Stones (1983) and Jeffcoate (1982), and useful regular reviews of children's books will be found in magazines such as *Books for Keeps* and *Signal*.

10  See Dickinson (1976).

11  See, for example, Jeffcoate (1982), Dixon (1977) and Lyons (1978)

12  For a fuller discussion of these points, see Wray (1989a).

13  Jackson (1986) is particularly interesting on this point.

14  It is difficult to find a balanced account of the 'poetry debate'. Most contributions are partisan, but Styles and Triggs (1988) provide the most comprehensive review of modern children's poetry. See Rosen (1984) for a short response to his critics and Rosen (1989) for an excellent handbook on getting children to produce the direct, personal poetry for which Rosen is renowned.

15  Bennett (1979) combines a powerful treatise on the place of children's literature in early reading with a useful list of suitable picture books.

16  For more ideas of this kind see Roeder and Lee (1982).

## 4 The emergence of literacy

1   The work of Downing and Thackray (1975) was most influential in establishing the concept of reading readiness, which they defined as, 'the stage in development when, either through maturation or through previous learning, or both, the individual child can learn to read easily and profitably'. They devised the *Reading Readiness Inventory* checklist as a means of assessing the readiness of individual children (Downing and Thackray, 1976).

2  In the United Kingdom an early challenge to the readiness view came from the work of Margaret Clark (1976). Other, very influential, international work is reported in Ferreiro and Teberosky (1983) and in Goelman, H., Oberg, A. and Smith, F. (1984).
3  The best review of the area is provided by Hall (1987).
4  An interesting analysis of young children's writing will be found in Newman (1984).
5  The seminal work in this area is that by John Downing (1969) and Jesse Reid (1966). The area is reviewed comprehensively in Yaden and Templeton (1986).

~  Vetta Goodman (1983) makes an important point about the
            ~f children's print concept knowledge. 'Children can use
                    '~ context but when asked to define the same
                            '~ part of the task we have given
                                    - book, wave it back
                                            ~~ olds


early ...
study of particula. -
(1984) who take a pronounced ..

8  The phrase comes from Clay (1979).
9  This example comes from Fox (1988).
10 This was one of the most important conclusions from the Bristol Language Development study. See Wells (1987).
11 From Heath (1982).
12 This analysis of language acquisition processes is taken from Cambourne (1988) who terms them 'conditions'.
13 The term 'engagement' comes from Smith (1983), Chapter 11.
14 The role of expectation, and the self-fulfilling prophecy, is most famously illustrated in the work of Rosenthal and Jacobson (1968). Although this research has been heavily criticised, the self-fulfilling prophecy still occupies an important place in educational theory.
15 From Smith (1983), page 105.
16 This exchange comes from the work of David McNeill. It is quoted in Crystal (1987), page 234.
17 See Britton (1970).
18 The term 'inner speech' comes from Vygotsky (1962).
19 This position is best illustrated by the work of Halliday (1978, p.54), who says, 'a child who is learning language is learning 'how to mean'; that is, he is developing a semantic potential, in respect of a set of functions in language that are in the last resort social functions'. For a thorough review of current theories of language acquisition see Lock and Fisher (1984).

## 5 Literacy in the early years of schooling

1   This basis for this analysis is again Cambourne's (1988) conditions.
2   See Hall *et al.* (1987).
3   In a paper given at the 1988 United Kingdom Reading Association conference, but unfortunately not yet published, Katharine Perera suggested that boys are more likely to read aloud in a monotone than girls simply because the model of reading aloud they receive is usually female. When given reading aloud tasks for which the model is normally male (e.g. reading football results) boys can show greater awareness of intonation and emphasis. Perera suggests that all children need reading aloud models from both sexes, which may involve extensive use of tape-recorded stories.
4   A damning critique of traditional strategies for introducing children to writing is given in the report of the Foundations of Writing project (Committee on Primary Education, 1986).
5   Smith (1983).
6   This issue is discussed by Vernon (1972). A thorough review of the research on the relationship between topic interest and children's reading comprehension, which has significant implications for teachers, will be found in Asher (1980).
7   Topping (1985) suggests modelling as one of the prime factors that account for the success of schemes in which parents are encouraged to become involved in their children's reading development. Children, he suggests, want to 'be like grown-ups', and the most significant grown-ups in their lives are their parents. If these parents can be encouraged to demonstrate an interest in reading to their children, then these children will become interested in reading also.
8   The effects upon reading progress of personal counselling were demonstrated by Lawrence (1972), but have been little investigated since. This is a promising area for future research.
9   Several of the chapters in Hall (1989) demonstrate the ways the use of journals, especially dialogue journals, can encourage the writing development of young children.
10  This separation of composing and transcribing activities is one of the most significant recommendations of the Foundations of Writing project (Committee on Primary Education, 1986).
11  This suggestion extends Graves' (1983) concept of conferencing to include reading. The procedure is also strongly recommended in the report of the Extending Beginning Reading project (Southgate, Arnold and Johnson, 1981).
12  See Chapter 1, Note 3.
13  These concepts come from Vygotsky (1962) and have been taken up, somewhat belatedly, by many theorists of social learning.
14  Best explained in Waterland (1985).
15  The best explanation of this shared-book approach will be found in Holdaway (1979).
16  Bennett (1979) sets the scene for the real books approach. Wade (1990) contains several insightful accounts of it in operation.

17  For a thorough treatment see Wray (1988).
18  For an account of developments in children's understandings about the spelling system see Gentry (1982) and Robinson (1988)
19  For some insights into the development of punctuation see Robinson (1988) and Cazden, Cordeiro and Giacobbe (1985).

## 6  The teaching of reading

1   Bryant and Bradley (1985).
    ~~dence for this, and for a great many of the basic principles
    ~~ psycho-linguistic approach to reading, comes from the
    ~~ uses the fact that fluent readers read at
    ~~ue convincingly that they cannot
    ~~r basis (Kolers, 1973).
    ~ is discussed

5   This p~~
    of reading put ~~
    evidence for this theory, ac~~
    in Gollasch (1982).
        The principle, however, can be seen in a simpl~ ~~ .
    following:

    The city of Paris is a
    a lovely place for a holiday.

    This may require a couple of readings before the point that reading is not a word-by-word process is appreciated.
6   The importance of cohesion in reading has been the subject of extensive research by Chapman. See Chapman (1983) and Chapman (1987) for summaries.
7   The fact that written language is different from speech is suggested by Smith (1977) as one of the most significant insights children need in order to learn to read. The nature of the difference is treated comprehensively in Rubin (1980).
8   The extent of some children's confusion over the syntactic structures commonly used in reading books specially written for them is well demonstrated by Reid (1970).
9   Well-known models of this kind are those of Gough (1972) and the 'automaticity' model of LaBerge and Samuels (1974). In both cases, the originators of these models have admitted to problems within them, stemming largely from their linearity. Both models have been revised to take into account the interactive and recursive nature of reading. See Singer and Ruddell (1985) for a thorough treatment of theoretical models of reading.

10 See Cambourne (1979)
11 Gough (1972).
12 The most influential model of this kind has been that of Goodman, presented in Gollasch (1982) (Volume 1) in diagrammatic form on page 29, and described on pages 41–2.
13 Cambourne (1979).
14 This has been one conclusion of the research work of Peter Bryant and his colleagues. They also argue that experience and knowledge of nursery rhymes in very young children is positively linked with later phonemic awareness. This finding usefully supports what many teachers of young children do already. See Maclean, Bryant and Bradley (1987), Bradley and Bryant (1983) and Bryant and Bradley (1985).
15 See Rumelhart (1985) for the clearest description of his interactive model.
16 A detailed description of the ways in which English orthography relates to speech sounds and to meaning units will be found in Chapters 5 and 6 of Downing (1979).
17 These principles are taken from Goodacre (1971).
18 The story method approach is described in detail in Moyle (1982). Moyle claims to have found a way to combine the benefits of language experience with those of story method, as exemplified by his 'Language Patterns' reading programme.
19 The individualised reading system has been popularised by the regular publications of Cliff Moon through the University of Reading. In his most recently published work, Moon himself (1985 and 1988) has argued against the concept of grading (and colour coding) which was at the heart of his system.
20 Wade (1989) is the best source for a full explanation and discussion of the real books approach. See also Moon (1985).
21 The apprenticeship approach has been popularised by Waterland (1985).
22 Bloom (1987) has noted the growth in parental involvement programmes and the gradual shift there has been in the planned role of parents, from a simple 'listening ear' for children reading aloud, to a wider concept of book-sharing.
23 The current 'reading debate' is summarised in Wray (1989b).
24 Reported in Farquhar (1987).
25 D.E.S. (1975).
26 D.E.S. (1975), paragraph 7.31.
27 Smith (1973), after 12 much-quoted 'easy ways to make learning to read difficult' gives one difficult rule for making learning to read easy, that is, 'to make reading easy'.
28 Southgate et al. (1981).
29 This suggestion is made strongly in Southgate et al. (1981) and repeated in Arnold (1982).
30 Holdaway (1979) refers to this as 'shared-book experience'.
31 Shared reading of this kind is well explained in Young and Tyre (1985).

32 Paired reading stems from the work of Morgan (1986). It is analysed in detail in Topping and Wolfendale (1985).
33 Described in Young and Tyre (1985).
34 See particularly Sandby-Thomas (1983).
35 Topping and Wolfendale (1985)

## 7 Writing: purpose and process

1 The term 'inner speech' comes from Vygotsky (1962) who uses it to signal the process by which thought moves from the social to the individual. Moffett (1981) uses the phrase 'revising inner speech' to ~ost highly developed kind of writing ('true authorship'). his hierarchy are 'crafting conventional or ~marising, plagiarising' and

Wray
6 Graves (1983) sugg~
   come to be able to revise. The su~,
   supports this by suggesting that children fina u~
   much more difficult than either resequencing or adding in u~
7 For an exploration of some of the issues involved in introducing peer group editing and revision see Wray and Gallimore (1986).
8 It has often been assumed that audience awareness was relatively late to develop in children. Robinson, Hall and Crawford (1990) produce evidence from the writing of very young children to suggest that this may not be so.
9 This is a revised version of the classification of audiences produced by the Schools Council Writing research team. See Britton et al. (1975).
10 The term 'conferencing' comes from the work of Graves (1983).
11 See Bloom (1988) for a fuller treatment of writing for the community.
12 It should not be thought that the tremendous results obtained by the pioneers of this movement (e.g. Langdon (1961) and Marshall (1974)) are being criticised here. What Gareth Owen is satirising are the extremes to which some teachers went in their quest for 'creative' writing.
13 See Britton et al. (1975).
14 Britton et al. (1975).
15 See Britton (1982).
16 The model originates from the work of Kinneavy (1971) but is elaborated by Beard (1984).
17 Further suggestions for the creation of good writing environments will be found in Wray (1988).

18 The idea of giving children choice for writing topics was one of the most influential aspects of the work of Graves (1983)
19 Many useful suggestions for responding to children's writing will be found in National Writing Project (1989b)
20 See Wray (1988) for a more extended account of the possibilities in teacher-modelling of writing.

## 8 Developing literacy across the curriculum

1 It was not until the late 1970s that this belief began to be challenged, which led to the setting up of two very influential research projects. One examined the reading experience of 7 to 9 year olds (Southgate *et al*, 1982), and the other that of 9 to 15 year olds (Lunzer and Gardner, 1979). Even today, however, many junior teachers will not see the teaching of reading and writing as really part of their job, unless children have special difficulties.
2 The H.M.I. Primary Survey (D.E.S., 1978) defined these 'advanced reading skills' as 'the efficient use of dictionaries and reference books, skimming passages for quick retrieval of information, scanning passages to establish the main points, the interpretation of context cues and the capacity to make sense of difficult passages'.
3 From *English in the National Curriculum* (D.E.S., 1989a).
4 This term was coined by Lunzer and Gardner (1984), whose research and book, while aimed mainly at secondary teachers has much of relevance to primary teachers. Studies have also been done on the use of DARTS with infant children (Davies, 1989; Filer, 1989).
5 These principles are derived from the work of Russell Stauffer (1969) whose seminal research and writing on the use of reading–thinking activities did not receive the attention it deserved from British teachers.
6 The technique of modelling was invented by John Merritt (1975). It has received some research evaluation (Sheldon, 1984) which found the use of it to improve the comprehension performance of poor readers. Sheldon (1986) explains this by suggesting that in trying to represent texts diagrammatically, readers were forced to *reflect* on what they read. Many classroom applications of semantic mapping are given by Heimlich and Pittelman (1986).
7 William Gray (1960) conceptualised comprehension as having three levels: 'the ability to read the lines, to read between the lines, and to read beyond the lines'.
8 For a secondary perspective on reading in science lessons see Davies and Greene (1984).
9 The distinction between logically and chronologically structured texts comes from Perera (1984) but has since become enshrined in National Curriculum documents.
10 A useful exercise is to analyse the readability of commonly used mathematics textbooks using a standard readability formula. This usually produces figures which suggest the textbook is a year or more ahead in reading difficulty than the children who are asked to use it.

### 9  Literacy for learning

1  Taken from *English in the National Curriculum* (D.E.S., 1989a).
2  A much fuller treatment of many of the points made in this chapter is given in Wray (1985a).
3  *English in the National Curriculum* (D.E.S., 1989a).
4  Taken from *English for Ages 5 to 16* (D.E.S., 1989b).
5  Evidence for this comes from the 'Effective Use of Reading' project as reported in Lunzer and Gardner (1979), but it is a very common thing to find in children and adults. Perry (1959) even found a similar ̇ ̇ ̇nomenon among American University students.
  ̇ ̇ ̇ ̇es a thorough overview of the bias in print issue and
  ̇ ̇ help children cope with it.
  ̇ ̇l ideas on the use of writing to
  ̇ 1989a), the first of a

Hamilto.. .
reported difficultes ...
from notice boards' to 'taking ..
others in this group had problems but did ..
9  Heath (1983).
10  This system derives from the work of John Merritt (1974) and was u.. as the basis for the renowned Open University Reading Development course (Open University, 1973).

### 10  The use of the computer to develop language and literacy

1  A more detailed discussion of these criteria will be found in Wray (1986).
2  The 'hospital model' of learning is contrasted with other models characterised by particular uses of the computer in Chandler (1984).
3  Some tentative research evidence for this has been produced by Potter and Walker (1984). They found that children seemed to talk more to each other when using the computer in groups of four than in groups of three or five. They go on to suggest some practical organisational responses to this.
4  For a fuller discussion see Wray (1985b).
5  An extended rationale together with several practical examples of the use of desktop publishing will be found in Wray and Medwell (1989).
6  See especially Govier (1985) and Johnston (1985b) for analyses of the use of the full version of TRAY, and Haywood and Wray (1988) for a study using the infant version.
7  Johnston (1985a).

8 The seminal text here is Papert (1980), but Anderson (1986) is also particularly useful.

9 Books on this topic which will be found extremely useful include Chandler and Marcus (1985) and Blows and Wray (1989).

## 11 Assessing language and literacy development

1 The list of purposes for assessment given here comes from Pumfrey (1977). Pumfrey (1985) also summarises these points and gives a useful catalogue of assessment procedures and tests for reading. An alternative view, and a wider perspective on testing in language and literacy is given in Neville (1988) which reports the results of the Scottish National Assessment of English research project.

2 This is a bold claim, and our evidence for it is personal rather than objective. It does seem to be the case, however, that schools are more likely to select teaching materials because they fit their current philosophy of teaching, are attractively presented or are more 'modern' than materials currently in use, than because there is well-documented research that they increase children's achievement.

3 For a much more extensive and more general treatment of assessment issues see Desforges (1989).

4 The terms 'formative' and 'summative' come from Scriven (1967).

5 See Neville and Pugh (1975) for one small piece of this evidence.

6 This figure emerged from the research commissioned by the Bullock Committee (D.E.S., 1975). The same research revealed that almost 35 per cent of primary schools were using the Burt Word Reading Test, similar in design to the Schonell test. Clearly many schools were using both. Even in the secondary sector the Schonell test was used by 48 per cent of schools.

7 This was demonstrated by Kenneth Goodman in one of his earliest research studies (Goodman, 1965) when he showed that even 6 year old children were able to read words in context significantly better than in isolation. The study has been replicated many times. More recently, Hudson and Haworth (1983) showed that children's abilities to read the words in the Schonell Graded Word Reading Test were greatly improved when they were given these words within a meaningful context.

8 Miscue analysis was invented and has been extensively researched by Kenneth and Yetta Goodman. Gollasch (1982) contains a collection of their most significant articles and papers.

9 The full miscue analysis system is explained in Goodman, Watson and Burke (1987). An alternative, simpler approach is given in Arnold (1982).

10 Yetta Goodman has coined the term 'kid-watching' for the essential observation processes which form the basis for teacher assessment (Goodman, 1978).

# References

`· ⌐⌐ough:`

`Aun....`
   *the Sociology of Basu ~~.*
Barnes, D. (1976) *From Communication ~*
   Penguin.
Beard, R. (1984) *Children's Writing in the Primary School,* Sevenoaks:
   Hodder & Stoughton.
Bellack, A., Kliebard, H., Hyman, R., and Smith, F. (1966) *The Language
   of the Classroom,* Columbia: Teachers College Press.
Bennett, J. (1979) *Learning to Read Through Picture Books,* Stroud: Thimble
   Press.
Benton, M. and Fox, G. (1985) *Teaching Literature: Nine to Fourteen,*
   Oxford: Oxford University Press.
Berdiansky, B., Cronell, B. and Koehler, J. (1969) *Spelling-sound relations
   and primary form-class descriptions for speech comprehension vocabularies of
   6-9 year olds,* Los Alamitos, California: Southwest Regional Laboratory
   (Technical report No. 15).
Bereiter, C. and Engelmann, S. (1966) *Teaching Disadvantaged Children in
   the Pre-school,* New Jersey: Prentice Hall.
Bernstein, B. (1971) *Class, Codes and Control,* London: Routledge and
   Kegan Paul.
Bloom, W. (1987) *Partnership with Parents in Reading,* Sevenoaks: Hodder
   & Stoughton.
Bloom, W. (1988) 'A community of authors' in Wray, D. (ed.) *Developing
   Children's Writing,* Leamington Spa: Scholastic.
Blows, M. and Wray, D. (1989) *Using Computers Effectively,* Leamington
   Spa: Scholastic.

Bradley, L. and Bryant, P. (1983) 'Categorising sounds and learning to read: a causal connection' in *Nature* No. 301, pp. 419–21.

Britton, J. (1970) *Language and Learning*, Harmondsworth: Penguin.

Britton, J., Burgess, T., Martin, N., McLeod, A. and Rosen, H. (1975) *The Development of Writing Abilities 11–18*, London: Macmillan.

Britton, J. (1982) 'Spectator role and the beginnings of writing' in Pradl, G. (ed.) *Prospect and Retrospect: Selected Essays of James Britton*, London: Heinemann.

Bruner, J. and Haste, H. (1987) *Making Sense: The Child's Construction of the World*, London: Methuen.

Bryant, P. and Bradley, L. (1985) *Children's Reading Problems*, Oxford: Basil Blackwell.

Cambourne (1979) 'How important is theory to the reading teacher?' in *Australian Journal of Reading*, Vol. 2, No. 2.

Cambourne, B. (1988) *The Whole Story*, Auckland, N.Z.: Ashton Scholastic.

Cazden, C., Cordeiro, P. and Giacobbe, M. (1985) 'Spontaneous and scientific concepts: young children's learning of punctuation' in Wells, G. and Nicholls, J. (eds) *Language and Learning: An Interactional Perspective*, Lewes: Falmer Press.

Chandler, D. (1984) *Young Learners and the Microcomputer*, Milton Keynes: Open University Press.

Chandler, D. and Marcus, S. (1985) *Computers and Literacy*, Milton Keynes: Open University Press.

Chapman, J. (1983) *Reading Development and Cohesion*, London: Heinemann.

Chapman, J. (1987) *Reading: From 5–11 Years*, Milton Keynes: Open University Press.

Cheetham, J. (1976) 'Quarries in the primary school', in Fox, G., Hammond, G., Jones, T., Smith, F. and Sterck, K. (eds) *Writers, Critics and Children*, London: Heinemann.

Clark, M. (1976) *Young Fluent Readers*, London: Heinemann.

Clay, M. (1979) *The Early Detection of Reading Difficulties*, London: Heinemann.

Committee on Primary Education (1986) *Foundations of Writing*, Edinburgh: Scottish Curriculum Development Service.

Corson, D. (1988) *Oral Language Across the Curriculum*, Clevedon: Multilingual Matters.

Craft, M. (ed.) (1970) *Family, Class and Education*, London: Longman.

Crystal, D. (1984) *Who Cares About English Usage?*, Harmondsworth: Penguin.

Crystal, D. (1987) *The Cambridge Encyclopaedia of Language*, Cambridge: Cambridge University Press.

Davies, J. (1989) 'Using reading-thinking activities with infant children'. Unpublished M.Ed. dissertation, University of Wales..

Davies, F. and Greene, T. (1984) *Reading for Learning in the Sciences*, Edinburgh: Oliver and Boyd.

Department of Education and Science (1975) *A Language for Life*, H.M.S.O.

Department of Education and Science (1978) *Primary Education in England*, H.M.S.O.

Department of Education and Science (1988) *Report of the Committee of Inquiry into the Teaching of English Language*, H.M.S.O.

Department of Education and Science (1989a) *English in the National Curriculum*, H.M.S.O.

Department of Education and Science (1989b) *English for Ages 5 to 16*, H.M.S.O.

Desforges, C. (1989) *Testing and Assessment*, London: Cassell.

Dickinson, P. (1976) 'A defence of rubbish', in Fox, G., Hammond, G., Jones, T., Smith, F. and Sterck, K. (eds) *Writers, Critics and Children*, Heinemann Educational.

*Them Young: Sex, Race and Class in Children's*

MacGibbon and Kee.

Reading

Driver, R. (1985)

Press.

Edwards, A. and Westgate, D. (1987) *Investigating*

Falmer Press.

Edwards, D. and Mercer, N. (1987) *Common Knowledge: The Development of Understanding in the Classroom*, London: Methuen.

Edwards, V. (undated) *Language Variation in the Multicultural Classroom*, Reading: Centre for the Teaching of Reading, University of Reading.

Farquhar, C. (1987) 'Little read books' in *Times Educational Supplement*, 8 May 1987.

Ferreiro, E. and Teberosky, A. (1983) *Literacy before Schooling*, London: Heinemann.

Filer, M. (1989) 'Using DARTs with infants'. Unpublished M.Ed. dissertation, University of Wales.

Flanders, N. (1970) *Analysing Teacher Behaviour*, Reading, Mass.: Addison-Wesley.

Fourlas, G. and Wray, D. (1990) 'Children's oral language: a comparison of two classroom organisational systems' in Wray, D. (ed.) *Emerging Partnerships: Current Research in Language and Literacy*, Clevedon: Multilingual Matters.

Fox, C. (1988) 'Poppies will make them grant' in Meek, M. and Mills, C. *Language and Literacy in the Primary School*, Basingstoke: Falmer Press.

Francis, H. (1982) *Learning to Read: Literate Behaviour and Orthographic Knowledge*, London: Allen and Unwin.

Gahagan, D. and Gahagan, J. (1970) *Talk Reform*, London: Routledge and Kegan Paul.

Gentry, R. (1982) 'An analysis of developmental spelling in GYNS AT WORK', in *The Reading Teacher*, Vol. 36, pp. 192–201.

Giles, H. (1971) 'Our reactions to accent', in *New Society*, 14 October 1971.

Goelman, H., Oberg, A. and Smith, F. (eds) (1984) *Awakening to Literacy*, London: Heinemann.

Gollasch, F. (ed.) (1982) *Language and Literacy: The Selected Writings of Kenneth S. Goodman*, 2 Vols, Boston: Routledge and Kegan Paul.

Goodacre, E. (1971) *Children and Learning to Read*, London: Routledge and Kegan Paul.

Goodman, K. (1965) 'A linguistic study of cues and miscues in reading' in *Elementary English*, Vol. 42, No. 6, reprinted in Gollasch (1982) Vol. 1.

Goodman, K. (1967) 'Reading: a psycholinguistic guessing game' in *Journal of the Reading Specialist*, Vol. 6, No. 4, pp. 126–35, reprinted in Gollasch (1982) Vol. 1.

Goodman, Y. (1978) 'Kid-watching: an alternative to testing' in *Journal of National Elementary Principals*, Vol. 57, No. 4, pp. 41–5.

Goodman, Y. (1983) 'Beginning reading development: strategies and principles', in Parker, R. and Davis, F. (eds) *Developing Literacy: Young Children's Use of Language*, Newark, Delaware: International Reading Association.

Goodman, Y., Watson, D. and Burke, C. (1987) *Reading Miscue Inventory*, New York: Richard Owen Publishers.

Gough, P. (1972) 'One second of reading' in Kavanagh, J. and Mattingley, I. (eds) *Language by Ear and by Eye*, Cambridge, Mass.: MIT Press.

Govier, H. (1985) 'DEVELOPING TRAY – a sample run' in M.E.P. (ed.) *Language Development in the Primary School*, London: Council for Educational Technology.

Graves, D. (1983) *Writing: Teachers and Children at Work*, London: Heinemann.

Gray, W. (1960) 'The major aspects of reading', in Robinson, H. (ed.) *Sequential Development of Reading Abilities*, Supplementary Educational monographs, No. 90, Chicago: University of Chicago Press.

Gregory, R. (1977) 'Psychology: towards a science of fiction', in Meek, M., Warlow, A., and Barton, G. (eds) *The Cool Web*, London: The Bodley Head.

Gregory, A. and Woollard, N. (1985) *Looking into Language: Diversity in the Classroom*, Stoke: Trentham Books.

Hall, N. (1987) *The Emergence of Literacy*, Sevenoaks: Hodder & Stoughton.

Hall, N. (ed.) (1989) *Writing with Reason: The Emergence of Authorship in Young Children*, Sevenoaks: Hodder & Stoughton.

Hall, N., May, E., Moores, J., Shearer, J. and Williams, S. (1987) 'The literate home corner' in Smith, P. (ed.) *Parents and Teachers Together*, Basingstoke: Macmillan.

Halliday, M. (1978) *Language and Social Semiotic*, London: Edward Arnold.

Hamilton, M. and Stasinopoulos, M. (1987) *Literacy, Numeracy and Adults*, ALBSU.

Harste, J., Woodward, V. and Burke, C. (1984) *Language Stories and Literacy Lessons*, Portsmouth, New Hampshire: Heinemann.

Haywood, S. and Wray, D. (1988) 'Using TRAY, a text reconstruction program, with top infants', in *Educational Review*, Vol. 40, No. 1, pp. 29–39.

Heath, S. B. (1982) 'What no bedtime story means: narrative skills at home and at school', in *Language and Society*, No. 6, pp. 49–76.

Heath, S. B. (1983) *Ways with Words*, Cambridge: Cambridge University Press.

Heimlich, J. and Pittelman, S. (1986) *Semantic Mapping: Classroom Applications*, Newark, Delaware: International Reading Association.

Holdaway, D. (1979) *The Foundations of Literacy*, Gosford, New South Wales: Ashton Scholastic.

Honey, J. (1983) *The Language Trap: Race, Class and 'Standard English' in British Schools*, Kenton, Middlesex: National Council for Educational

- - - - - London: Edward Arnold.

' - - - - - - nition', in

J - - - - - -

language development', - - -,
Cardiff.

Johnston, V. (1985b) 'Introducing the microcomputer into English: an evaluation of TRAY as a program using problem-solving as a strategy for developing reading skills', in *British Journal of Educational Technology*, Vol. 16, pp. 208–18.

Jones, A. and Buttrey, J. (1970) *Children and Stories*, Oxford: Blackwell.

Kinneavy, J. (1971) *A Theory of Discourse*, Englewood Cliffs, New Jersey: Prentice Hall.

Kolers, P. (1973) 'Three stages of reading' in Smith, F. (ed.) *Psycholinguistics and Reading*, New York: Holt, Rinehart and Winston.

LaBerge, D. and Samuels, S. (1974) 'Toward a theory of automatic information processing in reading', in *Cognitive Psychology*, Vol. 6, pp. 293–323.

Labov, W. (1969) 'The logic of non-standard English', *Georgetown Monographs on Language and Linguistics*, No. 22, Washington, D.C.: Georgetown University Press.

Langdon, M. (1961) *Let the Children Write*, London: Longman Group.

Lavender, R. (1978) 'Living by fact or fiction', in Grugeon, E. and Walden, P. (eds) *Literature and Learning*, London: Ward Lock Educational.

Lawrence, D. (1972) 'The effects of counselling on retarded readers' in Reid, J. (ed.) *Reading: Problems and Practices*, London: Ward Lock.

Linguistics Minority Project (1983) *Linguistic Minorities in England: Summary Report*, London: London Institute of Education.

Lock, A. and Fisher, E. (eds) (1984) *Language Development*, London: Croom Helm.

Lunzer, E. and Gardner, K. (1979) *The Effective Use of Reading*, London: Heinemann.

Lunzer, E. and Gardner, K. (1984) *Learning from the Written Word*, Edinburgh: Oliver and Boyd.

Lyons, H. (1978) 'Some second thoughts on sexism in fairy tales', in Grugeon, E. and Walden, P. (eds) *Literature and Learning*, London: Ward Lock.

Maclean, M., Bryant, P. and Bradley, L. (1987) 'Rhymes, nursery rhymes and reading in early childhood', in *Merrill-Palmer Quarterly*, No. 33, pp. 255–81.

Mandler, J. and Johnson, N. (1977) 'Remembrance of things parsed: story structure and recall' in *Cognitive Psychology*, 9, pp. 111–15.

Marchbanks, G. and Levin, H. (1965) 'Cues by which children recognise words', in *Journal of Educational Psychology*, Vol. 56, No. 2, pp. 57–61.

Marshall, S. (1974) *Creative Writing*, London: Macmillan.

Meek, M. (1988) *How Texts Teach what Readers Learn*, Stroud: Signal Press.

Mercer, N. (ed.) (1988) *Language and Literacy from an Educational Perspective*, (2 volumes) Milton Keynes: Open University Press.

Merritt, J. (1974) *What Shall We Teach?* London: Ward Lock.

Merritt, J. (1975) 'Reading: 7-11', in *Education 3–13*, No. 3, pp. 29–35.

Miller, G. (1977) *Spontaneous Apprentices: Children and Language*, New York: Seabury.

Moffett, J. (1981) 'Integrity in the teaching of writing', in Moffett, J. *Coming on Center: English Education in Evolution*, Upper Montclair, New Jersey: Boynton/Cook.

Moon, C. (1985) (ed.) *Practical Ways to Teach Reading*, London: Ward Lock.

Moon, C. (1988) 'Reading: where are we now?' in Meek, M. and Mills, C. *Language and Literacy in the Primary School*, Lewes: Falmer Press.

Morgan, R. (1986) *Helping Children Read*, London: Methuen.

Moyle, D. (1982) *Children's Words*, London: Grant McIntyre.

Murphy, R. (1973) *Adults Functional Reading Study*, United States Office of Education.

National Writing Project (1989a) *Writing and Learning*, Walton-on-Thames: Nelson.

National Writing Project (1989b) *Responding to Children's Writing*, Walton-on-Thames: Nelson.

Neville, M. (1988) *Assessing and Teaching Language*, Basingstoke: Macmillan.

Neville, M. and Pugh, A. (1975) 'Reading ability and ability to use a book: a study of middle school children', in *Reading*, Vol. 9, No. 3, pp. 23–31.

Newman, J. (1984) *The Craft of Children's Writing*, Richmond Hill, Ontario: Scholastic – TAB Publications.

Open University (1973) *Reading Development*, Milton Keynes: Open University Press.

Opie, I. and Opie, P. (1959) *The Lore and Language of Schoolchildren*, Oxford: Oxford University Press.

Papert, S. (1980) *Mindstorms: Children, Computers and Powerful Ideas*, London: Harvester Press.

Perera, K. (1984) *Children's Reading and Writing*, London: Blackwell.

Perry, W. (1959) 'Students' use and misuse of reading skills: a report to a faculty', in *Harvard Educational Review*, Vol. 29, No. 3.

Potter, F. and Walker, S. (1984) 'Using language programs with groups', in Potter, F. and Wray, D. (eds) *Micro-explorations (1): Using Language and Reading Software*, Ormskirk: United Kingdom Reading Association.

Pumfrey, P. (1977) *Measuring Reading Abilities*, Sevenoaks: Hodder & Stoughton.

Pumfrey, P. (1985) *Reading: Tests and Assessment Techniques*, Sevenoaks: Hodder & Stoughton.

Pand. M. (1984) 'Story schema: theory, research and practice', in *The Vol. 37, pp. 377–82.

reading', in *Educational Research*,

Roeder, H. ....
encourage voluntary reading , ...
J., and Mercer, N. (eds) *Children, Language* an...
Keynes: Open University Press.

Rosen, C. and Rosen, H. (1973) *The Language of Primary School Children*, Harmondsworth: Penguin.

Rosen, M. (1984) 'Memorable speech', in *Times Educational Supplement*, 9 March 1984.

Rosen, M. (1989) *Did I Hear You Write?* London: Andre Deutsch.

Rosenthal, R. and Jacobson, L. (1968) *Pygmalion in the Classroom*, New York: Holt, Rinehart and Winston.

Rubin, A. (1980) 'A theoretical taxonomy of the differences between oral and written language' in Spiro, R., Bruce, B. and Brewer, W. (eds) *Theoretical Issues in Reading Comprehension*, Hillsdale, New Jersey: Lawrence Erlbaum.

Rumelhart, D. (1980) 'Schemata: the building blocks of cognition' in Spiro, R., Bruce, B. and Brewer, W. (eds) *Theoretical Issues in Reading Comprehension*, Hillsdale, New Jersey: Lawrence Erlbaum.

Rumelhart, D. (1985) 'Toward an interactive model of reading' in Singer, H. and Ruddell, R. (eds) *Theoretical Models and Processes of Reading*, Newark, Delaware: International Reading Association.

Sandby-Thomas, M. (1983) 'The organisation of reading and pupil attainment', in *Journal of Research in Reading*, Vol. 6, No. 1, pp. 29–40.

Scriven, M. (1967) 'The methodology of evaluation', in Tyler, R., Gagne, R. and Scriven, M. (eds) *Perspectives on Curriculum Evaluation*, Chicago: Rand McNally.

Sheldon, S. (1984) 'Comparison of two methods for teaching reading comprehension', in *Journal of Research in Reading*, Vol. 7, No. 1, pp. 41–52.

Sheldon, S. (1986) 'Representing comprehension', in Root, B. (ed.) *Resources for Reading*, London: Macmillan.

Sinclair, J. and Coulthard, M. (1975) *Towards an Analysis of Discourse: The Language of Teachers and Pupils*, London: Oxford University Press.

Singer, H. and Ruddell, R. (1985) (eds) *Theoretical Models and Processes of Reading*, Newark, Delaware: International Reading Association.

Smith, F. (1973) (ed.) *Psycholinguistics and Reading*, New York: Holt, Rinehart and Winston.

Smith, F. (1977) 'Making sense of reading and of reading instruction', in *Harvard Educational Review*, Vol. 47, No. 3, pp. 386–95.

Smith, F. (1978) *Reading*, Cambridge: Cambridge University Press.

Smith, F. (1982) *Writing and the Writer*, London: Heinemann.

Smith, F. (1983) *Essays into Literacy*, Portsmouth, New Hampshire: Heinemann.

Smith, F. (1988) *Joining the Literacy Club*, London: Heinemann.

Southgate, V., Arnold, H. and Johnson, S. (1981) *Extending Beginning Reading*, London: Heinemann.

Stauffer, R. (1969) *Teaching Reading as a Thinking Process*, New York: Harper & Row.

Stones, R. (1983) *Pour Out the Cocoa, Janet: Sexism in Children's Books*, York: Longman.

Styles, M. and Triggs, P. (1988) *Poetry 0–16*, London: Books for Keeps.

Tann, S. (1990) 'Developing listening' in Wray, D. (ed.) *Talking and Listening*, Leamington Spa: Scholastic Publications..

Tizard, B. and Hughes, M. (1984) *Young Children Learning*, London: Fontana.

Tizard, B., Hughes, M., Carmichael, H. and Pinkerton, G. (1983) 'Language and social class: is verbal deprivation a myth?', in *Journal of Child Psychology and Psychiatry*, Vol. 24, No. 4, pp. 533–42.

Topping, K. (1985) 'Parental involvement in reading: theoretical and empirical background' in Topping, K. and Wolfendale, S. (eds) *Parental Involvement in Children's Reading*, London: Croom Helm.

Topping and Wolfendale (1985) (eds) *Parental Involvement in Children's Reading*, London: Croom Helm.

Trudgill, P. (1975) *Accent, Dialect and the School*, London: Edward Arnold.

Upton, C., Sanderson, S. and Widdowson, J. (1987) *Word Maps: A Dialect Atlas of England*, London: Croom Helm.

Vernon, M. (1972) 'The effect of motivational and emotional factors on learning to read' in Reid, J. (ed.) *Reading: Problems and Practices*, London: Ward Lock.

Vygotsky, L. (1962) *Thought and Language*, Cambridge, Mass.: MIT Press.

Wade, B. (ed.) (1985) *Talking to Some Purpose*, Birmingham: Educational Review.

Wade, B. (ed.) (1990) *Reading for Real*, Milton Keynes: Open University Press.

Walker, R. and Adelman, C. (1976) 'Strawberries' in Stubbs, M. and Delamont, S. (eds) *Explorations in Classroom Observation*, London: Wiley.

Waterland, L. (1985) *Read With Me*, Stroud: Thimble Press.

Wells, G. (1987) *The Meaning Makers*, London: Heinemann Educational.

Wertsch, J. (ed.) (1985) *Culture, Communication and Cognition: Vygotskian Perspectives*, Cambridge: Cambridge University Press.

Willes, M. (1981) 'Children becoming pupils: a study of discourse in nursery and reception classes' in Adelman, C. (ed.) *Uttering, Muttering*, London: Grant McIntyre.

Wray, D. (1985a) *Teaching Information Skills through Project Work*, Sevenoaks: Hodder & Stoughton.

Wray, D. (1985b) 'The adventurous way to use the computer', in Ewing, J. (ed.) *Reading and the New Technologies*, London: Heinemann Educational.

         ‐ ‐‐ᴸ ‐oftware? An update on computer-assisted ‐‐ ᴸ ᴼᴼ ᴺᴼ 9 pp.

Wray, D. (1990b) ‐ ‐ ‐
    Potter, F. *Communication and Learning*, Oxford: ᴸ‐‐‐

Wray, D. and Gallimore, J. (1986) 'Drafting in the classroom', in *Primary Teaching Studies*, Vol. 1, No. 3, pp. 65–77.

Wray, D. and Medwell, J. (1989) 'Using desk-top publishing to develop literacy' in *Reading*, Vol. 23, No. 2, pp. 62–8.

Yaden, D. and Templeton, S. (eds) (1986) *Metalinguistic Awareness and Beginning Literacy*, Portsmouth, New Hampshire: Heinemann.

Young, P. and Tyre, C. (1985) *Teach Your Child to Read*, London: Fontana.

Zimet, S. (1976) *Print and Prejudice*, Sevenoaks: Hodder & Stoughton.

# Index